DK EYEWITNESS

D0544619

TOP 10
LONDON

Top 10 London Highlights

The Top 10 of Everything

CONTENTS

London Area by Area

Streetsmart

Within each Top 10 list in this book, no hierarchy of quality or popularity is implied. All 10 are, in the editor's opinion, of roughly equal merit.

Title page, front cover and spine Panoramic view of the Shard and the Tower Bridge by river Thames
Back cover, clockwise from top left Autumn in Hyde Park; Big Ben and the Houses of Parliament; The Ship & Shovell pub; Tower Bridge and Shard; London Eye

The rapid rate at which the world is changing is constantly keeping the DK Eyewitness team on our toes. While we've worked hard to ensure that this edition of London is accurate and up-to-date, we know that opening hours alter, standards shift, prices fluctuate, places close and new ones pop up in their stead. So, if you notice we've got something wrong or left something out, we want to hear about it. Please get in touch at **travelguides@dk.com**

Welcome to
London

River city. Royal city. City of palaces and pubs, museums and monuments. The world's first National Park City. Hotbed of art. Shopping mecca. Financial powerhouse. London is all these things and more... so who could argue when we say that it's the world's most exciting metropolis? With DK Eyewitness Top 10 London, it's yours to explore.

We love London: the culture, the history, the diversity. What could be better than strolling along the cobbled streets of **Covent Garden**, sailing along the Thames between the **Houses of Parliament** and **Tate Modern**, browsing the cutting-edge boutiques of **Spitalfields** and scouting the stalls for a bargain, walking in one of the city's 3,000 parks, or time-travelling back to Shakespeare's England at the **Globe Theatre**? It's all here, packed into a few square miles of the world's most energetic streetscape.

This city is a cultural colossus, with a buoyant theatre district, a bar or restaurant on every corner, and a packed calendar of eye-catching ceremonies and festivals, including the **Notting Hill Carnival**. It does history and pageantry like nowhere else, but for all its pomp and ceremony, London has always been a cosmopolitan capital. The city is a paradise for foodies, where you can sample street food from around the world, as well as dine in an enticing array of Michelin-starred restaurants.

Whether you're coming for a weekend or a week, our Top 10 guide brings together the best of everything that London can offer, from hip **Hoxton** to sophisticated **St James's**. The guide has useful tips throughout, from seeking out what's free to places off the beaten track, plus 13 easy-to-follow itineraries, designed to tie together a clutch of sights in a short space of time. Add inspiring photography and detailed maps, and you've got the essential pocket-sized travel companion. **Enjoy the book, and enjoy London.**

Clockwise from top: **British Museum, Big Ben, Red telephone boxes, St Paul's and the Millennium Bridge, Westminster Abbey, Tate Britain, Kew Gardens**

Exploring London

For things to see and do, visitors to London are spoiled for choice. Whether you're here for a short stay or you just want a flavour of this great city, you need to make the most of your time. Here are some ideas for two and four days of sightseeing in London.

Shakespeare's Globe is a replica of the original Globe Theatre.

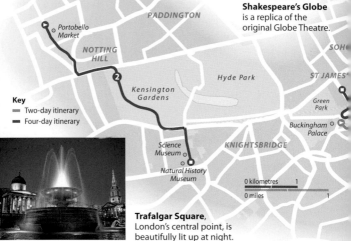

Key
— Two-day itinerary
— Four-day itinerary

Trafalgar Square, London's central point, is beautifully lit up at night.

Two Days in London

Day ❶

MORNING
Take a Beefeater tour of the **Tower of London** *(see pp38–41)*, then visit St Paul's Cathedral *(see pp42–5)*.

AFTERNOON
Cross **Millennium Bridge** *(see p64)*, for a panorama of the River Thames. Explore the **Tate Modern** *(see pp28–9)* before walking along the South Bank past **Shakespeare's Globe** *(see p89)*.

Day ❷

MORNING
Begin at **Buckingham Palace** *(see pp24–5)*, and then take a stroll through **St James's Park** *(see p119)*. Afterwards, head to **Westminster Abbey** *(see pp34–5)* to see the monuments of English monarchs.

AFTERNOON
After lunch, spend 2 hours at the **National Gallery** *(see pp16–17)* in Trafalgar Square. Then take a "flight" on the **London Eye** *(see pp26–7)*.

Four Days in London

Day ❶

MORNING
Start with a full morning exploring the **Tower of London** *(see pp38–41)*, then cross the imposing **Tower Bridge** *(see p141)* and stroll along the river past **HMS** *Belfast (see pp64–5)*.

AFTERNOON
Take lunch at **Borough Market** *(see p91)*, just around the corner from the towering **Shard** *(see p27)*. Roam the **Tate Modern** *(see pp28–9)* before enjoying an alfresco evening meal on the South Bank.

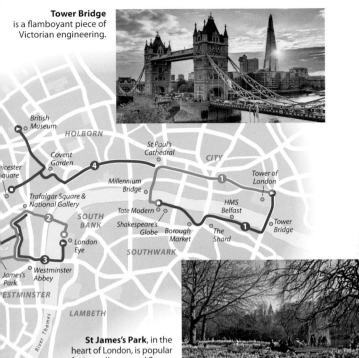

Tower Bridge is a flamboyant piece of Victorian engineering.

St James's Park, in the heart of London, is popular for its well-groomed flower beds and great views.

Day ❷
MORNING
Begin in Notting Hill, with a morning turn around **Portobello Road** market (see pp126–7). Walk south from there through the stately expanse of **Kensington Gardens** (see p54).
AFTERNOON
Exit the park into South Kensington's museum quarter, for an afternoon exploring the **Science Museum** (see pp22–3) and the **Natural History Museum** (see pp20–21).

Day ❸
MORNING
Choose between the **London Eye** (see pp26–7) or **Westminster Abbey** (see pp34–5). Not far away is **Trafalgar Square** (see p95), where you can admire Nelson's Column before taking in the old masters at the **National Gallery** (see pp16–17).

AFTERNOON
Meander through **St James's Park** (see p119) before enjoying afternoon tea at St James' Café. Peek through the gates at **Buckingham Palace** (see pp24–5), then hit swish **St James's** (see pp118–23) for dinner and cocktails.

Day ❹
MORNING
Start at the **British Museum** (see pp12–15), a two-million-year trove of human endeavour, then head down to **Covent Garden** (see pp104–11) for a leisurely stroll around the Apple Market and stop for lunch at one of the area's many eateries.
AFTERNOON
St Paul's Cathedral (see pp42–5) is a short way by Tube. In the evening, return west to **Leicester Square** (see p97), where the bright lights of London's Theatreland await.

Top 10 London Highlights

The blue whale skeleton at Hintze Hall, Natural History Museum

TOP 10 London Highlights

A city of infinite colour and variety, London is both richly historic, tracing its roots back over 2,000 years, and unceasingly modern, at the forefront of fashion, music and the arts. A selection of the best London has to offer is explored in the following chapter.

British Museum ①

The oldest national public museum in the world contains a rich collection of treasure and artifacts (see pp12–15).

② National Gallery and National Portrait Gallery

The nation's most important art collections are held here, including this 1581 miniature of Sir Francis Drake (see pp16–19).

③ Natural History Museum

The enormous and varied collection here explores the history of life on Earth (see pp20–21).

Science Museum ④

A huge museum with fascinating interactive exhibits that explain and demonstrate the wonders of science (see pp22–3).

⑤ Buckingham Palace

The official home of the Queen, where the Changing the Guard takes place (see pp24–5).

6 London Eye
The giant cantilevered observation wheel offers stunning views of the city *(see pp26–7)*.

7 Tate Modern and Tate Britain

London's two Tate galleries house collections of British and modern international art *(see pp28–31)*.

8 Westminster Abbey and Parliament Square
This royal abbey has, since 1066, been the place where all Britain's monarchs have been crowned *(see pp34–7)*.

9 Tower of London
The Tower has been a royal palace, fortress and prison, and is the home of the Crown Jewels *(see pp38–41)*.

10 St Paul's Cathedral
Sir Christopher Wren's Baroque masterpiece still stands out and takes pride of place on the City skyline *(see pp42–5)*.

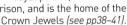

TOP 10 ⭐ British Museum

The world's oldest national public museum has over 8 million items spanning the history of the world's cultures, from the stone tools of early man to 21st-century artworks. The collection was started with the bequest of a physician and antiquarian, Sir Hans Sloane, in 1753. In the 18th and 19th centuries, travellers and emissaries, such as Captain James Cook, Lord Curzon and Charles Townley, added treasures from around the world. The present building was completed in 1852; the magnificent central courtyard is used as a public space.

Parthenon Sculptures ①
This spectacular 5th-century BC frieze from the Parthenon **(right)** was made under Pericles and shows a procession in honour of the goddess Athena. It was obtained in 1801 by Lord Elgin, Ambassador to Constantinople.

② Mummified Cat
Cats and sacred cows were mummified in Ancient Egypt. This cat **(left)** comes from Abydos and dates from the 1st century AD. Many Egyptian deities took on animal shapes, as seen on wall paintings and other artifacts.

③ Ram in a Thicket
Decorated with shells, gold leaf, copper and lapis lazuli, this priceless ornament comes from Ur in Sumer, one of the world's earliest civilizations. Games and musical instruments are also displayed.

④ Double-Headed Serpent Mosaic
Carved in wood and covered with turquoise mosaic, this Aztec ornament was probably worn on the chest on ceremonial occasions.

⑤ Rosetta Stone
In 196 BC Egyptian priests wrote a decree about Ptolemy V on this granite tablet in Greek, in demotic and in Egyptian hieroglyphics. Found in 1799, it proved crucial in deciphering Egyptian pictorial writing.

⑥ Portland Vase
It is not known where and when this 1st-century blue-and-opaque-glass vase was found. In 1778, it was purchased by Sir William Hamilton, Britain's ambassador to Naples, who sold it to the Duchess of Portland. It had to be reassembled after a visitor smashed it into 200 pieces in 1845.

⑦ David Vases
These blue and white porcelain altar vases dating from c 1351, were made in Jingdezhen, China. They feature elephant handles in addition to various motifs.

⑧ Mildenhall Treasure

Some of the greatest early English treasures are these silver plates **(left)** from the 4th century, found at Mildenhall in Suffolk. Their decorations include sea nymphs, satyrs and Hercules.

Ramesses II ⑨

This is all that remains of the colossal granite statue **(right)** of Ramesses II (c 1279 BC) from his memorial temple at Thebes. Its arrival in England in the 19th century is said to have inspired the poet Shelley to write the poem *Ozymandias*.

British Museum

Ram in a Thicket ❸

Mildenhall Treasure ❽

Mummified Cat ❷

Portland Vase ❻

Key to Floorplan
- Ground floor
- Upper floor

❿ Lewis Chessmen

❹ Double-Headed Serpent Mosaic

David Vases ❼

Ramesses II ❾

Parthenon Sculptures ❶

❺ Rosetta Stone

❿ Lewis Chessmen

These 12th-century carved chess pieces originate from Norway and were discovered in Scotland's Western Isles. The Lewis Chessmen set includes seated kings, queens, bishops, knights and standing warders, which are fashioned from walrus ivory.

NEED TO KNOW

MAP L1 ■ Great Russell St WC1 ■ 020 7323 8000 ■ www.britishmuseum.org

Open 10am–5:30pm Sat–Thu, 10am–8:30pm Fri.

Adm for major temporary exhibitions

Free guided tours

....

■ The Great Court's Reading Room is closed to public.

■ There are three cafés, a pizzeria and the fine-dining Great Court Restaurant.

■ Highlights tours (£14) introduce the collection.

■ The British Museum shop sells reproduction artifacts, books, jewellery and gifts.

Museum Guide

The museum has three floors with multiple levels.

Free maps are available and guides are on sale at the information desks. Otherwise start to the left of the main entrance with the Assyrian, Egyptian, Greek and Roman galleries. The upper floor has Egyptian mummies. The Asian collection provides a change from Classical material, as do the early British, medieval and Renaissance galleries on the east side.

British Museum Collections

 Middle East
Some 6,000 years of history start with the spectacular carved reliefs depicting a variety of scenes from the Assyrian palace of Nineveh.

2 Ancient Egypt and Sudan
An extraordinary array of mummies and sarcophagi are among thousands of objects in one of the world's greatest collections.

3 Africa
The museum holds 350,000 objects from indigenous peoples around the world. The Africa gallery holds an interesting collection of sculpture, textiles and graphic art.

4 Asia
Buddhist limestone reliefs, Chinese porcelain, Islamic pottery and a Japanese collection that includes a Samurai suit of armour.

 Greece and Rome
There are several rooms covering the marvels of the Classical world (c 3000 BC to c AD 400). The sculptures that once decorated the outside of the Parthenon are a particular highlight.

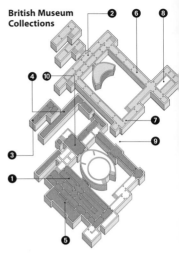

British Museum Collections

Ancient Greek vase

6 Prehistory and Europe
Covering a long period from prehistoric cave dwellers to the modern day, this collection includes Lindow Man, the body found preserved in a peat bog of a man who died some time between 2 BC and AD 119, and fine decorative arts, including medieval jewellery and Renaissance clocks.

7 Money
The exhibit traces the history of money over 4,000 years - from shell currency to digital payment methods.

8 Islamic World
This stunning display of objects ranges from West Africa to Southeast Asia covering the period from the 7th century to the present.

9 Enlightenment
This exhibition features the museum's 18th-century collections from around the world.

10 Life and Death
An imposing Easter Island carved head, Hoa Hakananai'a is the centrepiece of this themed display.

THE GREAT COURT

A magnificent glass-roofed addition encloses the heart of the British Museum. Opened in December 2000, the Great Court was designed by architect Sir Norman Foster. In the centre of the Court is the domed Reading Room, built in 1857. It once held one of the world's most important collections of books and manuscripts and was the workplace of some of London's greatest writers. It was used to host exhibitions from 2007 to 2013, after the Reading Room's collection was moved to a purpose-built building in St Pancras. Europe's largest covered public square, the Great Court has shops, cafés and the British Museum's main ticket and information desk.

The Reading Room, at the centre of the Great Court was designed by Sir Norman Foster.

The Great Court, at the centre of the museum, has a tesselated roof constructed out of 3,312 unique panes of glass. It surrounds the Reading Room.

TOP 10
LIBRARY READERS

1 Karl Marx
(1818–83), German revolutionary

2 Mahatma Gandhi
(1869–1948), Indian leader

3 Oscar Wilde
(1854–1900), playwright and wit

4 Virginia Woolf
(1882–1941), Bloomsbury novelist

5 W B Yeats
(1865–1939), Irish poet and playwright

6 Thomas Hardy
(1840–1928), English novelist

7 George Bernard Shaw
(1856–1950), Irish playwright

8 E M Forster
(1879–1970), English novelist

9 Rudyard Kipling
(1865–1936), Poet, novelist and chronicler of the British Empire

10 Leon Trotsky
(1879–1940), Russian revolutionary

TOP 10 ★ National Gallery

The National Gallery houses one of the world's greatest collections of European paintings. The collection was established in 1824, when a small group of paintings was gifted to the nation, and after rapid expansion it was moved to the present building in Trafalgar Square in 1838. The gallery is now home to over 2,300 paintings dating from the 13th to the 20th centuries. The Sainsbury Wing, built in 1991, showcases the gallery's outstanding collection of early Renaissance paintings and provides space for temporary blockbuster exhibitions.

1 The Virgin of the Rocks

This Renaissance masterpiece by Leonardo da Vinci (1452–1519) was originally painted as an altarpiece for a church in Milan. The Virgin and Child, with St John the Baptist and an angel, are depicted within a strange cavernous landscape.

2 The Arnolfini Portrait

One of the most famous paintings from the extensive Flemish collection is this unusual portrait of an Italian banker and his wife in Bruges. Jan van Eyck (c 1385–1441) brought oil painting to a new and colourful height.

3 The Ambassadors

Symbols, such as the foreshortened skull foretelling death, abound in this painting by Hans Holbein (1533).

4 The Wilton Diptych

A highlight of Gothic art, this exquisite English royal painting (right), by an unknown artist, shows Richard II being recommended to the Virgin by saints John the Baptist, Edward and Edmund.

5 The Rokeby Venus

Painted in Rome to replace a lost Venetian painting, *The Rokeby Venus* (right) is the only nude by Diego Velázquez (1599–1660), court painter to Spain's Philip IV. Venus, the goddess of love is depicted here with her son, Cupid, who holds a mirror up for her to see her reflection and that of the viewer.

6 A Young Woman Standing at a Virginal

Dutch painter Johannes Vermeer's (1632–75) works carry a sense of calm. Many of his interiors were painted in his home.

7 Samson and Delilah

This painting by Rubens (1577–1640) depicts the Old Testament legend and its theme of love and betrayal. Delilah caresses Samson while soldiers wait in the doorway to blind him.

8 The Sunflowers

Van Gogh (1853–90) painted this work **(right)** in Arles, France during a period of rare optimism while he was awaiting the arrival of his hero, the avant-garde painter Paul Gauguin.

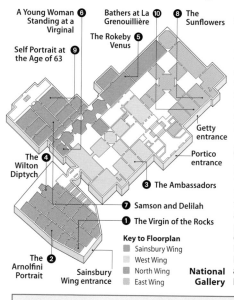

- 6 A Young Woman Standing at a Virginal
- 9 Self Portrait at the Age of 63
- 10 Bathers at La Grenouillière
- 8 The Sunflowers
- 5 The Rokeby Venus
- Getty entrance
- Portico entrance
- 4 The Wilton Diptych
- 3 The Ambassadors
- 7 Samson and Delilah
- 1 The Virgin of the Rocks
- 2 The Arnolfini Portrait
- Sainsbury Wing entrance

Key to Floorplan
- Sainsbury Wing
- West Wing
- North Wing
- East Wing

National Gallery

9 Self Portrait at the Age of 63

Rembrandt's (1606–69) self-portrait, created in the last year of his life, is among his most poignant works. He painted many self-portraits during his lifetime, and two of these are on display at the National Gallery.

10 Bathers at La Grenouillière

Claude Monet (1840–1926), the original Impressionist, explored the effect of light on water at La Grenouillière, a popular bathing spot on the Seine close to Bougival to the west of Paris, where he worked alongside fellow painter Pierre-Auguste Renoir.

NEED TO KNOW

MAP L4 ■ Trafalgar Sq WC2 ■ 020 7747 2885 ■ www.nationalgallery.org.uk

Open 10am–6pm daily (until 9pm Fri)

Adm for major temporary exhibitions

Free guided tours at 2pm Mon–Fri (1 hr; meet at the Sainsbury Wing entrance)

■ There is a café, an espresso bar and a good fine-dining restaurant, The National Dining Rooms.

■ The Sainsbury Wing has an excellent art bookshop.

■ Audio tours are available and trails can be downloaded from the museum's website.

■ Short talks are held at 1pm Mon, Wed and first Fri evening of every month.

Gallery Guide
The gallery is divided into four areas. The Sainsbury Wing contains the Early Renaissance collection. The West Wing displays works from 1500 to 1600, the North Wing 1600–1700, and the East Wing 1700 to early 1900s. Although the main entrance is on Trafalgar Square, the Sainsbury Wing makes a more sensible starting point.

🔟 ⭐ National Portrait Gallery

Founded in 1856 and unrelated to the neighbouring National Gallery, this museum showcases Britain's most famous and historically important figures through a series of portraits. There are some fascinating paintings from Tudor times through to the present day. Royalty is depicted, from Richard II (1367–1400) to Queen Elizabeth II, and the collection also holds a 1554 miniature, England's oldest self-portrait in oils. The gallery will be closed for major refurbishment until 2023, however the works from the collection will be on display at various galleries across the UK.

Queen Elizabeth I
This anonymous portrait **(right)** is one of several of Elizabeth I, who presided over England's Renaissance (1533–1603). The Tudor rooms feature portraits of central figures of the period, from courtiers to dramatists.

2 Prince Charles Edward Stuart
Known the world over as Bonnie Prince Charlie (1720–1788), this portrait was painted by Louis Gabriel Blanchett and was a splendid piece of propaganda for the Jacobite cause.

3 William Shakespeare
This is the only portrait **(below)** of the famous playwright known with certainty to have been painted during his lifetime (1564–1616).

4 The Whitehall Mural
The cartoon of Henry VIII and his father Henry VII by Hans Holbein (1537) was drawn for a large mural in the Palace of Whitehall. The mural was lost when the palace burnt down in 1698.

5 George Gordon Byron, 6th Baron Byron
Made in 1813, this oil painting of Lord Byron (1788–1824) by Richard Westall depicts the poet aged 25. He died while supporting Greek insurgents in their fight against the Ottoman Empire.

Key to Floorplan
- ■ Ground floor
- ■ First floor
- ■ Second floor

National Portrait Gallery

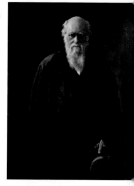

6 Horatio Nelson

The 1800 portrait by Sir William Beechey is considered to be a great likeness of the admiral, who died leading Britain to victory at the Battle of Trafalgar in 1805. Apart from Queen Victoria and the Duke of Wellington, Nelson was painted more than any other British figure in history.

7 Oliver Cromwell

Robert Walker's oil painting shows Oliver Cromwell (1599–1658) posing in armour. The portrait is believed to date from 1649 – the year Charles I, whose death warrant Cromwell signed, was executed. Cromwell went on to become the Lord Protector of Great Britain.

8 Queen Victoria

Painted by Aaron Edwin Penley (c 1840), this pretty watercolour miniature **(below)** shows the young queen near the beginning of her reign. Her early devotion to her husband, Prince Albert, whom she married in the year of this picture, is shown by the bust of him to her left. Prince Albert's image can frequently be found in portraits of Queen Victoria made before and after his death.

9 Charles Darwin

This portrait of the eminent scientist **(above)** was painted in 1883 by John Collier and completed a year before Darwin's death. It is a replica of a portrait at the Linnaean Society and was donated to the gallery by Darwin's eldest son.

10 Mary Seacole

Painted by Albert Charles Challen, this portrait is the only known oil painting of Mary Seacole, a Jamaican nurse who went to extraordinary lengths to care for the sick and wounded during the Crimean War.

NEED TO KNOW

MAP L3 ■ St Martin's Place WC2 ■ 020 7306 0055 ■ www.npg.org.uk

Closed until 2023

■ Works from collection will be displayed across galleries, including the National Gallery.

■ The Portrait Restaurant on the top floor has great views across Trafalgar Square to Parliament.

■ The bookshop stocks a range of fashion, history and biography titles.

■ The ground-floor gift shop has good postcards.

■ A range of talks take place at lunchtimes, and evening events known as Friday Lates take place every week from 6pm.

Gallery Guide
The three floors are arranged chronologically.

The second floor houses the Tudor and Stuart galleries (1–8). Men and women of industry, science and art from the 18th and early 19th centuries are in rooms 9 to 20. The first floor covers the Victorian period to the 20th century. The ground-floor galleries display contemporary portraiture and temporary exhibitions; closed for major redevelopment until 2023, check website for updates.

🔟 ⭐ Natural History Museum

There are some 80 million specimens in the Natural History Museum's fascinating collections. Originally the repository for items brought home by Charles Darwin and Captain Cook's botanist, Joseph Banks, among others, the museum combines traditional displays with innovative, hands-on exhibits. It remains one of London's most popular museums and has a number of attractions for kids, such as the impressive dinosaur collection and the life-sized model of a blue whale. A hot-house of research, it employs more than 300 scientists and librarians.

3 Treasures Gallery

Treasures is an apt title for this extraordinary collection, from a rare first edition of Darwin's *On the Origin of Species* to the dinosaur teeth that led to the discovery that giant reptiles once walked the Earth. The exhibits on display here **(right)** were chosen for their scientific and historical importance and are true movers and shakers of natural history.

4 Model Baby

A giant model of an unborn baby in the Human Biology galleries demonstrates sounds heard in the womb. Other hands-on exhibits test abilities and reactions and show how physical characteristics are inherited.

5 Images of Nature Gallery

This gallery showcases the museum's collection of historic and modern artworks, including prints from micro-CT scanners, watercolours and photographs. More than 110 exhibits span 350 years to the present day.

1 Fossils

Marine reptiles that existed at the time of the dinosaurs have survived as some remarkable fossils **(above)**, such as the pregnant female Ichthyosaur, found in a Dorset garden, which lived 187–178 million years ago.

Hintze Hall 2

After a major renovation in mid-2017, the museum's cathedral-like hall **(right)** replaced "Dippy", the Diplodocus skeleton cast, with a giant blue whale skeleton. In alcoves along the sides of the hall are other stars of the museum, including an American mastodon.

6 Spirit Collection

Get a fascinating glimpse of the museum's vast collection of zoological specimens preserved in spirit, including creatures collected by Charles Darwin.

7 Darwin Centre

One of the centre's many attractions is the eight-storey Cocoon, a permanent exhibition where visitors can see insect specimens as well as world-leading scientists at work.

8 Blue Whale

The Mammal gallery houses this fascinating exhibit, where both modern mammals and their fossil relatives are dwarfed in comparison to the astounding life-sized model of a blue whale, the largest mammal on the planet.

Key to Floorplan
- Ground floor
- First floor
- Second floor

9 Dinosaurs

T. Rex, one of the museum's life-like anim-atronic models, lurches and roars in this popular gallery. More traditional exhibits of fossilized skeletons are also on display. Taking pride of place in the Earth Hall is 6-m (19.5-ft) *Sophie*, **(above)** the most intact Stegosaurus fossilized skeleton ever found.

10 Attenborough Studio

On the ground floor of the Darwin Centre, the Attenborough Studio is a state-of-the-art audio-visual facility with 64 seats. The venue hosts events, films and talks covering all aspects of life on earth as well as scientific discovery.

Natural History Museum

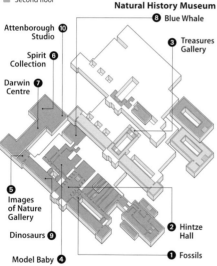

- **8** Blue Whale
- Attenborough **10** Studio
- Spirit **6** Collection
- Darwin **7** Centre
- **3** Treasures Gallery
- **5** Images of Nature Gallery
- Dinosaurs **9**
- **2** Hintze Hall
- Model Baby **4**
- **1** Fossils

NEED TO KNOW

MAP B5 ■ Cromwell Rd SW7 ■ 020 7942 5000 ■ www.nhm.ac.uk

Open 10am–5:50pm daily. Last admission 5:30pm

Closed 24–26 Dec

Adm for some special exhibitions

■ There is a restaurant in the green zone, and several cafés and snack bars.

■ A number of different self-guided trails are available, and you can visit the outdoor Wildlife Garden. Details at the Central Hall information desk.

Museum Guide

The Natural History Museum is divided into four zones: the blue zone, which includes the dinosaur gallery and Images of Nature; the green zone, with the ecology and creepy-crawlies galleries; the orange zone, with the Darwin Centre and a wild-life garden; and the red zone, incorporating the geological displays.

The Cromwell Road entrance leads to the Hintze Hall with its grand staircase.

An additional entrance on Exhibition Road leads to the red zone.

TOP 10 ⭐ Science Museum

Packed with hands-on exhibits, this museum explores the world of science through centuries of scientific and technological development. The collection showcases how Britain led the Industrial Revolution, with looms and steam engines, navigation and early flight. It also has displays on contemporary science, climate change, mathematics, space and cutting-edge technologies, with many interactive exhibits in the hi-tech Wellcome Wing.

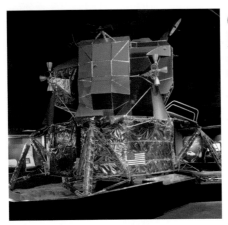

5 Apollo 10 Command Module

The Apollo 10 Command Module, which went around the moon in May 1969, is on display, as is a replica of the Apollo 11 Lunar Lander **(left)**. Buzz Aldrin and Neil Armstrong stepped onto the moon from the original in July 1969 and became the first humans to set foot on the lunar surface.

6 Wonderlab: The Equinor Gallery

With its 50 hands-on exhibits, this interactive gallery captivates 5- to 15-year-olds, to whom it primarily caters. From the friction slide to the magnetic sculpture, learning about science has never been so much fun.

1 Exploring Space

Rockets, satellites, space probes and landers can all be explored, and you can learn about Sputnik, the world's first satellite, how we sent spacecrafts to other planets and walked on the moon.

2 Information Age

The Queen opened this fascinating gallery with her first tweet in October 2014. It is divided into six themes and covers 200 years of communication and modern information technology from the earliest telegraph messages to the internet and mobile phones.

3 Medicine: The Wellcome Galleries

Five galleries hold one of the world's greatest medical collections. Highlights include stories from both patients and practitioners.

4 Puffing Billy

Puffing Billy **(below)** is the world's oldest remaining steam locomotive. It was built in England in 1813 and used to transport coal. George Stephenson's famous 1829 *Rocket*, the first locomotive engine to pull passenger carriages, is also on display.

7 Who Am I?

The continually updated Who Am I? gallery presents the latest in brain science and genetics through interactive exhibits and object-rich displays.

8 Fly Zone

This zone offers three kinds of flight simulators. With the virtual reality Space Descent, experience a journey from the International Space Station to Earth.

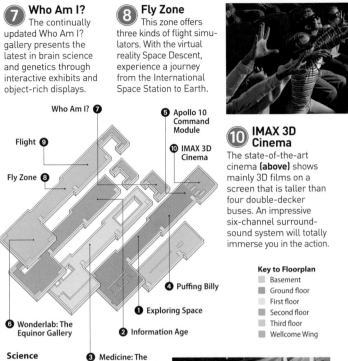

Who Am I? **7**

5 Apollo 10 Command Module

Flight **9**

10 IMAX 3D Cinema

Fly Zone **8**

10 IMAX 3D Cinema

The state-of-the-art cinema (above) shows mainly 3D films on a screen that is taller than four double-decker buses. An impressive six-channel surround-sound system will totally immerse you in the action.

4 Puffing Billy

1 Exploring Space

6 Wonderlab: The Equinor Gallery

2 Information Age

Science Museum

3 Medicine: The Wellcome Galleries

Key to Floorplan
- Basement
- Ground floor
- First floor
- Second floor
- Third floor
- Wellcome Wing

9 Flight

This gallery is filled with extraordinary aircraft reflecting both UK and international achievements in aviation. Highlights include Amy Johnson's *Gipsy Moth* and the *Vickers Vimy* (right), which first crossed the Atlantic in 1919.

NEED TO KNOW

MAP B5 ■ Exhibition Rd SW7 ■ 020 7942 4000 ■ www.science museum. org.uk

Open 10am–6pm daily (last entry 5:15pm)

Closed 24–26 Dec

Adm for special exhibitions, Wonderlab, simulator rides and IMAX cinema

■ There is a restaurant, several cafés and two picnic areas.

■ Printed maps with a guide provide details of exhibits.

■ The museum store is good for innovative gifts.

Museum Guide
The museum is spread over seven floors, however, the fourth and fifth floors are closed for renovation. Space exploration, steam engines and the IMAX cinema are on the ground floor. Information Age, Mathematics and London's connection to science are on the second floor. Flight and the interactive games and simulators can be found on the third floor along with Wonderlab.

⭐ Buckingham Palace

London's most famous residence, and one of its best recognized landmarks, Buckingham Palace was built as a townhouse for the first Duke of Buckingham around 1705. In 1825, George IV commissioned John Nash to extend the house into a substantial palace, and its first resident was Queen Victoria who moved in upon her accession to the throne in 1837. The palace is now home to the present Queen, though the State Rooms and the Palace Garden are open to the public during summer. Many royal parks and gardens in London are also accessible to the public.

1 The Balcony
On special occasions, the Queen and other members of the Royal Family step on to the palace balcony to wave to the crowds below.

2 Queen's Gallery
The gallery hosts a changing programme of exhibitions of the Royal Collection's master-pieces, including works by artists such as Johannes Vermeer and Leonardo da Vinci.

3 Changing the Guard
The Palace guards, in their red tunics and tall bearskin hats (below), are changed at 11am daily from May to July (and alternate days from August to April, weather permitting). The guards march to the palace from the Wellington Barracks.

Façade of Buckingham Palace

4 State Rooms
The Ambassadors' Entrance leads into the Grand Hall. From here the Grand Staircase, with gilded balustrades, rises to the first floor where the regal State Rooms are found.

5 Throne Room
This houses the thrones of Prince Philip and Queen Elizabeth used for the coronation. Designed by John Nash, the room has a highly ornamented ceiling and magnificent chandeliers.

6 Picture Gallery
One of the largest rooms in the palace it has a barrel-vaulted glass ceiling and a number of paintings from the Royal Collec-tion, including works by Rembrandt, Rubens and Van Dyck.

8 State Ballroom
Banquets for the visiting heads of state are held in this opulent ballroom **(left)**. The annual Diplomatic Reception hosted here, is attended by over 1,500 dignitaries from nearly 130 countries.

7 Brougham
Every day a horse-drawn Brougham carriage sets out to collect and deliver royal packages between Buckingham Palace and St James's Palace.

PALACE LIFE

The official business of the monarchy takes place in Buckingham Palace, which employs over 800 staff. Several members of the royal family have offices in the palace but due to ongoing restoration work, these have had to move to temporary premises. The work is due to finish in 2027. The most senior member of the Royal Household is the Lord Chamberlain. The Master of the Household and the Palace's domestic staff organize many functions every year, including Investitures for recipients of awards which are given by the Queen.

10 Royal Mews
The finest working stables in Britain care for horses that pull the royal coach on state occasions. The collection of coaches, motorcars and carriages includes the Gold State Coach, used at every coronation since 1821.

9 Palace Garden
The 16-ha (39-acre) Palace garden is an oasis for wildlife and includes a 1-ha (3-acre) lake. It can be visited on tours. There are at least three Royal garden parties each year, attended by over 30,000 people **(below)**.

NEED TO KNOW

MAP J6 ▪ Buckingham Palace SW1 ▪ 030 3123 7300 ▪ royalcollection.org.uk

Under 5s free; Combined tickets available

State Rooms: open end-Jul–Aug: 9:30am–7:30pm daily (last adm 5:15pm), Sep: to 6:30pm daily (last adm 4:15pm); Adm: adults £26.50, students & over 60s £24, under 17s £14.50; family £67.50

Royal Mews: open Apr–Oct: 10am–5pm daily (last adm 4:15pm), Feb, Mar & Nov: 10am–4pm daily (last adm 3:15pm); Adm: adults £13, students and over 60s £11.80, under 17s £7.50, family £33.50

Queen's Gallery: open 10am–5:30pm daily (last adm 4:15pm), end-Jul–Sep: 9:30am; Adm: adults £13.50, students £10.80, over 60s £12.20, under 17s £6.70, family £33.50

🔟 ⭐ London Eye

An amazing feat of engineering, the impressive cantilevered observation wheel offers fascinating views over the whole of London. Towering over the Thames opposite the Houses of Parliament, it was built to celebrate the millennium year, and has proved enormously popular. Its 32 enclosed capsules each hold up to 28 people and offer total visibility in all directions. A rotation on the London Eye takes 30 minutes and, on a clear day, you can see up to 40 km (25 miles) across the capital and the south of England.

2 Houses of Parliament

The London Eye rises high above the Houses of Parliament (see p36) on the far side of the Thames. From here you can look down on Big Ben (left) and see the Commons Terrace, where Members of Parliament and the House of Lords drink, dine and discuss policy by the river.

1 BT Tower

Built for the Post Office in 1961–4, this 190-m (620-ft) tower is now a TV, radio and tele-communications tower. It was given Grade II Listed Building status in 2003, meaning its defunct antennas needed special permission to be removed.

3 One Canada Square

With its distinctive pyramid roof, One Canada Square is located in the heart of Docklands which is the East London business and finance centre. It stands in the middle of the Isle of Dogs.

The London Eye, South Bank

5 Alexandra Palace

The BBC transmitted the world's first high-defini-tion public television broadcasting service from Alexandra Palace on 2 November 1936. There are exhibition halls and an ice rink here.

4 Wren Churches

The enormous dome of St Paul's Cathedral (left) stands out as the star of the City churches (see pp42–5). Pricking the sky around it are the spires of some of Wren's other churches, including St Bride's, which has a tiered design that has inspired wedding cakes, and Wren's favourite, St James's on Piccadilly.

6 Crystal Palace

This TV and radio transmission mast, to the south of the city, is near the site of the 1851 Great Exhibition "Crystal Palace." It was moved here from Hyde Park in 1852 and burned down spectacularly in 1936.

7 The Shard
Designed by Renzo Piano, this towering 306-m (1,004-ft) glass spire **(left)** rises from London Bridge station and gives the city skyline a new defining point. The 95-storey building houses offices, restaurants and a hotel. There is an observation deck on the 72nd floor.

MILLENNIUM LEGACY

The London Eye was one of a number of nationwide projects designed for the Millennium. The focus in London was on the enormous Millennium Dome, a spectacular structure that was built in Greenwich to house a national exhibition. Other projects included Tate Modern *(see pp28–9)* as well as the Millennium Bridge, the Waterloo Millennium Pier, the Great Court at the British Museum *(see pp12–15)* along with the inauguration of Somerset House *(see p105)*.

10 Heathrow
To the west of the city, London's main airport is one of the busiest international airports in the world. The Thames acts as a kind of runway, as planes line up overhead to begin their descent.

NEED TO KNOW

MAP N5 ■ South Bank SE1

■ www.londoneye.com

Open 10am–8:30pm daily (times vary seasonally, check website for detailed timings); closed 25 Dec and 2 weeks in Jan; ticket office opens 9:30am

Adm: adults £31, children £27.50, under 3s free; online tickets are cheaper

Timed tickets every 15 minutes

■ There are cafés in County Hall and on the South Bank.

■ Tickets are available on the day but advance booking is advisable to avoid standing in long queues.

8 Queen Elizabeth II Bridge
On a clear day you can just make out the lowest downstream crossing on the Thames, a huge suspension bridge at Dartford, some 32 km (20 miles) away. Traffic flows north in a tunnel under the river, south over the bridge.

9 Windsor Castle
Windsor Castle **(below)** sits by the Thames to the west of London. The largest occupied castle in the world, it is still a favourite residence of the royal family.

🔟 ⭐ Tate Modern

Looming over the southern bank of the Thames, Tate Modern is one of London's most exciting galleries and is housed in the former Bankside power station. In 2016, the Blavatnik Building was added to this site. The galleries provide an airy space for the collection of international modern art and installations, and includes works by Dalí, Picasso, Matisse, and Pollock, as well as work by many acclaimed contemporary artists. With an increased focus on the global art scene, the displays are changed frequently.

1 Three Dancers

Pablo Picasso (1881–1973) was noted for the different painting styles he mastered as he pushed the boundaries of Modern Art. The energetic, unsettling painting **(above)** *Three Dancers* (1925) followed the most serene stage of his work, and marked the beginning of a radical phase of distortion and emotional violence in his art.

2 Black on Maroon

Sombre and meditative, the *Black on Maroon* was painted in 1958 and later donated to the Tate. One of a series of large contemplative abstracts by the artist Mark Rothko (1903–70), it is a large unframed oil painting with different pigments of maroon.

3 Turbine Hall Installations

The power station's original and vast turbine hall is an iconic space used for large-scale as well as specially commissioned monumental art installations, which are very often interactive. With a new installation each year, the Turbine Hall has hosted some of the world's most acclaimed works and revolutionized public perceptions of 21st-century contemporary art.

4 Whaam!

Inspired by an image from *All American Men of War*, published by DC Comics in 1962, Roy Lichtenstein (1923–97) created *Whaam!* **(below)** in 1963. He was inspired by comics and advertisements, presenting powerful or emotive scenes in an impersonal and detached style.

The Tate Modern

5 Lobster Telephone

This iconic Surrealist work by Salvador Dalí (1904–1989) is made from steel, plaster, rubber, resin and paper. Created in 1936, this combination of objects with sexual overtones is one that Dalí returned to many times. For Dalí, such objects could reveal desires of the unconscious.

6 Fountain

One of the most iconic works of 20th-century art on display, Marcel Duchamp's much discussed *Fountain* is a urinal simply signed 'R. Mutt 1917'. This is a 1964 replica – the original, which consisted of a standard urinal, is lost. Made from glazed earthenware, it was painted to resemble the original porcelain. The ordinary object, presented largely unchanged but out of its usual context, is often used as an example to debate what constitutes a "work of art".

7 The Snail

This 1953 collage is one of Henri Matisse's (1869–1954) final works, completed while he was bedridden. The paper shapes represent a snail's shell.

10 Babel

The modern Tower of Babel (2001) is a creation of Brazilian artist, Cildo Meireles (b 1948). The immense pillar **(above)** of hundreds of radios produce a constant hum of noise as they all broadcast different frequencies. This installation is a part of Tate's themed exhibit Media Networks.

8 Top of the Tower

The fascinating Blavatnik Building's 360-degree viewing platform on level 10, offers breathtaking views of the city, across the river, including the grand St Paul's Cathedral and beyond. The restaurant on level 9 also offers similar views.

9 Composition B (No. II) with Red

The Dutch painter Piet Mondrian (1872–1914) gradually refined his art to a rigorous and pure abstract language of straight lines and squares of primary colours, an example of which is this painting, completed in 1935.

NEED TO KNOW

MAP R4 ▪ Bankside SE1 ▪ 020 7887 8888 ▪ www.tate.org.uk

Open 10am–6pm Sun–Thu, 10am–10pm Fri & Sat; closed 24–26 Dec

Adm for temporary exhibits

▪ Stores in both buildings have a wide selection of art and culture books.

▪ A Tate-to-Tate boat service from Bankside connects the Tate Modern with the Tate Britain (see p30)

Gallery Guide

There are seven levels in the Natalie Bell Building and eleven levels in the Blavatnik Building. The main entrance on Holland Street, leads to the Turbine Hall on level 0, where the information and ticket offices, main shop and temporary installations are located. The other points of entry – River Entrance and Blavatnik Building Entrance – are on level 1.

The Start Display on level 2 of the Natalie Bell Building is an introduction to the collection. Special exhibitions are displayed on levels 2, 3 and 4 of both buildings and in The Tanks on level 0 of the Blavatnik Building.

Level 6 of the Natalie Bell Building and level 9 of the Blavatnik Building have restaurants, whereas level 10 is a viewing platform.

TOP10 ⭐ Tate Britain

Opened in 1897 as the National Gallery of British Art, the magnificent collection at London's first Tate gallery ranges from 1500 to the present day. It was founded by the sugar merchant, Henry Tate (1819–99). The collection has works by major British painters and was greatly added to by J M W Turner, one of Britain's most revered artists. Paintings are often moved to Tate's other galleries, loaned out or removed for restoration. The works on these pages, therefore, may not always be on display.

1 Norham Castle, Sunrise

J M W Turner (1775–1851) was the great genius of English landscape painting. This 1845 work **(above)** typifies his use of abstraction and luminosity of colour.

2 Pelagos

The elm and string hollowed-out sculpture by Barbara Hepworth (1903–75), evokes a wave of the sea, and was ins- pired by the coast off St Ives, where she lived and also had her studio.

3 Sunset: Carthorses Drinking at a Stream

Thomas Gainsborough's (1727–88) family groups in landscapes are among the finest "conversation pieces" in English art. This is one of his several paintings on the theme of peasants travelling to and from the market.

4 Works by William Blake

Poet, mystic, illustrator and engraver William Blake (1757–1827) claimed to be guided by visions. Tate has a large collection of his works on paper, and some will always be displayed in- cluding *Elohim Creating Adam*, which illustrates the Book of Genesis.

5 Ophelia

Detailed and accurate observation of nature was a key element of the Victorian Pre-Raphaelite painters, as in this tragic scene from Shakespeare's *Hamlet* **(above)** by John Everett Millais (1829–96), painted in 1852.

6 Flatford Mill

Painted near his home in Dedham Vale, and depicting a mill on the Stour, this **(left)** is one of the first land- scapes that John Constable (1776–1837) painted outdoors rather than in his studio.

7 The Cholmondely Ladies

One of the earliest works on display that dates from the early 1600s, this is a painting by an unknown artist of two almost identical noble women and their babies. Despite the strong likeness, there are subtle differences.

9 Carnation, Lily, Lily, Rose

John Singer Sargent (1856–1925) moved to London from Paris in 1885 and adopted Impressionist techniques. The title of this 1886 work **(right)** was taken from a popular song of the time.

10 Three Studies for Figures at the Base of a Crucifixion

Leading light of the Soho arts scene, Francis Bacon (1910–1992) was uncompromising in his view of life. When first shown, this triptych **(below)** caused an immediate sensation, shocking audiences with its savage imagery. It is now among his best-known works.

8 Recumbent Figure

Henry Moore (1898–1986) was a sculptor whose work is on public display around London. This 1938 work became a recurrent theme of Moore's prolific output.

NEED TO KNOW

MAP E5 ■ Millbank SW1 ■ 020 7887 8888 ■ www.tate.org.uk

Open 10am–6pm daily; Closed 24–26 Dec

Adm for temporary exhibitions

Tate-to-Tate boat service between Tate Britain and Tate Modern every 40 minutes from Millbank Pier

■ The excellent Djanogly café is located on the lower floor.

■ Free guided tours daily, weekly talks and films shown monthly.

■ The Tate's art bookshop is very comprehensive.

Gallery Guide

The permanent collection occupies most of the Main Floor. Starting in the north-west corner, it follows a broad chronological sweep from the 16th century to the present. Alongside the permanent collection are a smaller number of regularly changing displays focusing on individual artists, movements or topics. The Turner Collection – about 300 oil paintings and about 20,000 watercolours by J M W Turner – is displayed in the adjoining Clore Gallery.

Following pages Changing the Guard in front of Buckingham Palace

🔟 ⭐ Westminster Abbey

A glorious example of Medieval architecture on a truly grand scale, this former Benedictine abbey church stands on the south side of Parliament Square. Founded in the 11th century by Edward the Confessor, it survived the Reformation and continued as a place of royal ceremonials. Queen Elizabeth II's coronation was held here in 1953 and Princess Diana's funeral in 1997. It was also the venue for the wedding of Prince William to Catherine Middleton in April 2011.

① St Edward's Chapel

The shrine of Edward the Confessor (1003–66), last of the Anglo-Saxon kings, lies at the heart of Westminster Abbey. He built London's first royal palace at Westminster.

② Coronation Chair

This chair was made in 1301 for Edward I. It is placed in front of the high-altar screen on the 13th-century mosaic pavement when used for coronations. Four gilt lions **(above)** were added in 1727 and form the chair's legs.

③ Nave

At 32 m (102 ft), this is among the tallest Gothic naves **(right)** in England and took 150 years to build. Designed by the great 14th-century architect Henry Yevele, it is supported externally by flying buttresses.

④ Poets' Corner

This corner of the transept contains memorials to literary giants, including Shakespeare and Dickens.

⑤ Lady Chapel

The spectacular fan vaulting **(below)** above the nave of this eastern addition to the church is late Perpendicular in style. Built for Henry VII (1457–1509), it includes two side aisles and five smaller chapels and is the home of the Order of the Bath (see p38).

⑥ Tomb of Elizabeth I

England's great Protestant queen (1553–1603) is buried in a huge marble tomb complete with recumbent effigy on one side of the Lady Chapel. The tomb of her Catholic rival and first cousin once removed, Mary Queen of Scots (beheaded in 1587), is on the other side of the chapel. Mary's remains were brought to the abbey by James I in 1612.

7 The Queen's Diamond Jubilee Galleries

These grand galleries in the Abbey's medieval triforium display treasures reflecting its history. The triforium offers arresting views to the Houses of Parliament and into the church. Access to the galleries is via the Weston Tower by a spiral staircase or lift.

ABBEY HISTORY

A Benedictine monastery was established by St Dunstan (AD 909–988) on what was the marshy Isle of Thorney. King Edward the Confessor re-endowed the monastery, and founded the present church in 1065. William the Conquerer was crowned here in 1066. Henry III's architect Henry of Reyns rebuilt much of the church in 1245. The nave was completed in 1376. The eastern end of the church was extended by Henry VII, who had the Lady Chapel built. Finally, in 1734–45, the twin towers on the west front were completed by Nicholas Hawksmoor.

8 Tomb of the Unknown Warrior

The body of an unknown soldier from the battlefields of World War I was buried here in 1920. His grave **(above)** represents all those of have lost their lives in war.

9 Chapter House

This octagonal building with a 13th-century tiled floor is one of the largest in England and is where the abbey's monks once gathered. The House of Commons met here between 1257 and 1542. Run by the abbey, it can also be reached via Dean's Yard.

10 Cloisters

The cloisters were located at the heart of the former Benedictine monastery and would have been the monastery's busiest area. On the east side are the only remaining parts of the Norman church, the Undercroft and the Pyx Chamber, where coinage was tested in medieval times.

Westminster Abbey

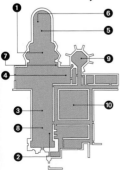

NEED TO KNOW

MAP L6 ■ 20 Dean's Yard SW1 ■ 020 7222 5152 ■ www.westminster-abbey.org ■ Guided tours (£7)

Adm: adults £22; concessions £17; children 6–16 £9; for family tickets see website; £5 (the Queen's Galleries)

Abbey: open 9:30am–3:30pm Mon–Fri, 4:30–6pm Wed, 9am–1pm Sat, Sun for worship only

Cloisters and Chapter House: open 9:30/10am–4:30pm Mon–Fri (until 4pm Sat; cloister: also 9:30am–4:30pm Sun)

■ Hear the choir sing at the 5pm Evensong service weekdays except Wednesday, 3pm on Saturdays and at Sunday services.

■ Listen to free organ recitals at 5:45pm every Sunday.

■ Stop for refreshment at the abbey's Cellarium Café and Terrace.

TOP 10 ★ Parliament Square

The spiritual and political heart of the city, the Palace of Westminster was built here a thousand years ago and has served as a royal household, seat of government and abbey. The square was planned as part of the rebuilding programme after a fire destroyed the palace in 1834. Usually known as the Houses of Parliament, the new Palace of Westminster stands opposite Westminster Abbey. On the north side of the square, Parliament Street leads to Whitehall and No.10 Downing Street.

1 Westminster Abbey
See pp34–5.

2 St Margaret's Church
Winston Churchill was among many eminent figures to marry in this 15th-century church **(below)**. William Caxton (c 1422–92), who set up the first printing press in England, and the writer and explorer, Sir Walter Raleigh, are both buried here. Charles I is also remembered.

3 Big Ben
The huge Elizabeth Tower of the Palace of Westminster is known as Big Ben **(left)**. The name refers to the clock's 13.5-tonne bell, thought to be named after Sir Benjamin Hall, Chief Commissioner of Works in 1858. It will only chime on special occasions until 2021.

4 Houses of Parliament
A Gothic Revival building by Sir Charles Barry and Augustus Welby Pugin, built between 1840 and 1870, the Houses of Parliament **(right)** cover 8 acres and have 1,100 rooms around 11 court-yards. The Commons chamber is where the elected MPs sit, while the Lords chamber is where the unelected MPs sit.

5 Westminster Hall
This lofty hall is all is about all of the original palace that remained after the 1834 fire. For centuries the courts of law sat beneath its grand 14th-century hammerbeam roof.

6 Central Hall
This large assembly hall, built in Viennese Baroque style, was funded by a collection among the Methodist Church to celebrate the centenary of their founder John Wesley (1703–91).

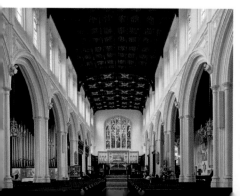

7 Jewel Tower

Built in 1365 to safeguard the treasure of Edward III, this **(left)** is an isolated survivor of the 1834 fire. A museum about the history of the tower is housed inside.

8 Winston Churchill Statue

This statue of the UK's wartime leader (1874–1965) is one of several in the square, including prime minister Benjamin Disraeli (1804–81) and Nelson Mandela (1918–2013).

PARLIAMENT

The 650 elected Members of Parliament sit in the House of Commons, where the Prime Minister and his or her government sits on the right-hand side of the Speaker, who ensures the House's rules are obeyed. The opposing "shadow" government sits on his left. The House of Lords seats around 800 members (most appointed by the government) who have limited powers. The Prime Minister attends a weekly audience with the Queen, who today has largely a symbolic role.

10 Dean's Yard

Buildings around this square were used by monks and included their school before Dissolution of the Monasteries in the 1530s. A new Westminster School was founded by Elizabeth I in 1560 and it is still one of the country's top public schools.

NEED TO KNOW

MAP M6 ■ Parliament Sq SW1
■ www.parliament.uk

Tours can be arranged through MPs at www.parliament.uk

■ Tickets for audio tours on Saturdays and during recess are available online, call 020 7219 4114, or book at the ticket office at Victoria Embankment (£19.50)

■ The Public Galleries at the Houses of Parliament have limited seating for visitors during debates. Check times online or call 020 7219 4272.

■ The basement café in Central Hall is a good place for a snack.

■ Big Ben is undergoing restoration, expected to be completed in 2021.

Parliament Square

9 Statue of Oliver Cromwell

Oliver Cromwell (1599–1658) presided over England's only republic, which began after the Civil War. He was buried in Westminster Abbey, but after the monarchy was restored in 1660, his corpse was taken to Tyburn and hanged as a criminal.

🔟 ⭐ Tower of London

London's great riverside fortress is usually remembered as a place of imprisonment, but it has a much more varied past. Originally a moated fort, the White Tower was built for William I (the Conqueror) and begun around 1078. It became home to the city arsenal, the Crown Jewels, a menagerie and the Royal Mint – and was enlarged by later monarchs, including Henry VIII, who sent two of his wives to their deaths on Tower Green.

3 The White Tower

The heart of the fortress is a sturdy keep, 30 m (90 ft) tall with walls 5 m (15 ft) thick. Constructed under William I, it was completed in 1097, and is the Tower's oldest surviving building. In 1240 it was whitewashed inside and out, hence its name.

4 Imperial State Crown

This is the most dazzling of a dozen crowns in the Jewel House. It contains 2,868 diamonds, and the sapphire at its top is from the reign of Edward the Confessor (r 1042–66). The crown was made for the coronation of George VI in 1937.

1 Yeoman Warders

The Tower's 37 Yeoman Warders **(above)** now include female Warders. They are former military officers with long service and good conduct medals. They organize guided tours of the Tower that is included in the ticket.

The Tower of London

5 Chapel of St John the Evangelist

The finest Norman place of worship in London **(left)**, which remains much as it was when it was built, is on the upper floor of the White Tower. In 1399, in preparation for Henry IV's coronation procession, 40 noble knights held vigil here. They then took a purifying bath in an adjoining room and Henry made them the first Knights of the Order of the Bath. It is still used as a royal chapel today.

2 The Bloody Tower

The displays here explore the dark history of the Bloody Tower where murderous deeds, including the alleged killing of the little princes, took place.

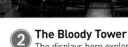

6 Ravens

The saying goes that when ravens leave the Tower the building and the monarchy will fall. There are seven ravens in residence, looked after by the Ravenmaster.

Tower of London

9 The Line of Kings

Drawn from the Royal Armouries' collection, this exhibition showcases the arms and armours of centuries of monarchs, displayed on and alongside sculpted horses.

NEED TO KNOW

MAP H4 ■ Tower Hill EC3 ■ www.hrp.org.uk

Open Mar–Oct: 9am–5:30pm Tue–Sat, 10am–5:30pm Sun & Mon; Nov–Feb: 9am–4:30pm Tue–Sat, 10am–4:30pm Sun & Mon (last adm: 30 min before closing); closed 24–26 Dec

Adm: adults £27.50; children 5–15 £13.10 (under 5s free); family (1 adult, 3 children) £44, (2 adults; 3 children) £76.90

■ You can buy cheaper advance tickets online.

7 Traitors' Gate

The oak and iron water gate in the outer wall **(right)** was used to bring many prisoners to the Tower, and became known as Traitors' Gate.

8 Beauchamp Tower

The walls here are engraved with graffiti made by real prisoners of the Tower, including Lady Jane Grey. The tower takes its name from Thomas Beauchamp, Earl of Warwick, who was imprisoned here between 1397–9 by Richard II.

10 Tower Green

The place of execution for nobility, including Lady Jane Grey (1554) and two of Henry VIII's wives – Anne Boleyn (1536) and Katherine Howard (1542).

Tower Prisoners

1 Bishop of Durham
The first political prisoner to be held in the White Tower was Ralph de Flambard, Bishop of Durham. Locked up by Henry I in 1100, he was seen as responsible for the unpopular policies of Henry's predecessor, William II.

2 Henry VI
During the Wars of the Roses, between the rival families of York and Lancaster, Henry VI was kept in Wakefield Tower for five years, until restored to power in 1470.

3 The Little Princes
The alleged murder of Edward, 12, and Richard, 10, in 1483, gave the Bloody Tower its name. It is thought their uncle, Richard III, was responsible.

4 Sir Thomas More
Chancellor Thomas More's refusal to approve Henry VIII's marriage to Anne Boleyn led to his imprisonment in the lower Bell Tower. He was beheaded in 1535.

Sir Thomas More

5 Henry VIII's Wives
Some of the Tower's most famous victims, such as the

Anne Boleyn

beheaded wives of Henry VIII, Anne Boleyn and Katherine Howard, are buried in the Chapel Royal of St Peter ad Vincula.

6 Lady Jane Grey
In 1554 Lady Jane Grey was queen for just nine days. Aged 16, she was held in the gaoler's house on Tower Green and later executed by order of Queen Mary I.

7 Catholic Martyrs
Under the reign of Elizabeth I (1558–1603), many Catholics were executed. Most, including Jesuits, were held in the Salt Tower.

8 John Gerard
Jesuit priest Gerard escaped from the Cradle Tower with a fellow prisoner in 1597, using a rope strung over the moat by an accomplice.

9 Guy Fawkes
The most famous of the Catholic conspirators, Guy Fawkes tried to blow up King James I and Parliament in 1605. He is burned in effigy each year on 5 November.

10 Rudolf Hess
The Tower's last prisoner was Hitler's deputy. He was held in the Queen's House in 1941, after flying to the UK to ask for peace.

Sites of Imprisonment

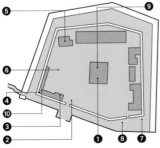

THE CROWN JEWELS

The lavish, bejewelled items that make up the sovereign's ceremonial regalia are all in the care of the Tower of London. The collection dates from 1661 when a new set was made to replace those destroyed by Cromwell following the execution of Charles I in 1649. St Edward's Crown was the first subsequent crown to be made of pure gold, and is the oldest of the 10 crowns here. Other coronation jewels on display include a gold, jewel-studded orb, made in 1661,

and a sceptre containing the 530-carat Cullinan 1, the biggest cut diamond in the world. The Sovereign's Ring, made for William IV, is sometimes called "the wedding ring of England".

**TOP 10
JEWELS**

1 Imperial State Crown
2 St Edward's Crown
3 Imperial Crown of India
4 Queen Victoria's Crown
5 Royal Sceptre
6 Jewelled State Sword
7 George V's Crown
8 The Sovereign's Ring
9 The Sovereign's Orb
10 The Sovereign's Sceptre

The Imperial State Crown is heavily encrusted with 2,868 diamonds, 17 sapphires, 11 emeralds, 4 rubies and 269 pearls. It was designed for the coronation of George VI in 1937.

Queen Elizabeth II wore the Imperial State Crown at her coronation on 2 June 1953.

TOP 10 ⭐ St Paul's Cathedral

This is the great masterpiece of Christopher Wren, who rebuilt the City's churches after the Great Fire of 1666. Completed in 1711, it was England's first purpose-built Protestant cathedral, but the exterior design shares similarities with St Peter's in Rome, most notably its ornate dome. One of its bells, Great Paul, was the largest in Europe until the bell cast for the 2012 Olympics. The hour bell, Great Tom, strikes the hour and marks the death of royalty and senior church officials. The cathedral is renowned for its music and draws its choristers from St Paul's Cathedral School.

3 Dome
One of the largest domes in the world **(left)**, it is 111 m (365 ft) high and weighs 65,000 tonnes. The Golden Gallery at the top, and the larger Stone Gallery, both have great views.

Whispering Gallery **4**
Inside the dome is the famous Whispering Gallery **(right)**. Words whispered against the wall can be heard on the gallery's opposite side.

1 Quire
The beautiful stalls and organ case in the Quire are by Grinling Gibbons. Handel and Mendelssohn both played the organ, which dates from 1695.

5 St Paul's Watch Memorial
Set in the nave, this memorial honours those who saved St Paul's from destruction during the Blitz by fighting fires started by bombs dropped on and near it.

2 The Light of the World
This painting by the Pre-Raphaelite artist William Holman Hunt shows Christ knocking on an overgrown door that opens from inside, meaning that God can enter our lives only if we invite Him in.

6 West Front and Towers
The imposing West Front **(right)** is dominated by two huge towers. The pineapples at their tops are symbols of peace and prosperity. The Great West Door is 9 m (29 ft) high and is used only for ceremonial occasions.

High Altar 7

The magnificent High Altar **(right)** is made from Italian marble, and the canopy, constructed in the 1950s after the cathedral was bombed during World War II, is based on one of Wren's sketches.

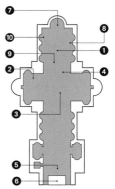

Tijou Gates 8

The French master metal worker Jean Tijou designed these ornate wrought-iron gates in the South and North Quire, along with the Whispering Gallery balcony and other cathedral metalwork.

Mosaics 9

Colourful mosaic ceilings were installed in the Ambulatory and Quire in the 19th century. They are made with glass tesserae, angled so that they sparkle.

Moore's Mother and Child 10

This piece is one of a growing number of works of art that have been introduced into St Paul's since the 1960s. The sculptor, Henry Moore, is commemorated in the crypt.

ST PAUL'S HISTORY

The first known church dedicated to St Paul was built on this site in AD 604. Made of wood, it burned down in 675 and a subsequent church was destroyed by Viking invaders in 962. The third church was built in stone. Following another fire in 1087, it was rebuilt under the Normans as a much larger cathedral, with stone walls and a wooden roof. This was completed in 1300. In 1666 Sir Christopher Wren's plans to restore the building had just been accepted when the Great Fire of London burned the old cathedral beyond repair.

St Paul's Cathedral

NEED TO KNOW

MAP R2 ■ Ludgate Hill EC4 ■ 020 7246 8350 ■ www.stpauls.co.uk

Adm: adults £20; children 6–17 £8.50 (under 6s free); students & over 60s £17.50; family £48.50; for group adm and discounts, check website. Services are free.

Cathedral: open 8:30am–4:30pm Mon–Sat

Galleries: open 9:30am–4:15pm Mon–Sat

■ **Guided tours usually take place at 10am, 11am, 1pm, 2pm and are included in the admission. Reserve a place at the guiding desk.**

■ There is a charming tearoom in the crypt.

■ You can hear the choir during the very popular choral evensong service (usually at 5pm daily).

■ Multimedia guides are also available and included in the price of admission.

St Paul's Monuments

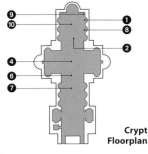

Crypt Floorplan

1 Tomb of Christopher Wren

St Paul's architect, Christopher Wren's (1632–1723), tomb inscription reads, *"Lector, si monumentum requiris, circumspice"* – "Reader, if you seek a monument, look around you".

2 Wellington's Tomb

The UK's great military leader and prime minister, Arthur Wellesley, 1st Duke of Wellington (1769–1852), lies in the crypt. He also has a monument in the nave.

3 John Donne's Memorial

The metaphysical poet John Donne (1572–1631) was made Dean of St Paul's in 1621. His memorial is in the Dean's Aisle in the Ambulatory on the cathedral floor.

4 Nelson's Tomb

Preserved in brandy and brought home from Trafalgar, sea hero Admiral Lord Nelson's (1758–1805) black sacrophagus is in the centre of the crypt.

5 American Memorial

Behind the High Altar on the cathedral floor, the American Memorial Chapel's roll of honour lists the US servicemen killed while stationed in the UK in World War II.

Detail, American roll of honour

6 Gallipoli Memorial

This memorial is dedicated to those who died in the 1915 Gallipoli campaign of World War I.

7 Churchill Memorial Gates

These gates commemorate Sir Winston Churchill (1874–1965), who during the 1940–41 Blitz said "at all costs, St Paul's must be saved".

8 The Worshipful Company of Masons Memorial

This City guild's plaque near Wren's tomb reads, "Remember the men who made shapely the stones of Saint Paul's Cathedral".

9 Turner's Tomb

The great painter J M W Turner is buried in the OBE chapel.

10 OBE Chapel

At the eastern end of the crypt is a chapel devoted to those appointed to the Order of the British Empire, an honour established in 1917, and the first to include women.

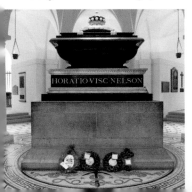

Nelson's Tomb, St Paul's Cathedral

ST PAUL'S ROLE IN HISTORY

St Paul's, as the Cathedral for the Diocese of London, belongs to the parishes all across London, as well as to the nation. It is run by a Dean and Chapter of priests. One of the cathedral's main functions is as a place of national mourning and celebration. In the 19th century, 13,000 people filled the cathedral for the funeral of the Duke of Wellington. Queen Victoria's Jubilee was a spectacular occasion held on the steps of the cathedral. The Prince of Wales and Lady Diana Spencer chose to be married at St Paul's rather than the royal Westminster Abbey. The decision helped to portray the couple as the people's prince and princess.

TOP 10
MOMENTS IN ST PAUL'S HISTORY

1 Elizabeth II's Diamond Jubilee (2012)

2 Prince Charles' and Lady Diana's wedding (1981)

3 Winston Churchill's funeral (1965)

4 Martin Luther King Jr preaches (1964)

5 Cathedral bombed (1940)

6 Queen Victoria's Diamond Jubilee (1897)

7 Duke of Wellington's funeral (1852)

8 Nelson's funeral (1806)

9 First service (1697)

10 Gunpowder Plotters executed in the churchyard (1606)

The wedding of Prince Charles and Lady Diana Spencer, 1981

The Duke of Wellington's funeral at St Paul's Cathedral

The Top 10 of Everything

**The Lady Chapel,
Westminster Cathedral**

🔟 Moments in History

Painting depicting Charles I being taken for his execution

1 **AD 43: Roman Invasion**
The Romans built a bridge across the Thames from Southwark and encircled Londinium with a wall, fragments of which are still visible in the City *(see pp140–45)*. Their forum was near Cornhill and their amphitheatre lies beneath the Guildhall.

2 **1066: Norman Conquest**
The next successful invasion of England came from northern France. It was led by William the Conqueror, Duke of Normandy, who was crowned King of England in the newly completed Westminster Abbey *(see pp34–5)* on Christmas Day 1066.

3 **1240: First Parliament**
The first parliament sat in Westminster and became a seat of government separate from the mercantile City, which continued to expand on the former Roman site.

4 **1534: The Reformation**
A quarrel between Henry VIII and Pope Clement VII over the king's divorce led to Henry breaking with Rome and declaring himself head of the church in England. Today, the sovereign remains the head of the Church of England.

5 **1649: Charles I Executed**
Charles I's belief in the divine right of kings led to civil war. The royalist cause was lost and the king was beheaded in 1649. After 11 years of the Commonwealth, his son Charles II returned to the throne to preside over the Restoration.

6 **1666: Great Fire of London**
Much of the city, including the medieval St Paul's Cathedral *(see pp42–5)* and 87 parish churches, were destroyed in the fire, which raged for nearly five days. Afterwards, Sir Christopher Wren replanned the entire city, including the cathedral.

7 **1863: First Underground**
The Metropolitan Line was the world's first underground railway, operating between Paddington and

Baker Street underground station

Farringdon Street. Carriages were pulled by steam locomotives until the start of the 20th century.

8 1940–41: The Blitz

Between September 1940 and May 1941, German air raids left 30,000 Londoners dead. The bombers destroyed much of the docks, the East End and the City. The House of Commons, Westminster Abbey and the Tower of London were all hit. Many Londoners sought shelter in Underground stations at night.

An air warden watching for bombers

9 2012: Olympic Games

The Olympic and Paralympic Games were held in London in 2012, with many of the city's iconic landmarks including Horse Guards Parade playing host to sporting events. Part of Stratford was transformed into a world-class Olympic Park, with a magnificent stadium and velodrome, and a spectacular aquatic centre with a wave-shaped roof.

10 2016–2021: Brexit

In a critical referendum in June 2016, Londoners vote to remain in EU, however, the country as a whole supports the leave campaign. On 31 January 2020, after more than three years of divisive debate and with the terms of departure being agreed upon, the UK enters a year-long transition period negotiating its future relationship with the EU.

TOP 10 CULTURAL HIGHLIGHTS

The Great Exhibition of 1851

1 Shakespeare Arrives
The first mention of William Shakespeare (1564–1616) as a London dramatist was recorded in 1595.

2 Van Dyck Knighted
The Flemish artist Anthony Van Dyck was knighted by Charles I in 1632 for his service as the king's principal royal portrait painter.

3 Purcell's Appointment
The greatest English composer of his time, Henry Purcell was appointed organist at Westminster Abbey in 1679.

4 Handel's Water Music
George Friedrich Handel composed *Water Music* for a performance on King George I's royal barge in 1717.

5 Great Exhibition
In 1851, the expanding Empire was celebrated in an exhibition held in a massive glass structure in Hyde Park.

6 J M W Turner Bequest
Turner's paintings *(see pp30–31)* were left to the nation on condition that they be displayed together.

7 Royal Opera Highlight
In 1892 Gustav Mahler conducted the first UK performance of Wagner's *Ring* at the Royal Opera House.

8 First Radio Broadcast
The BBC made its first broadcast on New Year's Day in 1922.

9 Festival of Britain
In 1951, the Festival of Britain was held at the South Bank to mark the centenary of the Great Exhibition.

10 Royal National Theatre
The National Theatre company was founded in 1963 and temporarily housed at the Old Vic in Waterloo under Laurence Olivier (later Lord Olivier).

TOP 10 Churches

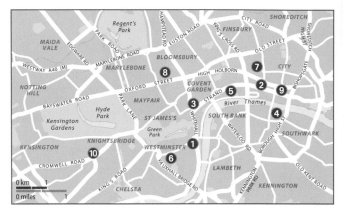

1 Westminster Abbey
See pp34–5.

2 St Paul's Cathedral
See pp42–5.

3 St Martin-in-the-Fields
MAP L4 ■ Trafalgar Sq WC2
■ Open 8:30am–6pm Mon–Fri, 9am–6pm Sat & Sun ■ www.stmartin-in-the-fields.org
Buckingham Palace's parish church is famous for its music. There's been a church on the site since the 13th century, and the present building was designed by James Gibbs in 1726. The crypt café is award-winning.

St Martin-in-the-Fields

4 Southwark Cathedral
MAP G4 ■ London Bridge SE1 ■ Open 9am–5pm Mon–Fri, 9:30am–3:45pm & 5–6pm Sat, 12:30–3pm & 4–6pm Sun ■ www.cathedral.southwark.anglican.org
This priory church became a cathedral in 1905. It has many connections with local Elizabethan theatres, and with Shakespeare, who is commemorated in a memorial and a stained-glass window. US college founder John Harvard was baptised here and is remembered in the Harvard Chapel.

5 Temple Church
MAP P2 ■ Inner Temple Lane EC4 ■ Check website for opening times ■ Adm ■ www.templechurch.com
This circular church was built in the 12th century for the Knights Templar. Effigies of the knights are embedded in the floor. A chancel was added in the 13th century. The church has been maintained by the Inns of Court since 1608, and was rebuilt after wartime bomb damage in 1958.

6 Westminster Cathedral
MAP E5 ■ 42 Francis St SW1 ■ Cathedral: open 7am–7pm Mon–Fri, 7:30am–8pm Sat & Sun ■ Tower: open 9:30am–5pm Mon–Fri (until 6pm Sat & Sun); adm ■ www.westminstercathedral.org.uk
The main Roman Catholic church in England, Westminster Cathedral was designed in Byzantine Revival style by John Francis Bentley and completed in 1903. Intricate mosaics and over 100 varieties of marble decorate the interior, while the exterior features horizontal bands of white stone across red brickwork. Take the lift to the top of the tower for spectacular views.

Inside St Bartholomew-the-Great

7 St Bartholomew-the-Great

A survivor of the Great Fire, this is London's only Norman church apart from St John's Chapel in the Tower of London. It was founded in 1123 by the monk Rahere, a courtier of Henry I, and its solid pillars and Norman quire have remained unaltered since. The 14th-century Lady Chapel, restored by Sir Aston Webb in 1890, once housed a printing press where US statesman Benjamin Franklin worked. The church *(see p144)* has also featured in films, including *Four Weddings and a Funeral* and *Shakespeare in Love*.

8 All Saints Margaret Street

MAP J1 ▪ 7 Margaret St W1 ▪ Open 7am–7pm daily (from 8:30am Wed & 11am Sat) ▪ www.asms.uk

Reredos detail, All Saints Margaret Street

Designed by William Butterfield and completed in 1859, this is a fine example of High Victorian Gothic architecture, with a patterned brick exterior and an interior decorated with inlaid marble, mosaics and stained glass.

9 St Stephen Walbrook

MAP G3 ▪ 39 Walbrook EC4 ▪ Open 10am–4pm Mon, Tue & Thu, 11am–3pm Wed, 10am–3:30pm Fri ▪ www.ststephenwalbrook.net

Unspectacular on the outside, the interior of St Stephen Walbrook is the best-preserved and most beautiful of all Wren's churches – it was his own parish church. Designed at the same time as St Paul's Cathedral, the space is dominated by its deep, coffered dome with ornate plasterwork, which is raised above a set of twelve Corinthian columns. A simple, white modern altar by Henry Moore sits in the centre of the church.

10 Brompton Oratory

MAP C5 ▪ Brompton Rd SW7 ▪ Open 6:30am–8pm daily ▪ www.bromptonoratory.co.uk

Renowned for its rich musical tradition, this Italianate church was established by a Catholic convert, Henry Newman (1801–90). He introduced to England St Philip's Oratory, a community of Catholic priests and lay brothers founded in 16th-century Rome. The building, by Herbert Gribble, opened in 1884, and houses many Italian treasures.

Rich interior of Brompton Oratory

Royal London

Main entrance to Hampton Court

Hampton Court

The finest piece of Tudor architecture in Britain, Hampton Court *(see p153)* was given to Henry VIII by the king's ally Cardinal Wolsey. It was enlarged by Henry and then later rebuilt by William and Mary, who employed Christopher Wren as architect. Its many rooms include a huge kitchen, the Cumberland Art Gallery, the Chapel Royal and royal apartments. The stunning gardens, with their famous maze, are as much an attraction as the palace.

2 Buckingham Palace
(see pp24–5).

3 Kensington Palace

An intimate royal palace in Kensington Gardens, famous as the home of Princess Diana, its first sovereign residents were William and Mary in 1689, and Queen Victoria was born here in 1819. The interior has displays of regal fashion and focuses on the lives of past residents including William and Mary, Victoria and Diana *(see p125)*. The Kensington Place Pavillion is delightful for tea.

4 St James's Palace

Although closed to the public, St James's Palace *(see p119)* has a key role in royal London. Its classic Tudor style sets it in the reign of Henry VIII, and while it has had many royal residents, every monarch since Victoria has lived at Buckingham Palace.

5 Kew Palace and Queen Charlotte's Cottage

Kew, Surrey TW9 ■ Palace: open Apr–Sep: 10:30am–5:30pm daily; Cottage: open Apr–Sep: 11am–4pm Sat, Sun & public hols ■ Adm ■ www.hrp.org.uk

The smallest royal palace, Kew was built in 1631 and was a residence of George III and Queen Charlotte. Queen Charlotte's Cottage *(see p153)* was used for picnics and housing pets. The palace is in Kew Gardens.

6 Banqueting House

MAP L4 ■ Whitehall SW1 ■ Open 10am–5pm daily ■ Adm ■ www.hrp.org.uk

Built by Inigo Jones, this magnificent building is particularly noted for its

Formal garden, Kensington Palace

Rubens ceiling. It was commissioned by Charles I, who stepped from the Banqueting House onto the scaffold for his execution in 1649.

7 Queen's House
Romney Rd SE10 ■ Train to Greenwich; DLR Cutty Sark, Greenwich ■ Open 10am–5pm daily ■ www.rmg.co.uk

This delightful home in the middle of Greenwich Park was the first Palladian building by Inigo Jones, and once home to the wife of Charles I. Restored to its 17th-century glory, it houses the National Maritime Museum's *(see p56)* art collection.

Queen's House, Greenwich

8 Royal Mews
(see p25).

9 Queen's Chapel
MAP K5 ■ Marlborough Rd SW1

This royal chapel is open only to its congregation (visitors welcome as worshippers). Built by Inigo Jones and operational from 1626, its furnishings include a beautiful altarpiece by Annibale Carracci.

10 Clarence House
MAP K5 ■ St James's Palace SW1 ■ Tours: check website for hours ■ Adm ■ www.rct.uk

Designed by John Nash for the Duke of Clarence, William IV, who lived here after becoming king in 1830. It was home to the Queen Mother until her death in 2002, and since to the Prince of Wales and Duchess of Cornwall.

TOP 10 ROYAL MONUMENTS AND MEMORIALS

Albert Memorial, Kensington

1 Albert Memorial
Prince Albert, beloved consort of Queen Victoria, has a splendid memorial *(see p125)* in Kensington Gardens.

2 Queen Anne's Gate
A delightful small Westminster street with a statue of the queen who gave her name to a style of furniture.

3 Queen Elizabeth I's Statue at St Dunstan-in-the-West
Originally located at Ludgate, this is one of the only statues to have been sculpted during Elizabeth's reign.

4 Duke of York Steps
A statue of the "Grand Old Duke of York", subject of the nursery rhyme, is elevated above these steps off Pall Mall.

5 Queen Victoria Statue at Blackfriars
This regal statue at the northern end of Blackfriars Bridge shows a middle-aged Victoria holding her sceptre and orb.

6 Queen Elizabeth II's Birthplace Plaque
At 17 Bruton Street in Mayfair, a simple plaque marks the Queen's birthplace.

7 George VI and Queen Elizabeth Memorial
A statue of the Queen Mother was positioned next to that of her husband, George VI, on the Mall in 2009.

8 Charles I Statue, Whitehall
Over the road from Trafalgar Square is a mounted Charles I.

9 The Henry VIII Gate at St Barts
The only outdoor statue of Henry VIII in London is in St Bartholomew's Hospital.

10 Princess Diana Memorial Fountain
This popular man-made stream in Kensington Palace opened in 2004.

TOP 10 Parks and Gardens

Tazza Fountain in the Italian Gardens, Kensington Gardens

1 Kensington Gardens
MAP B4 ▪ W8 ▪ Open 6am–dusk daily ▪ www.royalparks.org.uk

A succession of queens living in Kensington Palace between 1689 and 1837 appropriated parts of Hyde Park for their palace gardens. Since opening in 2000, the Diana, Princess of Wales Memorial Playground has proved a great hit with children. The park is also home to the Serpentine Galleries *(see p59)*.

2 St James's Park
London's oldest and most elegant park *(see p119)* was redesigned by John Nash in 1828. Its lake is home to some 15 varieties of waterfowl. It has an attractive restaurant and, in summer, lunchtime concerts are given at a bandstand.

3 Hyde Park
MAP C4 ▪ W2 ▪ Open 5am–midnight daily ▪ www.royalparks.org.uk

One of the most popular features of this huge London park is its lake, the Serpentine, with boats for hire and a swimming area. Horses can be rented and ridden in the park. On Sunday mornings at Speakers' Corner, near Marble Arch, you can get up on a soapbox and address the crowds who gather there.

4 Green Park
MAP D4 ▪ SW1 ▪ Open all day, year-round ▪ www.royalparks.org.uk

Originally called Upper St James's Park, it was enclosed by Charles II in 1668 to create a link between Hyde Park and St James's Park. There are deckchairs for hire in summer.

5 Regent's Park
Home to London Zoo, an open-air theatre and a boating lake, Regent's Park *(see p135)* is surrounded by John Nash's Classical terraces. The fragrant Queen Mary's Garden is a delight.

The bandstand at Regent's Park

6 Richmond Park

Kingston Vale TW10 ■ **Open 7am–dusk daily (winter: from 7:30am)** ■ **www.royalparks.org.uk**

Covering an area of 10 sq km (4 sq miles), this is by far the largest Royal Park. Herds of red and fallow

Fallow deer, Richmond Park

deer roam freely across the heath. In late spring, the Isabella Plantation is a blaze of colourful azaleas, camellias and rhododendrons, plus many rare shrubs. The Royal Ballet School has a base in the Palladian White Lodge.

7 Victoria Tower Gardens

MAP E5 ■ **SW1** ■ **Open all day, year-round** ■ **www.royalparks.org.uk**

Although little heralded, this small pocket of green just south of Parliament's Victoria Tower is utterly charming. Beyond the entrance, which features a statue of suffragette Emmeline Pankhurst, is a replica of Rodin's *The Burghers of Calais*.

8 Primrose Hill

MAP C1 ■ **NW1** ■ **Open 5am–dusk daily** ■ **www.royalparks.org.uk**

North of Regent's Park, Primrose Hill offers spectacular views of the city skyline from its 63-m (207-ft) summit. Once a popular venue for duels, this small park was purchased by the Crown in 1841 to provide outdoor space for the poor of North London.

9 Bushy Park

Hampton Court Rd, Hampton TW11 ■ **Hours vary** ■ **www.royalparks.org.uk**

Chestnut Sunday in May, when the trees' blossoms are out, is one of the best times to come to Bushy

Park, near Hampton Court. Highlights include the bronze Diana Fountain and the Upper Lodge Water Gardens. Deer also roam this park.

10 Greenwich Park

SE10 ■ **Open 6am–dusk daily** ■ **www.royalparks.org.uk**

The 0° longitude meridian passes through the Royal Observatory Greenwich, located on a hill in this sprawling 74-ha (183-acre) family park. There are great views of the Old Royal Naval College *(see p153)*, the River Thames and over London.

The expansive Greenwich Park

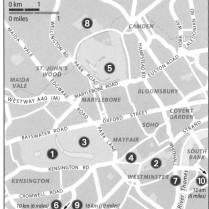

TOP 10 Museums

Main entrance of the British Museum

1 British Museum

The oldest national public museum in the world, and one of the most fascinating in London, the British Museum *(see pp12–15)* contains treasures from far and wide.

2 Natural History Museum

Life on Earth and the Earth itself are vividly explained here *(see pp20–21)* using hundreds of traditional and interactive exhibits.

3 Science Museum

This exciting museum traces centuries of scientific and technological development *(see pp22–3)*, with impressive and educational displays throughout.

4 Victoria and Albert Museum

One of London's great pleasures, this museum of art and design *(see p125)* contains astonishingly eclectic collections covering many periods and styles. Highlights include the Medieval and Renaissance Galleries, with their remarkable collections, and

Chalice, V&A

the rooms full of Indian and Far Eastern treasures. There are also displays of ornate jewellery, fashion, textiles, metalwork, glass, paintings, prints and sculpture.

5 Museum of London

This museum *(see p142)* provides a detailed account of London life from prehistoric times to the present day. It is particularly strong on Roman Londinium, but also has a model of Shakespeare's Rose Theatre, an original 18th-century prison cell with graffiti by its prisoners and a reconstruction of a Victorian street.

6 National Maritime Museum

Greenwich SE10 ■ Open 10am–5pm daily (last adm 4:30pm) ■ www.rmg.co.uk

The world's largest maritime museum, part of the Maritime Greenwich World Heritage Site *(see p153)*, depicts Britain's seafaring past and the continuing effects of the oceans. One of the most famous exhibits is the coat that was worn by Nelson at the Battle of Trafalgar, complete with a bullet hole on the left shoulder. Four galleries opened in 2018, examining British and European sea exploration from the 15th century to the present day.

Spitfire, Imperial War Museum

7 Imperial War Museum

Housed in part of the former Bethlehem ("Bedlam") Hospital for the Insane, some of the larger highlights in the four-level atrium of this museum *(see p89)* include aircraft suspended from the ceiling, armoured vehicles and missiles, along with hundreds of smaller items in exhibitions covering each era of modern wafare. The objects on display range from weapons, uniforms and equipment to diaries and letters, photographs and art. A highlight is the walk through a "trench" with a Sopwith Camel fighter plane swooping low overhead.

8 Design Museum

Located in a 1960s architectural landmark with beautifully converted interiors, this museum *(see p128)* is the only one in Britain devoted solely to 20th- and 21st-century British and international design. New inventions draw attention, such as the 3D printers and objects made by them. The regularly changing exhibitions feature the very best of modern design, including both product and graphic design, fashion, furniture and engineering.

9 London Transport Museum

In this former flower-market building *(see p106)*, the history of London's transport system is illustrated with posters, photographs, films and examples of early buses, Tube carriages and horse-drawn vehicles. There are activities available for children of all ages.

Exhibit, London Transport Museum

10 Sir John Soane's Museum

The former home *(see p113)* of Neo-Classical architect John Soane is filled with his collection of paintings, sculptures and ancient artifacts. An Act of Parliament negotiated by Soane preserves the house and collection as he left it, for the benefit of students.

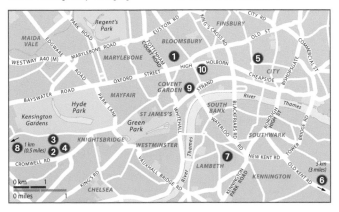

TOP 10 Art Galleries

Tiger in a Tropical Storm (Surprised!) by Rousseau, National Gallery

1 National Gallery

Located adjacent to the National Portrait Gallery, this Neo-Classical building with a "pepper pot" dome, houses one of the world's finest collections of European Art *(see pp16–17)*. Masterpieces from the mid-13th century to the early 20th century are also on display.

2 Tate Modern

Housed in a huge converted power station *(see pp28–9)*, this exciting gallery with a new extension covers modern international art from 1900 to the present day. The exhibits are curated thematically, with an increasing focus on artists from across the globe.

3 Tate Britain

The oldest Tate gallery *(see pp30–31)* focuses on British art from 1500 to the present, has, among its many treasures, the largest collection of J M W Turner paintings.

4 Dulwich Picture Gallery

If you have time, this suburban gallery is well worth a short train journey. England's oldest public art gallery *(see p154)*, it was opened in 1817. The important collection includes Murillo's *Flower Girl*, Poussin's *The Triumph of David* and Rembrandt's *Girl at a Window*.

5 Wallace Collection

This wonderful Victorian mansion *(see p135)* belonged to Sir Richard Wallace (1818–90). In 1897, his widow bequeathed the house and the amazing art collection inside it to the nation. Covering two floors, the 25 public rooms are beautifully furnished with one of the best collections of French 18th-century pictures, porcelain and furniture in the world. The paintings are rich and ornate – notable works include Nicolas Poussin's *A Dance to the Music of Time* and Frans Hals' *The Laughing Cavalier*. There are English portraits by Gainsborough and Reynolds.

6 National Portrait Gallery

Tucked away at the back of the National Gallery, is the world's most extensive collection of portraits. The National Portrait Gallery *(see pp18–19)*, home to some 10,000 paintings, drawings, sculptures and photographs, is a virtual "Who's Who" of important British people.

Jan van Eyck's Portrait of a Man, National Portrait Gallery

7 Serpentine Galleries

MAP B4 ■ Kensington Gardens W2 ■ Open 10am–6pm daily ■ www.serpentine galleries.org

Opened in 1970 and 2013, respectively, these two contemporary art galleries located on either sides of the Serpentine lake have a reputation of promoting avant-garde works. Designed by the renowned architect Zaha Hadid, the Serpentine Sackler Gallery hosts temporary exhibitions while the original Serpentine Gallery is famous for its summer pavilion installations, in which leading architects design large temporary structures in the gallery's outdoor space.

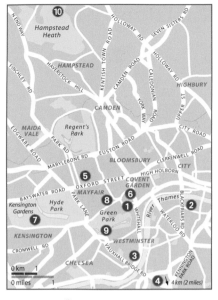

Façade of the Serpentine Galleries

8 Royal Academy of Arts

The Royal Academy's *(see p119)* continual big-name temporary exhibitions draw the crowds, and it is often necessary to reserve a ticket in advance. The traditional Summer Exhibition, which both established and unknown artists can apply to enter, is also extremely popular.

9 Queen's Gallery, Buckingham Palace

Established in 1962, this fascinating gallery showcases the incredible selection of paintings and other pieces collected by British monarchs *(see p24)* over the last 500 years.

10 Kenwood House

This majestic mansion with a library designed by Robert Adam has a small but important collection comprising 17th-century Dutch and Flemish works, 18th-century English portraits, and examples of French Rococo. There are statues by Henry Moore and Barbara Hepworth in the landscaped grounds *(see p148)*, which border Hampstead Heath.

Henry Moore piece, Kenwood House

TOP 10 Literary London

Writer and poet Oscar Wilde

1 Oscar Wilde
Dublin-born Wilde (1854–1900) dazzled London audiences with his plays, and society with his wit. He fell from grace when he was convicted of homosexual activity. His plays, such as *Lady Windermere's Fan* (1892) and *The Importance of Being Earnest* (1895), are frequently revived.

2 Dr Johnson
Dr Johnson's House: MAP P2; 17 Gough Sq EC4; Open 11am–5pm Mon–Sat (May–Sep: until 5:30pm); adm; www.drjohnsons house.org

"When a man is tired of London, he is tired of life," said Dr Samuel Johnson (1709–84). A towering literary figure, he lived in this house from around 1748 to 1759 and compiled much of his famous dictionary here. His satirical poem, *London* (1738), attacked poverty in the city.

Geoffrey Chaucer
Chaucer (c 1343–1400) was plomat and son of a London ner. His *Canterbury Tales* is a classic piece of English literature, and follows a group of pilgrims travelling from Southwark to Canterbury. In 17,000 lines the characters tell their rollicking tales.

4 Samuel Pepys
The extraordinary *Diary* of Samuel Pepys (1633–1703) begins on New Year's Day, 1660, and ends on May 31, 1669. He vividly describes contemporary life, the Plague and the Great Fire, and a naval attack on England by the Dutch. The work was written in shorthand and only deciphered and first published in 1825.

5 Virginia Woolf
Woolf (1882–1941) and her sister Vanessa Bell lived in Gordon Square, where the influential pre-war Bloomsbury Group grew from social gatherings. She developed an impressionistic stream of consciousness in novels such as *Mrs Dalloway* (1925) and *To The Lighthouse* (1927).

6 Alan Bennett
The Yorkshire-born playwright lived in Camden for some 40 years. *The Lady in the Van* is his touching and amusing account of an eccentric elderly woman who spent 15 years living in an old yellow van parked in the author's driveway.

Playwright and author Alan Bennett

Novelist and essayist Zadie Smith

Zadie Smith

Her first novel, *White Teeth*, made Smith (b 1975) an overnight sensation in 2000. Wickedly funny, it has remarkably well-drawn portraits of London life.

8 Martin Amis

Darling of the London literary scene in the 1970s and 1980s, Amis (b 1949) had a famous literary father and a precocious talent. His first novel, *The Rachel Papers* (1973), won a prestigious award for young writers and his novels such as *Money* (1984) and *London Fields* (1989) are set in London.

9 Charles Dickens

London provided the setting for many of Dickens' novels (1812–70). He drew inspiration from his experiences while writing. For instance, working in a factory gave him an insight into London's poverty, his job in a law firm helped him write *Bleak House* (1853). He also used many familiar places in his works, such as the debters' prison in *Little Dorrit* (1855).

10 John Betjeman

A devoted Londoner, with a disdain for bureaucracy, mediocrity and hideous architecture, Betjeman (1906–84) was made Poet Laureate of the United Kingdom in 1972. His poems are full of wit and humour and he remains one of the country's favourite poets.

TOP 10 LITERARY SIGHTS

1 Strawberry Hill, Twickenham
The 18th-century home of Horace Walpole that inspired *The Castle of Otranto* (1764).

2 Platform 9 ¾, King's Cross
Popular with Harry Potter fans for photo opportunities.

3 Russell Square
This square inspired scenes for William Thackeray's *Vanity Fair* (1848) and Virginia Woolf's *Night and Day* (1919).

4 The George Inn, Southwark
Dickens visited this inn and it is also mentioned in *Little Dorrit* (1855).

5 St Giles' Cripplegate
This was the parish church of Daniel Defoe and John Bunyan, and the burial place of poet John Milton.

6 Rose Theatre, Bankside
The excavated, original Tudor theatre is where Shakespeare's and Marlowe's plays were staged.

7 The Senate House, Bloomsbury
This 1930's building inspired the Ministry of Truth in George Orwell's novel *Nineteen Eighty Four* (1948).

8 The Criterion, Piccadilly Circus
A plaque commemorates how Dr Watson was to meet Holmes in *A Study in Scarlet* (1887).

9 Kensington Park Gardens
Said to be the inspiration for the Darling Family home in J M Barrie's novel *Peter Pan and Wendy* (1911).

10 The Old Curiosity Shop, Portsmouth Street
Claimed to be the subject of Dickens' novel of 1841 and is one of the oldest shops in London. It's now an artisan shoe shop.

The Old Curiosity Shop

TOP 10 Famous Residents

1 John Keats

The London-born Romantic poet (1795–1821) lived in Hampstead from 1818 to 1820 (see p147) before leaving for Italy to try to cure his fatal tuberculosis. After falling in love with his neighbour's daughter, Fanny Brawne, he is said to have written his famous and beautiful *Ode to a Nightingale* in the garden.

2 Florence Nightingale

Famously known as the "lady with the lamp", Florence Nightingale (1820–1910) tended to wounded soldiers during the Crimean War. After the war, she returned to London and established the first professional nursing school at St Thomas's hospital. The Florence Nightingale Museum (see p90) celebrates the life and works of this brilliant and revolutionary nurse.

3 Charles Dickens

The great Victorian novelist and social campaigner (1812–70) lived in Doughty Street for two years from 1837 (see p114). The house is his only surviving London home,

and he thought of it as "a frightfully first-class family mansion, involving awful responsibilities".

Statue of Millicent Fawcett

4 Millicent Fawcett

A campaigner for women's suffrage and founder of the National National Union of Women's Suffrage Societies in 1897, Millicent Fawcett (1847–1929) had been a resident at Gower Street for 45 years. There is a statue of Fawcett in the Parliament Square (see p36) holding a banner proclaiming her widely known phrase, "Courage calls to courage everywhere".

5 Sigmund Freud

The Viennese founder of psychoanalysis (1856–1939) spent the last year of his life in a north London house (see p147). A Jew, he had fled the Nazis before the onset of World War II, bringing his celebrated couch with him.

6 Lord Leighton

Yorkshire-born Frederic Leighton (1830–96) was one of the most successful artists in Victorian London

Charles Dickens

and president of the Royal Academy. He had exotic Leighton House *(see p127)* built for him between 1865 and 1895.

7 Amy Winehouse
The powerful lyricist with a soulful voice, Amy Winehouse (1983–2011) rose to fame in the 2000s. A bronze statue of her now stands in Stables Market, Camden *(see p147)*, where she lived.

8 The Duke of Wellington
Arthur Wellesley, 1st Duke of Wellington (1769–1852), lived at Apsley House *(see p120)*, popularly known as No. 1 London (the actual address is 149 Piccadilly), following his victories in the Napoleonic Wars.

9 George Frideric Handel
MAP D3 ■ Handel & Hendrix in London, 25 Brook St W1 ■ Open 11am–6pm Mon–Sat (last adm 5pm) ■ Adm ■ www.handelhendrix.org

The great German-born composer settled here in 1712. The attic apartment next door was occupied by Jimi Hendrix in 1968.

Portrait of William Hogarth

10 William Hogarth
Hogarth's House, Hogarth Lane W4 ■ Open noon–5pm Tue–Sun ■ Closed 1 Jan, Good Fri, Easter Sun, 25 & 26 Dec ■ www.hogarthshouse.org

The great painter of London life (1697–1764, *see pp30–31*) was used to the gritty life of the city and called his house near Chiswick "a little country box by the Thames".

TOP 10 BLUE PLAQUES

Wax figurine of Mozart

1 Wolfgang Amadeus Mozart
The Austrian German composer (1756–91) wrote his first symphony, aged eight, at No 180 Ebury Street.

2 Benjamin Franklin
The US statesman and scientist (1706–90) lived for a time at No 36 Craven Street.

3 Charlie Chaplin
The much-loved movie actor (1889–1977) lived at No 287 Kennington Road.

4 Charles de Gaulle
The exiled general (1890–1970) organized the Free French Forces from No 4 Carlton Gardens.

5 Mary Seacole
Jamaican nurse and heroine of the Crimean War (1805–81) lived at No 14 Soho Square.

6 Virginia Woolf
The great English novelist (1882–1941) lived and worked in three different houses in Bloomsbury between 1905 and 1912.

7 Mahatma Gandhi
The "father" of India's independence movement (1869–1948) lived as a law student at No 20 Baron's Court Road.

8 Jimi Hendrix
The American guitarist (1942–70) stayed in central London at No 23 Brook Street.

9 Henry James
The American writer (1843–1916) lived in Bolton Street, De Vere Gardens, and in Cheyne Walk, where he died.

10 Emmeline Pankhurst
The leading women's rights activist (1858–1928) lived at No 50 Clarendon Road during World War I.

🔟 River Sights

Morton's Tower, Lambeth Palace

central London river crossing to be built in over 100 years, and makes an apt approach to the Tate Modern.

4 Savoy Hotel

London's first luxury hotel (see p176) opened in 1889 on the site of the medieval Savoy Palace. Its Chinese lacquered "ascending rooms" were some of the first lifts in Europe. Oscar Wilde objected to the built-in plumbing: he wanted to ring for his hot water like a gentleman. Sip afternoon tea in the Thames Foyer or dine at Michelin-starred chef Gordon Ramsay's Savoy Grill. Attached is the historic Savoy theatre.

1 Lambeth Palace
MAP F5 ■ Lambeth Palace Rd SE1 ■ Open only for occasional tours ■ www.archbishopofcanterbury.org

The Archbishop of Canterbury's official London residence is a famous riverside landmark. Part of the palace dates from the 13th century, but it is the red-brick Morton's Tower or Gatehouse (1490) that gives the palace a distinctive appearance.

2 Houses of Parliament
See pp36–7.

3 Millennium Bridge
MAP R3

This blade-like, steel pedestrian-only suspension bridge links Tate Modern on Bankside with St Paul's Cathedral and the City opposite. It is the first

5 Shakespeare's Globe

This modern reconstruction (see p89) in oak, thatch and 36,000 handmade bricks is near the site of the original Globe Theatre, which burned down in 1613. The centre of the theatre is uncovered, so performances only happen during part of the year, but there are guided tours all year round, and there is a café, a restaurant and a bar with river views.

6 HMS Belfast
MAP H4 ■ The Queen's Walk SE1 ■ Open 10am–6pm daily (last entry 1 hr before closing) ■ Closed 24–26 Dec ■ Adm ■ www. iwm.org.uk

The last of the big-gun armoured ships, the nine-deck HMS *Belfast*

Millennium Bridge and St Paul's Cathedral at dusk

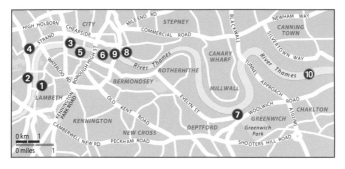

was launched in 1938 and saw active service in World War II and Korea. Retired in 1963, she was opened as a floating naval museum in 1971. Visitors can tour the huge engine rooms, the galley and the messdecks, where it is easy to get an idea of what life must have been like on board the ship.

The hull of the *Cutty Sark*

7 Cutty Sark
King William Walk SE10
■ Train to Greenwich; DLR Cutty Sark ■ Open 10am–5pm daily ■ Closed 24–26 Dec ■ Adm ■ www.rmg.co.uk

Launched in 1869, this is the last of the record-breaking tea-clippers that brought the leaves to thirsty London. The ship was reopened in 2012 by the Queen

after a serious fire in 2007. Its history and life onboard can be explored inside.

8 St Katharine Docks
The first piece of modern Docklands development was this handsome dock *(see p142)* beside Tower Bridge. Designed by Thomas Telford in 1824, it suffered severe bomb damage during World War II and was refurbished between the 1970s and 1990s. The area is now home to luxury apartments, shops and cafés.

9 Tower Bridge
A masterly piece of civil engineering, this bridge *(see p141)* is a Neo-Gothic wonder and was built in 1894 with steam pumps to raise its two halves. Tours of the tower include views from the top and the engine room.

10 Thames Barrier
This barrier spanning 520 m (1,700 ft) across the lower reaches of the Thames *(see p160)*, just past Greenwich, was built between 1974 and 1982 to prevent dangerous tidal surges from flooding central London. The Information Centre details historical flooding in London. The barrier has been raised over 190 times since it opened.

🔟 Off the Beaten Track

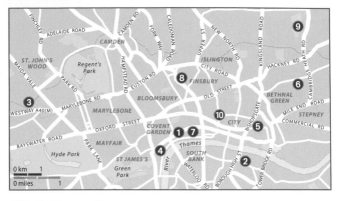

1 St Clement Danes

MAP N3 ■ Strand WC2 ■ 020 7242 8282 ■ Open 9am–4pm Mon–Fri, 10am–3pm Sat, 9:30am–3pm Sun ■ www.stclementdanesraf.org

Dating from 1681, this Wren church was bombed in the Blitz of 1941 and rebuilt by the Royal Air Force. Four times daily the bells peal out the tune of "Oranges and Lemons".

2 Old Operating Theatre

MAP K1 ■ 9a St Thomas St SE1 ■ 020 7188 2679 ■ Open 2–5pm Mon, 10:30am–5pm Tue–Fri, noon–4pm Sat & Sun ■ Adm ■ www.old operatingtheatre.com

Located on the site of the original St Thomas' Hospital, this restored operating theatre is a fascinating window on 19th-century medicine. Housed in the church attic of the old hospital, it is reached by a tightly

I**nterior of the Old Operating Theatre**

spiralling staircase. The theatre as well as the garret is stocked with remedies and surgical implements.

3 Puppet Theatre Barge

MAP P3 ■ Little Venice W2 ■ 020 7249 6876 ■ www.puppetbarge.com

From late October to July the narrowboats in the canal quarter of Little Venice include the Puppet Theatre Barge, putting on shows for children. It moves to the Thames at Richmond in August and September.

4 Benjamin Franklin House

MAP R2 ■ 36 Craven St WC2 ■ 020 7839 2006 ■ Historical Experience: noon, 1pm, 2pm, 3:15pm & 4:15pm Wed–Sun; Architectural Tour: same times Mon ■ Adm ■ www.benjamin franklinhouse.org

This seemingly modest townhouse was once a hotbed of invention – the great American statesman-scientist lived here from 1759 to 1775, dreaming up the lightning rod and measuring the Gulf Stream. A light and sound show explores his story.

5 Leadenhall Market

MAP J2 ■ Gracechurch St EC3 ■ Open all day, year-round ■ www. leadenhallmarket.co.uk

Leadenhall was once the site of the Roman forum, and it still dazzles

Crowds dining in Leadenhall Market

today, a warren of cobbled arcades encased in fancy ironwork. Gourmet butchers and cheesemongers vie with slick brasseries and bars for patrons.

6 E Pellicci

MAP P1 ■ 332 Bethnal Green Rd E2 ■ 020 7739 4873 ■ Open 7am–4pm Mon–Sat ■ www.epellicci.co.uk

Lauded as the grandest of all the East End's traditional "greasy spoon" cafés, E Pellicci has been run by the same Italian family for a century. The breakfasts are legendary.

7 Temple

MAP P3

This riverside campus in the heart of the city comprises two of the legal profession's four Inns of Court. A network of alleyways, gardens and medieval buildings make it an alluring spot to escape the West End crowds.

8 The Postal Museum

MAP F2 ■ 15–20 Phoenix Place WC1 ■ 030 0030 0700 ■ Open 10am–5pm daily ■ Adm ■ www.postalmuseum.org

Explore the history of the postal service in the UK through interactive displays, interesting exhibits and an exciting ride on the Mail Rail. The miniature train takes you on a short trip of the Post Office's London underground railway network.

9 London Fields

MAP R1 ■ London Fields Westside E8 ■ 020 8356 3000 ■ Open 24hrs ■ www.hackney.gov.uk/london-fields

Near Hackney Town Hall lies London Fields Lido, an Olympic-size heated outdoor pool. The park offers tennis courts, a summertime wildflower meadow and a paddling pool. The nearby Hackney Museum explores the area's rich cultural influences.

10 Postman's Park

MAP R2 ■ St Martin's Le-Grand EC1 ■ Open 8am–7pm (or dusk if earlier) ■ www.postmanspark.org.uk

The name of this picnic-friendly spot derives from its use by workers from the Post Office nearby. It houses the George Frederic Watts Memorial, honouring people who sacrificed their lives saving others'. Each is remembered on a hand-painted tile.

The picnic-friendly Postman's Park

🔟 Children's Attractions

Children looking at infinity mirrors in the Science Museum

 Science Museum
See pp22–3.

 Natural History Museum
See pp20–21.

 Mudchute City Farm
City farms are great places for families to enjoy and Mudchute City Farm (see p162) is one of Europe's largest inner city farms. This brilliantly conceived place in London's East End is home to more than 200 animals, from llamas and donkeys to chickens and ducks. For the really keen, farm tours are available, and there's also a riding school. Apart from the animals, the farm also has a diverse range of plants, wetlands and open meadows to be explored by the children. Make for the cracking café when the kids are getting hungry and tired.

 London Zoo
There's a full day out to be had in this 15-ha (36-acre) zoo (see p135). Home of the Zoological Society of London, the zoo emphasizes its important international role in conservation and research work. Walk-through exhibits include Penguin Beach, Gorilla Kingdom, Meet the Monkeys, In With The Lemurs, and the Land of the Lions enclosure.

Shark tank, Sea Life London Aquarium

 Sea Life London Aquarium
Located on London's South Bank, the aquarium (see p90) is home to thousands of marine creatures. A journey through 14 different zones shows them in all their glory. Crocodiles, green turtles and zebra sharks are among the sea life to be seen here. For some interactive fun, visit the rock pools to see crabs and starfish, with marine experts on hand.

...key at the Mudchute City Farm

6 Diana Memorial Playground

MAP A4 ■ Kensington Gardens W2
■ Open 10am–dusk daily ■ www.royalparks.org.uk

With its pirate galleon inspired by Peter Pan, the Diana Memorial Playground is the perfect place for imaginations to run wild.

7 V&A Museum of Childhood

This East End museum (see p161) has one of the world's largest toy collections, including dolls, teddies, games and children's clothes.

8 Coram's Fields

MAP F2 ■ 93 Guilford St WC1
■ Open daily ■ www.coramsfields.org

No adults admitted without a child, says the sign on the gate to this large park for children and teenagers. There's a paddling pool, play areas, adventure playground with zipwire and a small city farm.

9 Battersea Park

MAP D6 ■ Albert Bridge Rd SW11 ■ Zoo: open Easter–Oct: 10am–5:30pm (winter: until 4:30pm or dusk); adm; www.batterseaparkzoo.co.uk ■ www.batterseapark.org

This large south London park (see p156) is ideal for children, with an adventure playground, a boating lake and Recumbent bikes available to rent on weekends. It is also home to a children's zoo, with meerkats, otters, monkeys, pigs and emus, among others. Children are allowed to help in feeding some of the animals.

Torture chamber, London Dungeon

10 London Dungeon

MAP N6 ■ County Hall, Westminster Bridge Rd SE1
■ Open 10am–5pm Sun–Fri (from 11am Thu), 10am–6pm Sat
■ Adm ■ www.thedungeons.com

The scariest experience in town combines history and horror to celebrate an "orgy of grisly entertainment", with death, violence and gore at every turn. Follow in the bloody footsteps of the Victorian serial killer Jack the Ripper, bear witness to the Guy Fawkes Conspirators show or be condemned by Henry VIII on the fast-flowing Tyrant Boat Ride. Be warned that it's not for the very young or faint-hearted.

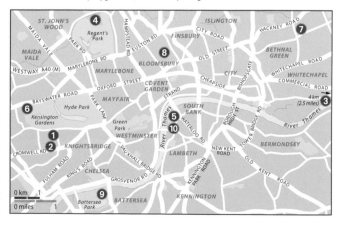

TOP 10 Performing Arts Venues

Performer at the Royal Opera House

concerts and exhibitions can all be seen here, and there are plenty of restaurants, cafés and bars to be enjoyed. The centre also contains a library and convention hall. The Guildhall School of Music and Drama is located nearby.

4 London Coliseum

London's other principal opera house (see p108) stages innovative productions sung in English by the English National Opera. Opened in 1904, it was restored to its Edwardian decor in 2004.

Globe above the London Coliseum

1 Royal Opera House

One of the greatest opera houses in the world, this theatre is home to the Royal Ballet company (see p105), and hosts international opera productions. Apart from the sumptuous main auditorium, there are the smaller Linbury Theatre and The Clore Studio Upstairs, which have music and dance. There are regular backstage tours and occasional big-screen live outdoor simulcasts of productions.

2 Southbank Centre

The centre (see p88) contains three concert venues – the Royal Festival Hall, Queen Elizabeth Hall and the Purcell Room – and the Hayward Gallery, Poetry Library, shops and restaurants. It hosts a range of events.

3 Barbican Centre

Home of one of the best music companies in the world – the London Symphony Orchestra – the Barbican (see p141) is the City's most important arts complex. Theatre, cinema, dance

5 National Theatre

MAP N4 ■ South Bank SE1
■ 020 7452 3000 ■ www.national theatre.org.uk

Seeing a play here takes you to the heart of London's cultural life. Within the concrete blocks of this innovative building, designed by Denys Lasdun and opened in 1976, you can see a musical, a classic play or a new production in one of its three theatres: the Olivier, the Lyttelton or the Dorfman. There are several themed theatre tours available. Reduced price tickets are sold from 9:30am on the day of the performance.

Exterior of the National Theatre

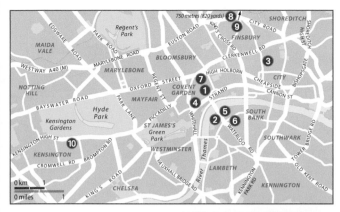

6 Old Vic
MAP P5 ■ The Cut SE1 ■ 0344 871 7628 ■ www.oldvictheatre.com

Famed for its associations with Laurence Olivier and other great British actors, this historic theatre has gained new verve in the last decade with groundbreaking productions and youth outreach initiatives. The programme usually includes modern revivals of neglected classics. A new wing, housing additional theatre spaces and a café-cum-bar, will be completed by 2022.

7 Donmar Warehouse
A little powerhouse, the intimate Donmar *(see p108)* has created some of the most dynamic productions in London in recent years, which have gone on to play in larger theatres and be acclaimed worldwide. Such is its reputation that productions often feature star actors such as Tom Hiddleston and Sinéad Cusack.

8 Almeida Theatre
MAP G1

One of the most renowned and award-winning fringe theatres in the city, this fantastic Islington venue *(see p150)* is committed to promoting an innovative and experimental programme of new British theatre, reimagined classics, and up-and-coming talent. This 325-seat theatre has brought to stage many notable productions.

Dancer at Sadler's Wells

9 Sadler's Wells
Having an unsurpassed reputation as London's best dance theatre, Sadler's Wells *(see p150)* has programmes for everyone. Ranging from creative re-interpretations of the classics by Matthew Bourne, to international dance styles and contemporary and hip-hop performances.

10 Royal Albert Hall
This circular building resembling a Roman amphitheatre, has a terracotta frieze around the exterior. The atmosphere inside makes it a treasured venue for every kind of concert, including the eight-week "Proms" season *(see p126)*, opera, ballet and Cirque du Soleil performances.

TOP 10 Live Music Venues

Ronnie Scott's, a famous jazz venue bustling with visitors

1 Ronnie Scott's

This legendary London jazz club *(see p99)* was opened by saxophonist Ronnie Scott (1929–96) in Gerrard Street in 1959. It moved to this location in Soho in 1965. Intimate lamplit tables surround a tiny stage that has hosted such stars as Ella Fitzgerald and Dizzy Gillespie, and continues to attract top names from the jazz world.

2 100 Club

MAP K2 ▪ 100 Oxford St W1 ▪ www.the100club.co.uk

An atmospheric jazz, blues, rock and pop venue that's open till 2am. Its heritage is legendary – the Rolling Stones played here, as did the Sex Pistols and other punk bands of the 1970s. Today it also hosts indie groups.

3 The Jazz Café

MAP D1 ▪ 5 Parkway NW1 ▪ www.thejazzcafelondon.com

Top performers from diverse genres, as well as great food, make this a popular venue. The best views are to be had from the balcony tables.

4 KOKO

MAP D1 ▪ 1a Camden High St NW1 ▪ www.koko.uk.com

Hosting mainly indie gigs and nightclubs as well as big names such as Kanye West and The Killers, KOKO is undergoing a major expansion and refurbishment, and is unlikely to reopen until late 2021.

5 O2 Academy, Brixton

211 Stockwell Rd SW9 ▪ Tube Brixton ▪ www.academymusicgroup.com/o2academybrixton

This is a great place to see acts from across the music spectrum. It holds nearly 5,000 but manages to retain an intimate atmosphere with good views of the performers from across the auditorium.

6 Roundhouse

This place has hosted the Rolling Stones, Jimi Hendrix, Led Zeppelin and other illustrious performers *(see p150)*. Originally a train shed, it was transformed into one of the leading performance arts venues of London. Headline acts here include the biggest names in music as well as emerging talent.

7 Eventim Apollo, Hammersmith

45 Queen Caroline St W6 ■ Tube Hammersmith ■ www.eventim apollo.com

This giant former cinema remains ever-popular and has hosted many of the city's most memorable gigs.

8 Union Chapel

MAP L2 ■ Compton Terrace, Islington, N1 ■ www.unionchapel. org.uk

Still a functioning church, this Gothic revival chapel hosts concerts and offers one of the most atmospheric gig experiences in London. Enjoy "daylight music" during lunch on Saturdays.

9 The O2

Peninsula Sq, North Greenwich SE10 ■ Tube North Greenwich ■ www. theo2.co.uk

Built as the Millennium Dome but later converted into a 20,000-seater concert venue in 2007, the O2 hosts some of the biggest names around. The 2,350-capacity indigo at The O2 is more intimate. Arriving via the Thames Clipper or Emirates Air Line is half the fun.

The O2 arena in Greenwich

10 The Troubadour

MAP A6 ■ 263–7 Old Brompton Rd SW5 ■ www.troubadour london.com

A coffee house club devoted to live music. All the great 1960s folk singers played here including Bob Dylan, and today there is a relaxed and enjoyable feel to the evenings of singing, poetry and comedy.

TOP 10 LONDON MUSICIANS

Stormzy performing at a concert

1 Stormzy
In 2019, the Croydon-born grime superstar became the first black solo artist to headline Glastonbury.

2 David Bowie
Brixton-born Bowie is arguably the most influential singer of his generation.

3 Adele
Hailing from Tottenham, Adele is one of the most successful singer/songwriters of the past decade.

4 George Michael
Originally part of Wham!, the late Finchley-born singer went on to sell millions as a solo artist.

5 Led Zeppelin
Formed in London in 1968, Led Zep are widely recognized as the progenitors of hard rock.

6 Chas & Dave
Popular duo whose fusion of music hall and rock gave rise to the term "rockney".

7 Adam Ant
Lead singer of the new wave group Adam and the Ants who developed a cult following in the 80s.

8 Marc Bolan
From Stoke Newington, Bolan was one of the pioneers of glam rock in the 70s.

9 Sex Pistols
Legendary 70s punk band formed in London in 1975.

10 Amy Winehouse
A statue in Camden honours the late singer, whose soulful voice won her legions of fans.

Best Places to Eat

1 The Barbary

With an informal setting, this restaurant *(see p111)* set in Neal's Yard in Covent Garden epitomizes all that is exciting about London dining. Enjoy watching the chefs flame the food while eating at the bar. Combining the best of ingredients, the flavours draw inspiration from North Africa and the Middle East.

2 Clarke's

A steady favourite since it opened in 1984, this simple yet elegant restaurant *(see p131)* serves wonderfully fresh Mediterranean food. The set no-choice menus that include roasted and baked dishes, are the focal point. There is also a daily changing selection of à la carte dishes and a well-chosen wine list. On most nights the owner, Sally, oversees every part of the operation.

3 Kricket

This modern restaurant *(see p101)*, which originated in a shipping container at a food market in Brixton, now occupies a chic spot in Soho. With a convivial atmosphere, it offers modern Indian cuisine and inventive cocktails. Don't miss out on samphire *pakora* (fritters) or Keralan fried chicken among other highlights.

4 Hakkasan

Alan Yau, the man behind the highly successful Wagamama chain, founded this seriously stylish dining experience *(see p117)*. Michelin-starred Cantonese-style food, such as sautéed sweet ginger and pineapple roasted duck, along with dim sum specialities, is served in the luxurious surroundings designed by Christian Liaigre. The cocktails are also sublime.

5 J Sheekey

Established in 1896, this legendary restaurant *(see p101)* still remains head and shoulders above any of the city's other fish and seafood restaurants. Take your seat inside one of the booths, or at the oyster bar, and tuck into tasty morsels such as herring roe or lobster thermidor.

6 Rules

London's oldest restaurant *(see p111)*, open since 1798, is like a Victorian time capsule. The walls above the velvet seats are covered in hunting trophies and portraits of forgotten figures. Game is a speciality, and this is also the place to go for classic English roast beef.

Fine decor at Rules, London's oldest restaurant

7 The Ledbury

Australian chef Brett Graham is brilliant – in only a short time his Notting Hill restaurant *(see p131)* has won two Michelin stars. Set menus are good value and there's also an outstanding eight-course tasting menu.

8 The Wolseley

Although it only opened in 2003, the Wolseley *(see p123)* has the feel of a 19th-century grand café-brasserie, and Londoners have taken to it as if it has been there forever. It's open from breakfast to dinner, serving finely prepared classic European dishes, and its giant windows offer a great view of Piccadilly.

The elegant interior of The Wolseley

9 Barrafina

One of the coolest tapas bars *(see p101)* around, using top-quality ingredients to excellent effect. Sit at the bar and watch the experts at work. There are also two branches in Covent Garden, and one at King's Cross.

10 St John

A great restaurant *(see p145)* near Smithfield meat market, in a converted smokehouse, the focus here is on nose-to-tail eating. Guests are served a delicious range of high-quality British cuisine, and the restaurant also has its own bakery *(see p163)*. Try the amazing Eccles cakes with Lancashire cheese. The bar-menu snacks are not expensive.

TOP 10 PLACES TO EAT WITH A VIEW

Seating at Galvin at Windows

1 Galvin at Windows
MAP D4 ▪ 22 Park Lane W1
▪ 020 7208 4021
Sumptuous cuisine, views of Hyde Park.

2 Hutong
MAP H3 ▪ The Shard, 31 St Thomas St SE1 ▪ 020 3011 1257
On level 33 of the Shard, with great views of the skyline. The speciality is Sichuan and northern Chinese food.

3 Le Pont de la Tour
MAP H4 ▪ 36D Shad Thames SE1
▪ 020 7403 8403
Modern French cuisine with a view over iconic Tower Bridge.

4 Tate Modern Restaurant
MAP R4 ▪ Blavatnik Building, Bankside SE1 ▪ 020 7401 5108
Panoramic views and great food.

5 Portrait Restaurant
MAP L4 ▪ National Portrait Gallery, St Martin's Place WC2 ▪ 020 7312 2490
Views over Trafalgar Square and Whitehall from this rooftop restaurant.

6 Blueprint Café
MAP H4 ▪ 28 Shad Thames SE1
▪ 020 7378 7031
A spectacular view of London Bridge.

7 Skylon
MAP N4 ▪ Royal Festival Hall SE1
▪ 020 7654 7800
One of the finest river views in town.

8 Swan at the Globe
MAP G4 ▪ New Globe Walk SE1
▪ 020 7928 9444
Look over to the City through mullioned windows.

9 Oxo Tower Restaurant
Terrific river views *(see p93)* from this South Bank landmark.

10 Coq d'Argent
MAP G3 ▪ 1 Poultry EC2 ▪ 020 7395 5000
Unparalleled views from this rooftop garden bar and French restaurant.

TOP 10 Pubs

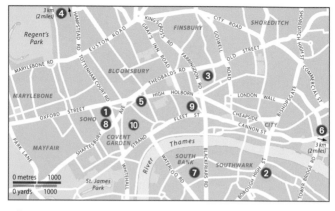

1 The Dog and Duck

Known to have been frequented by noted figures such as George Orwell and Madonna, this tiled Victorian pub *(see p100)* set in Soho. It has a tiny bar, where you might bump into art students and designers, and a blackboard with the latest selection of beers from all corners of England.

2 George Inn

Dating back to 1676 in parts, this is the only galleried coaching inn *(see p92)* left in London, and was given to the National Trust in the 1930s. You can enjoy excellent beers in its many old rooms with lattice windows and wooden beams, or in the courtyard.

The galleries of the George Inn

3 Jerusalem Tavern

This delightful little pub *(see p145)* was once an 18th-century coffee shop. It has a brown wooden interior with tiles, cosy booths and a small bar. It serves the full range of St Peter's in Suffolk. Light meals are also served during lunchtime, but note that the pub is closed on the weekend.

4 Spaniards Inn

This lovely 16th-century pub *(see p151)* on the northern edge of Hampstead Heath, with a large, attractive beer garden, is steeped in history and romance: the notorious 18th-century highwayman Dick Turpin is said to have drank here, along with literary luminaries Keats, Shelley and Byron and artist Sir Joshua Reynolds. Although the bar downstairs has been altered frequently over the decades, the small upstairs Turpin Bar is original.

5 Princess Louise

The Princess Louise is a beautifully restored 19th-century pub *(see p117)* with stained-glass windows, a mosaic floor, mirrors, nooks and alcoves. An unexpected bonus is the reasonably priced Sam Smiths beer, as well as the delicious pies and puddings that are served here.

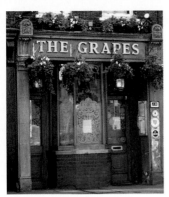

Entrance to The Grapes pub

6 The Grapes

This classic East End pub *(see p163)* has stood here since 1583 – although much of the current building dates from the 1720s – and it features in Charles Dickens' *Our Mutual Friend*. It is now owned by a group that includes actor Sir Ian McKellen, which seeks to maintain all its traditional charm, but which has added a very comfortable, high-quality restaurant on the first floor. It has a heated waterside deck overlooking the Thames.

7 Anchor & Hope

Located close to the young Vic theatre, this bustling gastropub *(see p92)* is worth the wait for the superior English fare such as hare ragout and gourmet sausages. No reservations are taken during the week; tables are on first-come-first-served basis. Sunday lunch is very popular, so book well in advance.

8 French House

This was once a meeting place for the French Resistance during World War II – hence the name. Gaining a reputation as a bohemian bolthole, French House *(see p100)* was also frequented by artists and poets such as Francis Bacon, Brendan Behan and Dylan Thomas. It is now well known for its refreshing Breton cider and fine wines.

9 Ye Olde Cheshire Cheese

In an alley off Fleet Street, this warren of rooms *(see p145)* still seems as if it should have sawdust scattered on the floors. Rebuilt in 1667, after the Great Fire of London, this was a favourite of Dr Johnson *(see p60)* and other writers. Never too crowded, its intimate corners make a good meeting place, made cosier with fires in winter. It is an ideal spot for enjoying good pub grub.

Pub sign

10 The Lamb and Flag

This old-world pub *(see p110)* tucked up an alley looks much as it did in Charles Dickens' day. In the heart of Covent Garden, it can get crowded – during the summer drinkers spill outside into the quiet alley. The 17th-century poet John Dryden was severely beaten up outside this pub, which was known as The Bucket of Blood because of the bareknuckle fights held here.

The Lamb and Flag, Covent Garden

🔟 Shops and Markets

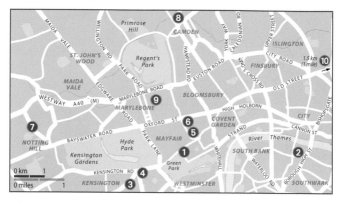

1 Fortnum & Mason

London's most elegant store *(see p122)* has hardly noticed the arrival of the 21st century. The ground-floor food hall is famous for its traditional English produce, and lavish picnic hampers can be found, along with a selection of fine wines, in the basement. The upper floors are good for designer men's and women's fashion and stylish gifts.

2 Borough Market

Nestled alongside Southwark Cathedral, London's oldest food market *(see p91)* is also one of its most atmospheric. It currently boasts over a hundred stalls selling

Artisan bread, Borough Market

high-quality produce from all across the country, as well as exceptional international specialities and snacks.

3 Harrods

London's most famous and exclusive department store *(see p129)* is more of an event than a shop. Covering seven floors, it is full of extraordinary things to buy – from pianos to children's racing cars – all with equally extraordinary prices. The children's toy department is excellent, and the store's food hall is rightly famous, with bars selling upmarket ice cream, pizzas and countless other treats.

4 Harvey Nichols

With its flagship store in Kinghtsbridge, this is a premium British designer emporium *(see p129)*. There are wall-to-wall designer labels, an extravagant perfume and beauty department and stylish homeware. The fifth floor has a food hall, sushi bar and the to-be-seen-in Fifth Floor Café.

5 Hamleys

The seven storeys of London's largest toyshop *(see p98)* contain just about anything a child might want, from traditional puppets and games to giant stuffed toys, models, arts and crafts supplies and all the latest

Hamleys toyshop on Regent Street

electronic gadgets. Of course, there are also many delights here for adults who haven't let go of their childhood.

6 Liberty

This handsome, half-timbered building *(see p98)* dates from 1925 and its fine wood-floored and panelled interior is part of the shopping experience. Long associated with the Arts and Crafts movement, it employed designers such as William Morris to create its fabrics. Great for its own Liberty floral fabrics, home furnishings, men's and women's fashions.

7 Portobello Road

West London's liveliest street *(see p126)* sells a mixture of antiques and bric-à-brac. As it heads north, there are food stalls, crafts, clothes and music. Shops and some stalls open daily but the main attraction, the antiques section, is open on Saturday.

8 Camden Market

A great place to spend a Saturday, this rambling market *(see p147)* around Camden Lock takes in several streets and buildings. Street fashion, jewellery and vintage world crafts. Do note that weekends are generally a crush.

9 Daunt Books

For all things travel-related, be it guidebooks, literature or maps, this stunning Edwardian bookshop *(see p138)*, featuring galleried balconies, conservatory ceiling and a stained glass window, is hard to beat. There are also branches at Cheapside, Hampstead and Holland Park.

10 Columbia Road Flower Market

A visit to this hugely popular flower and plant market *(see p160)* is one of the most delightful things to do on a Sunday morning in London. With an impressive range on offer, look out for bargains as the day wears on.

The handsome interior of Liberty department store

London for Free

1 South Bank Events
MAP N4 ■ www.southbank
centre.co.uk

Various free events are held along
the entire South Bank – from the
National Theatre *(see p70)* along
to the Royal Festival hall *(see p88)*.
These include regular Friday evening
concerts in the Queen Elizabeth
Hall foyer as well as monthly social
dances in the Festival Hall's Clore
ballroom. During summer many
stages and outdoor bars are set up
by the riverside.

2 Walking Tours
078 8925 9312 ■ www.free
londonwalkingtours.com

Free London Walking Tours offers
2-hour strolls around the city. Choose
from several tours, including Secrets
of London, Debauched London, Royal
London and the Changing the Guard
tour. There is no upfront charge, but
guides are only paid by tip, so do
leave one.

3 Museums and Art Galleries

Most of London's major public art
galleries and museums are free,
and it's easy to while away a whole
day at Tate Modern *(see pp28–9)*, the
British Museum *(see pp12–15)* or
the Natural History Museum *(see
pp20–21)*. Less well known is the
Royal Institution *(see p121)*, whose
Faraday Museum covers the history
of scientific endeavour since 1799,
the Wallace Collection *(see p135)* and
Kenwood House *(see p148)*, that have
their impressive collections displayed
as part of their stately home settings.

Pageantry at Horse Guards Parade

4 Changing the Guard
MAP L4 ■ Horse Guards Parade,
Whitehall SW1A

This ceremony is world-famous,
but it can be tricky to get a good view
at Buckingham Palace. The Horse
Guards Parade is more civilized, with
guardsmen arriving on horseback
at 11am (10am on Sundays) for the
mounted changeover ceremony.

5 Roman Amphitheatre

At the Guildhall Art Gallery
(see p142), the ruins of the city's
2,000-year-old colosseum lurk in a
dark basement. Built in c 74 AD and
capable of holding over 6,000 specta-
tors, the amphitheatre would have
featured animal hunts, executions and
gladiatorial combat. Sound effects
and spotlights bring the arena to life.

6 Sky Garden
MAP H3 ■ 20 Fenchurch St EC3
■ www.skygarden.london

A blot on the city skyline for some, the
"Walkie-Talkie" building is home to
London's highest public garden. Its
three levels harbour an abundance of
greenery, with plants and herbs from
the Mediterranean to South Africa;
grab a beer or cocktail from one of the
bars and soak up the stunning views.

The Mold Gold Cape, British Museum

7 Nature Watch at St James's Park

www.royalparks.org.uk

Like all the royal parks, St James's (see p119) is full of free entertainment, but the show-stealers are its pelicans. In 1664, the first pelicans arrived as a gift from the Russian ambassador. The birds are fed daily at 2:30pm near Duck Island.

8 Parliamentary Debates

MAP M6 ■ Palace of Westminster, St Margaret St SW1A ■ 020 7219 4114 ■ www.parliament.uk

You can view debates for free by queuing on Cromwell Green – see the website for times. There are free guided tours of the Palace of Westminster for UK citizens who book ahead by applying to their MP.

Westminster Abbey

9 Evensong

Westminster Abbey (see pp34–5) and St Paul's Cathedral (see pp42–5) are must-visits for many, but the admission fees are steep. Visit for free by attending evensong, and experience London's greatest churches the way they were intended – as places for worship and reflection.

10 Stand-up Comedy

MAP M1 ■ Camden Head, 2 Camden Walk, Islington N1 ■ www.angelcomedy.co.uk

Check out the stars of tomorrow at one of London's free comedy clubs. Angel Comedy at the Camden Head pub runs nightly, with a mix of open-mic sessions and established acts.

TOP 10 BUDGET TIPS

Music at the Southbank Centre

1 Look out for free concerts in churches (see pp50–51), and at various locations in the Southbank Centre.

2 Some museums are free and others have free late-afternoon or evening opening. The London Pass (www.londonpass.com) gives access to more than 80 major sights.

3 There is street entertainment all day at Covent Garden. Leicester Square and the South Bank are also good spots.

4 Cheap theatre tickets (for the same day only) are available at TKTS, a booth on the south side of Leicester Square.

5 You can get standby tickets for knock-down prices at the Royal Opera House, the National Theatre and the Royal Albert Hall.

6 London's numerous parks (www.royalparks.org.uk) offer lots of free entertainment, from exhibitions to bandstand concerts.

7 Santander Cycles (www.tfl.gov.uk) are a cheap way to get around the city. Bikes can be hired from as little as £2 – just bring your bank card to any docking station.

8 Check out the capital's plethora of street food venues, such as Dinerama, where you can feast on delicious food at bargain prices.

9 Enjoy free or reduced entry into more than 20 bars and clubs courtesy of the London Nightlife Ticket, which is available for two or seven days.

10 For cheap rooms in London, investigate universities (which rent rooms from June to September) and youth hostels (www.lhalondon.com).

TOP 10 Festivals and Events

1 Chinese New Year

Between late January and early February the Chinese community celebrate the New Year. Lanterns are hung above Chinatown (see p95), authentic markets pop up and a colourful parade takes place.

Fish figurine, Chinese New Year

2 RHS Flower Shows
www.rhs.org.uk

The summer months see the Royal Horticultural Society's (RHS) most prestigious annual show take place – the Chelsea Flower Show. Here you can see imaginative gardens in bloom and attend floral workshops – some can be found online too. The RHS also manage a number of gardens which can be visited throughout the year.

3 Foodie Festivals
www.london.tastefestivals.com ■ www.feriadelondres.com

There's a wealth of summer foodie festivals to choose from in the city. Taste of London is one of the largest, offering cooking classes and tasting sessions in Regent's Park. There's also Feria de Londres, which gives locals a taste of Spanish culture and cuisine.

4 Pride
www.prideinlondon.org

The UK's biggest pride event takes place in this buzzing capital in July. Vibrant parades fill the streets and locals gather to celebrate the LGBT+ community. Alongside the main parade, numerous parties, shows and virtual events take place.

5 Arty Events
www.royalacademy.org.uk

London is never short of blockbuster exhibitions but the Royal Academy of Arts Summer Exhibition always steals the show. Running since 1769, its eclectic and colourful display features around 1,100 works by emerging and established artists.

6 Music Mania
www.bbc.co.uk ■ www.south bankcentre.co.uk ■ www.efglondon jazzfestival.org.uk

One of the city's most well-known events, the BBC Proms at the Royal Albert Hall (see p126) boasts an eight-week summer programme of classical music. Other festivals include Meltdown, which is held at the Southbank Centre in June and curated by a famous artist, and the London Jazz Festival in November.

7 Notting Hill Carnival
www.nhcarnival.org

For two days in August, Notting Hill celebrates Caribbean music and culture. This is Europe's largest street festival, with steel bands, flamboyant floats, costumed dancers and DJs.

Striking costume, Notting Hill Carnival

8 Film Screenings
www.bfi.org.uk ■ www.somersethouse.org.uk

Hundreds of international films are shown across cinemas during the two-week BFI Film Festival, which is held in October. Outdoor cinema is also offered in abundance during the summer, with Somerset House curating a programme of indie and popular films for their outdoor screen event.

9 Guy Fawkes Night
Traditionally, effigies of Guy Fawkes, who attempted to blow up Parliament in 1605, are burned on bonfires across the country. These days the 5th November sees a flurry of firework displays, and London's parks host especially good shows.

Lord Mayor riding in a gilded coach

10 Ceremonious Events
A city known for its pomp and ceremony, London revels in traditional events. There's the Lord Mayor's show in November, which involves the new Lord Mayor riding through the Square Mile in a gilded state coach. This is the world's oldest and longest civic procession, and day-long entertainment is also organized. For a royal event, don't miss the Queen's birthday in June, which features a parade known as Trooping the Colour, where troops of the Household Division put on a display of marching and drilling.

TOP 10 SPORTS EVENTS

Rugby at Twickenham Stadium

1 The Six Nations
www.sixnationsrugby.com
Rugby contest between England, France, Ireland, Italy, Scotland and Wales.

2 Oxford and Cambridge Boat Race
www.theboatrace.org
The two universities' annual race covers some 6.5 km (4 miles).

3 The London Marathon
www.virginmoneylondon marathon.com
A 42-km (26.2-mile) road race from Greenwich Park to The Mall.

4 FA Cup Final
www.thefa.com
The much-anticipated last match of the Football Association Cup.

5 Test Matches
www.icc-cricket.com
Top-flight international cricket matches, with games lasting up to five days.

6 The Derby
www.thejockeyclub.co.uk
This is the historic highlight of the English flat horse-racing season.

7 Royal Ascot
www.ascot.co.uk
All London Society goes to the races in stylish hats and glamorous clothes.

8 The Wimbledon Championships
www.wimbledon.com
The world's premier grass-court tennis championships.

9 Rugby League Challenge Cup
www.rugby-league.com
The north of England comes to London for this bone-crunching final.

10 The London International Horse Show
www.olympiahorseshow.com
Lots of family fun can be found at this Christmas show.

London
Area by Area

Millennium Bridge and St Paul's
Cathedral lit up at night

TOP 10 Westminster, the South Bank and Southwark

Big Ben

This area is rich with sights, cultural institutions and experiences. Attractions range from Westminster Abbey and the Houses of Parliament to the Tate's art institutions, the Southbank Centre and Shakespeare's Globe. In between there's the *Golden Hinde II*, the fascinating Imperial War Museum, the London Eye and other entertainments around County Hall, former headquarters of the Greater London Council. Two footbridges – the twin Golden Jubilee footbridges and the Millennium Bridge – help to bring together the two sides of the river.

WESTMINSTER, THE SOUTH BANK AND SOUTHWARK

1 Houses of Parliament
The Palace of Westminster *(see pp36–7)* is the seat of the two Houses of Parliament – the Lords and the Commons. A Union flag flies on the Victoria Tower, replaced by the royal standard when the Queen is present.

2 Tate Modern
One of the great contemporary art galleries in the world, Tate Modern *(see pp28–9)* is located in the Bankside Power Station and the ten-storey Blavatnik Building extension. A boat service connects Tate Britain and Tate Modern.

3 London Eye
The large and spectacular cantilevered observational wheel offers amazing views of the city *(see pp26–7)*. Close by are the attractions in County Hall – the Sea Life London Aquarium *(see p90)*, London Dungeon and Shrek's Adventure.

South façade of Westminster Abbey

4 Westminster Abbey
London's most venerable and most beautiful church *(see pp34–5)* is the scene of coronations and royal weddings and the final resting place of monarchs.

5 Tate Britain
The best of British art is held at the Tate *(see pp30–31)*, with collections ranging from the 16th century to the present. While the contemporary installations add contrast and dynamism to the elegant spaces, the highlights are the collections of works by Turner and Blake. The atmosphere here is more relaxed than Tate Modern.

1	**Top 10 Sights** *see pp87–9*
①	**Restaurants** *see p93*
①	**Shopping** *see p91*
①	**The Best of the Rest** *see p90*
①	**Pubs and Cafés** *see p92*

Gallery in the Tate Britain

6 Downing Street
MAP L5 ■ Downing St SW1 ■ Closed to public

The official home and office of the UK's Prime Minister is one of four surviving houses built in the 1680s for Sir George Downing (1623–84) who went to America as a boy and returned to fight for the Parliamentarians in the English Civil War. The building contains a State Dining Room and the Cabinet Room, where a group of senior government ministers meets regularly to formulate policy. Next door, No. 11, is the traditional residence of the Chancellor of the Exchequer, with numbers 9 and 12 used for other government offices. Downing Street has been closed to the public for security reasons since 1989.

7 Churchill War Rooms
MAP L6 ■ Clive Steps, King Charles St SW1 ■ Open 9:30am–6pm daily (Jul & Aug: until 7pm) ■ Adm ■ www.iwm.org.uk

During World War II, Winston Churchill and his War Cabinet met in these War Rooms beneath the Government Treasury Chambers. They remain just as they were left in 1945, with spartan rooms and colour-coded phones. Take a guided audio tour through the rooms where ministers plotted the course of the war, and visit the Churchill Museum which records Churchill's life and career.

WHITEHALL AND HORSE GUARD PARADE

The wide street connecting Parliament Square and Trafalgar Square is named after the Palace of Whitehall, the main residence of the Tudor monarchs. The palace was guarded on the north side at what is now Horse Guard Parade, where the guard (below) is still mounted daily at 11am (10am on Sundays), with a dismounting inspection at 4pm.

8 Southbank Centre
MAP N4 ■ South Bank SE1 ■ www.southbankcentre.co.uk

The most accessible arts centre in London (see p70) still has the air of friendly, egalitarian optimism. The Royal Festival Hall and the renovated Queen Elizabeth Hall have diverse programmes, while the Hayward Gallery is a major venue for contemporary art exhibitions. The BFI Southbank, run by the British Film Institute, has a varied programme of films. The National Theatre's three stages (Olivier, Dorfman and

Map Room at the Churchill War Rooms

Lyttelton) are to the east along the river. Pedestrianized outdoor spaces host free performances, food markets and outdoor bars in summer.

Exterior of Shakespeare's Globe

⑨ Shakespeare's Globe

MAP R4 ■ 21 New Globe Walk, Bankside SE1 ■ Bookings (plays Apr–Oct only): 020 7401 9919 ■ Tours: from 9:30am daily (morning only on performance days; book online) ■ Adm ■ www.shakespearesglobe.com

To see a Shakespeare play at the reconstructed Globe (see p64) is a magical experience. The theatre is open to the skies, with seating in three tiers around the sides and standing in the central courtyard. A second, adjacent indoor venue, the candlelit Sam Wanamaker Playhouse, based on designs of early 17th-century indoor playhouses, has performances year-round – the behind the scenes guided tours are worthwhile as well.

⑩ Imperial War Museum

MAP F5 ■ Lambeth Rd SE1 ■ 020 7416 5000 ■ Open 10am–6pm daily ■ www.iwm.org.uk

This museum documents the social effects of war as much as the technology. Concerned with conflicts in the 20th and 21st centuries, it will appeal to anyone interested in wartime Britain. Extensive galleries document trench warfare in World War I, life in London during World War II, and the Holocaust (unsuitable for under 14s).

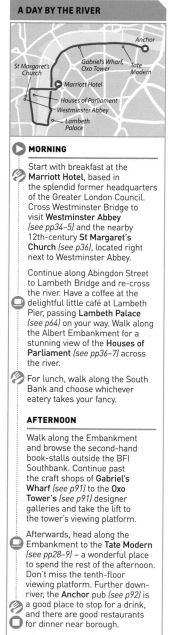

A DAY BY THE RIVER

▶ MORNING

Start with breakfast at the **Marriott Hotel**, based in the splendid former headquarters of the Greater London Council. Cross Westminster Bridge to visit **Westminster Abbey** (see pp34–5) and the nearby 12th-century **St Margaret's Church** (see p36), located right next to Westminster Abbey.

Continue along Abingdon Street to Lambeth Bridge and re-cross the river. Have a coffee at the delightful little café at Lambeth Pier, passing **Lambeth Palace** (see p64) on your way. Walk along the Albert Embankment for a stunning view of the **Houses of Parliament** (see pp36–7) across the river.

For lunch, walk along the South Bank and choose whichever eatery takes your fancy.

AFTERNOON

Walk along the Embankment and browse the second-hand book-stalls outside the BFI Southbank. Continue past the craft shops of **Gabriel's Wharf** (see p91) to the **Oxo Tower's** (see p91) designer galleries and take the lift to the tower's viewing platform.

Afterwards, head along the Embankment to the **Tate Modern** (see pp28–9) – a wonderful place to spend the rest of the afternoon. Don't miss the tenth-floor viewing platform. Further down-river, the **Anchor** pub (see p92) is a good place to stop for a drink, and there are good restaurants for dinner near borough.

The Best of the Rest

1 Clink Prison Museum
MAP G4 ■ 1 Clink St SE1
■ Open 10am–6pm Mon–Fri, 10am–
7.30pm Sat & Sun (closes later in
summer) ■ Adm ■ www.clink.co.uk
On the site of this medieval prison
there is a small exhibition devoted
to crime and punishment.

2 Sea Life London Aquarium
MAP N6 ■ County Hall SE1 ■ Open
10am–6pm Mon–Fri, 9:30am–7pm Sat
& Sun (last adm 1 hour before closing)
■ Adm ■ www.visitsealife.com/London
See thousands of marine creatures
at one of Europe's largest aquariums
(see p68) located on the South Bank.

3 The View from the Shard
MAP D4 ■ Joiner St SE1 ■ Open
10am–10pm daily ■ Adm ■ www.
theviewfromtheshard.com
At the top of the tallest tower in the city
are two floors of viewing platforms.
The 72nd floor is open to the sky, and
the views stretch beyond the city limits.

4 BFI IMAX
MAP N4 ■ South Bank SE1
■ Open daily (screening times vary)
■ Adm ■ www.bfi.org.uk
Giant-screen cinema that shows the
latest movies and documentaries.

BFI IMAX

5 London Dungeon
MAP N6 ■ County Hall SE1
■ Open 10am–5pm daily ■ Adm
■ www.thedungeons.com
This perennial favourite (see p69)
illuminates the capital's gory history.

6 Florence Nightingale Museum
MAP N6 ■ 2 Lambeth Palace Rd SE1
■ Open 10am–5pm daily ■ Adm
■ www.florence-nightingale.co.uk
A fascinating museum devoted to the
life and work of revolutionary 19th-
century nurse Florence Nightingale.

Florence Nightingale's writing case

7 Golden Hinde II
MAP G4 ■ St Mary Overie Dock,
Cathedral St SE1 ■ Open 10am–
6pm daily ■ Adm ■ www.goldenhinde.co.uk
A full-size replica of the ship in which
Sir Francis Drake circumnavigated
the world from 1577 to 1580.

8 Fashion and Textile Museum
MAP H4 ■ 83 Bermondsey St
SE1 ■ Opening times vary ■ Adm
■ www.ftmlondon.org
Founded by Zandra Rhodes, the
museum puts on well-curated
temporary exhibitions on fashion,
textiles and jewellery.

9 Young Vic Theatre
MAP Q6 ■ 66 The Cut SE1
■ www.youngvic.org
This independent theatre company
nurtures young thespian talent and
attracts diverse audiences with its
critically acclaimed productions.

10 Oxo Tower Wharf
MAP P4 ■ Bargehouse St SE1
■ Open daily ■ www.oxotower.co.uk
Take a lift to the viewing gallery
next to the restaurant (see p93)
for great city views.

Shopping

1 Houses of Parliament Shop
MAP L6 ▪ 12 Bridge St SW1
Buy the day's political reading, plus parliamentary-related prints.

2 Lower Marsh Market
MAP P6 ▪ Lower Marsh SE1
▪ Open 9am–5pm Mon–Sat ▪ www.lowermarshmarket.com
This market sells inexpensive music, clothes, hardware, food and has newer street food stalls.

3 BFI Shop
MAP N4 ▪ South Bank SE1
▪ Open 11am–8:30pm daily
This film shop selling DVDs, books and gifts is a must for movie buffs.

4 Southbank Centre
MAP N4 ▪ South Bank SE1
In addition to concert halls and art galleries (see p70), the Southbank Centre has great shops. The Festival Terrace and second-hand book stalls outside are a must-visit.

Shops in Gabriel's Wharf

5 Gabriel's Wharf
MAP P4 ▪ Gabriel's Wharf SE1
Shops in riverside Gabriel's Wharf sell glassware, jewellery and ceramics.

6 Bermondsey Fayre
MAP H5 ▪ 212 Bermondsey St SE1 ▪ Open noon–6pm Tue–Thu & Sat, 11am–6pm Fri, noon–5pm Sun ▪ www.bermondseyfayre.com
This boutique gallery sells appealing clothes and accessories made by local and independent designers.

Food stalls at Borough Market

7 Borough Market
MAP R4 ▪ 8 Southwark St SE1 ▪ Open 10am–5pm Mon–Thu, 10am–6pm Fri, 8am–5pm Sat ▪ www.boroughmarket.org.uk
Superb quality produce and hot food stalls come to this incredibly popular traditional market near Southwark Cathedral, from all over the country. Fewer stalls are open for business on Mondays and Tuesdays.

8 Bermondsey Antiques Market
MAP H5 ▪ Bermondsey Sq SE1 ▪ Open 6am–2pm Fri ▪ bermondseysquare.net
This Friday morning market offers jewellery, glassware, trinkets and all sorts of material curiosities. Get here early in the day for the best finds.

9 Oxo Tower Wharf
MAP P4 ▪ Bargehouse St SE1 ▪ Open 11am–6pm Tue–Sun
Three floors are given over to designers of fashion, jewellery and interiors. The gallery@oxo show-cases cutting-edge photography, art, design and architecture.

10 Konditor
MAP P5 ▪ 22 Cornwall Rd SE1 ▪ Open 10am–5pm Mon & Tue, 8am–7pm Wed–Fri, 8am–6pm Sat, 11am–5pm Sun
This urban village bakery has a cult following among the cake connois-seurs. Its brownies are legendary.

See map on pp86–7 ←

Pubs and Cafés

1 **The Southwark Tavern**
MAP G4 ▪ 22 Southwark St SE1

A popular pub with a wide range of food and drink. Upstairs is bright and airy, while the downstairs bar has exposed brick-walled booths.

2 **The Refectory Café**
MAP S4 ▪ Southwark Cathedral, London Bridge SE1

Opening onto a bright courtyard, the cathedral's Refectory is ideal for hot lunches or afternoon tea and homemade cakes.

3 **Anchor & Hope**
MAP Q5 ▪ 36 The Cut SE1

The food is among the best around. Great English ingredients make dining at this a gastropub *(see p74)* a wonderful experience.

4 **Monmouth Coffee Company**
MAP G4 ▪ 2 Park St SE1

Serving arguably the best coffee in London, this atmospheric café in the heart of Borough Market also has delicious pastries and snacks.

5 **The Anchor at Bankside**
MAP Q4 ▪ 34 Park St SE1

Snug, old English pub with a large terrace that offers outdoor seating in summer, makes it a popular venue for punters. The dining room upstairs serves traditional English food.

6 **Wheatsheaf**
MAP G4 ▪ 6 Stoney St SE1

The eclectic selection of British beers and a menu of burgers and roasts make this a great choice when exploring Borough Market.

7 **Scooter Caffe**
MAP P4 ▪ 132 Lower Marsh SE1

With resident cats and vintage furniture, this atmospheric little café is good for daytime coffee and drinks as well as an evening drink.

8 **Market Porter**
MAP G4 ▪ 9 Stoney St SE1

This popular, historic pub overlooks Borough Market and has been serving punters since the late 17th century.

9 **Rake**
MAP G4 ▪ 14a Winchester Walk SE1

A fine selection of beers is on offer at this tiny bar near Borough Market. The outdoor decking area is great for summer drinks.

10 **George Inn**
MAP G4 ▪ 77 Borough High St SE1

London's only surviving galleried coaching inn is a maze of plain, wood-panelled rooms and upstairs bars. Food is served from 11am to 10pm from Monday to Saturday and from noon to 9pm on Sundays. Courtyard tables are pleasant in the summer.

A vibrant Park Street pub, The Anchor

Restaurants

Tables at the Cinnamon Club

1 The Cinnamon Club
MAP E5 ■ Old Westminster Library, 30–32 Great Smith St SW1 ■ 020 7222 2555 ■ £££

Housed in a Grade II-listed former library, The Cinnamon Club serves innovative Indian cuisine.

2 Skylon
MAP N4 ■ Royal Festival Hall, Belvedere Rd, Southbank SE1 ■ 020 7654 7800 ■ £££

Named after the symbol of the 1950s Festival of Britain, the Southbank Centre's restaurant is a classy affair. Guests have a fine river view, along with classic British dining.

3 The Laughing Gravy
MAP Q6 ■ 154 Blackfriars Rd SE1 ■ 020 7998 1707 ■ ££

This cosy neighbourhood restaurant occupies the premises of an old foundry and serves delicious bistro fare. Don't miss out on the braised rabbit pappardelle ragout.

4 Roast
MAP G4 ■ The Floral Hall, Stoney St SE1 ■ 020 3006 6111 ■ £££

In the middle of Borough Market (see p91) is this handsome restaurant with views of St Paul's. It serves excellent and well-sourced British cooking.

5 The Archduke
MAP N5 ■ 153 Concert Hall Approach SE1 ■ 020 7928 9370 ■ ££

Set in beautifully converted railway arches, this restaurant serves steaks, burgers and cocktails. Open daily with live jazz gigs.

6 Footstool Restaurant
MAP E5 ■ St John's, Smith Sq SW1 ■ 020 7222 2779 ■ ££

Tasty, modern food is served in the hall's crypt at lunch on weekdays and on regular concert evenings.

7 Pizarro
MAP H5 ■ 194 Bermondsey St SE1 ■ 020 7378 9455 ■ £££

A classic Spanish restaurant serving a small menu of Iberian meat dishes.

Views from Oxo Tower Restaurant

8 Oxo Tower Restaurant, Bar and Brasserie
MAP G4 ■ Oxo Tower Wharf SE1 ■ 020 7803 3888 ■ Restaurant: £££ ■ Brasserie: £££

Delicious modern dishes in the restaurant; live jazz in the Brasserie.

9 Swan at the Globe
MAP R4 ■ 21 New Globe Walk SE1 ■ 020 7928 9444 ■ ££

Next to the Globe, this place has great views of St Paul's and a creative menu.

10 fish!
MAP G4 ■ Cathedral St, Borough Market SE1 ■ 020 7407 3803 ■ ££

Innovative fish dishes are served in this modern, stylish restaurant.

See map on pp86–7 ←

🔟 Soho and the West End

London's west end is an eclectic blend of theatre, live entertainment, nightlife, top-notch eating out and shopping. People flock here for the theatres of Shaftesbury Avenue and Charing Cross Road and the cinemas of Leicester Square. At its heart, the atmosphere of Soho is a big draw, its boutique shops and LGBT+ bars abuzz with activity as the night wears on. For a taste of East Asia, Chinatown boasts a wealth of restaurants. But this area isn't all about nightlife, Trafalgar Square is home to the National Gallery, the National Portrait Gallery and an excellent series of free lunchtime concerts at St Martin-in-the-Fields.

Statue on the Shaftesbury Memorial Fountain

SOHO AND THE WEST END

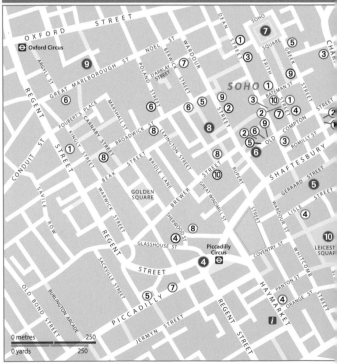

① National Gallery
See pp16–17.

② National Portrait Gallery
See pp18–19.

③ Trafalgar Square
MAP L4 ■ WC2

Trafalgar Square – once the royal mews – is a hub of the West End and a venue for public rallies and events. From the top of a 50-m (165-ft) column, Admiral Lord Nelson, who famously defeated Napoleon's fleet at the Battle of Trafalgar in 1805, looks down Whitehall towards the Houses of Parliament. The column is guarded at its base by four huge lions – the work of Edwin Landseer. At the northwest corner of the square, the Fourth Plinth features temporary artworks by leading

National Gallery, Trafalgar Square

national and international artists. On the north side of the square is the National Gallery *(see pp16–17)* and St Martin-in-the-Fields church *(see p50)*; to the south-west, Admiralty Arch leads to Buckingham Palace.

④ Piccadilly Circus
MAP K3 ■ W1

Designed by the architect John Nash as a junction in Regent Street, Piccadilly Circus is the endpoint of the street called Piccadilly. Its Anteros statue – often mistakenly called Eros – tops a memorial fountain to the Earl of Shaftesbury that is a familiar London landmark and a popular meeting place. The Circus is renowned for its neon advertising displays and the constant crowds at this busy junction. To the south is the Criterion Theatre, next to Lillywhites – a popular sporting-goods store.

⑤ Chinatown
MAP L3 ■ Sts around Gerrard St W1 ■ www.chinatown.co.uk

Chinese archways in Gerrard Street mark the entrance to Chinatown, an area of London that has, since the 1950s, been the focus of the capital's Chinese residents. Here you can shop at Chinese supermarkets and gift shops. The Chinese New Year celebrations in late January or early February are great for those travelling with family. Chinatown abounds with excellent-value restaurants.

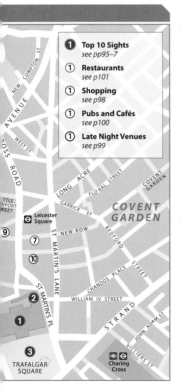

6 Old Compton Street
MAP L2

The main street in Soho is a lively thoroughfare both day and night. It is also the centre of London's LGBT+ scene, and the site of the popular gay pubs Comptons of Soho and the Admiral Duncan. Soho's vibrant streetlife spills into Frith, Greek and Wardour streets, where pubs, clubs, restaurants and cafés have pavement tables, often warmed by gas heaters in winter. Some, like Bar Italia on Frith Street and Balans Café on Old Compton Street, are open until the early hours. Everywhere fills up when the evening's performance at the Prince Edward Theatre ends. A delicious breakfast is to be had at Café Boheme at No. 13 Old Compton Street, and such long-standing shops as the Italian delicatessen I Camisa & Son, and the Vintage House (over 1,350 malt whiskeys in stock), give the area its village feel.

7 Soho Square
MAP K2

This pleasant square, crossed by footpaths lined with flowerbeds, is popular at lunchtime, after work and at weekends, especially in summer. Many of the buildings in the square have long been occupied

LGBT+ SOHO

Soho is undoubtedly the heartland of the city's LGBT+ community. It's a scene which has its roots at the turn of the 20th century when members of the community would meet in secret in the area's pubs. Today, a plethora of LGBT+ bars and clubs, such as Ku Bar (below) and Comptons of Soho, testify to the enduring popularity of the area among both residents and visitors.

by film, TV production and other media companies. On the north side is a church built in 1893 for French Protestants under a charter granted by Edward VI in 1550. The redbrick St Patrick's, on the east side, sometimes has music recitals. On the corner of Greek Street is the House of St Barnabas, a charitable foundation for the homeless in an 18th-century building, which is occasionally open for cultural events.

Mock-Tudor cottage, Soho Square

Stall at Berwick Street Market

8 Berwick Street Market
MAP K2

There has been a market on this street since the 18th century, and the daily fruit and vegetable stalls remain cheap and cheerful, though they are becoming increasingly foodie. The traders are usually Cockney and some still talk in old money ("ten bob" is 50p) and round things up to a "nicker" or a "quid" (£1). It operates between 8am to 6pm from Monday to Saturday.

9 The Photographers' Gallery
MAP D3 ▪ 16–18 Ramilies St W1
▪ Open 10am–6pm Mon–Sat, 10am–8pm Thu, 11am–6pm Sun ▪ Adm until 5pm ▪ www.thephotographers gallery.org.uk

Displayed across three floors of exhibition space are works from both emerging global talent and established artists, as well as pieces from the gallery's archives. There are also talks, workshops and courses, plus a bookshop and a café.

10 Leicester Square
MAP L3 ▪ Leicester Sq W1

This square was originally laid out in the 1670s. Celebrities of the 17th and 18th centuries who lived here included Sir Isaac Newton and the painters Joshua Reynolds and William Hogarth. Today the square forms the heart of London's West End entertainment district and houses the Empire and Art Deco Odeon cinemas. There is also a booth called "TKTS" to the south of the square where cut-price theatre tickets can be bought.

A WALK AROUND THE WEST END

▶ **MORNING**

Start the day in **Trafalgar Square** (see p95) at 8:30am when the fountains are switched on and view the latest art on the Fourth Plinth. You could spend a day at the **National Gallery** (see pp16–17), but limit yourself to an hour or two, perhaps just visiting the Impressionist galleries.

For coffee, head next door to the Portrait Restaurant at the top of the **National Portrait Gallery** (see pp18–19). It has fine views over Trafalgar Square. Head up Charing Cross Road to Leicester Square. Note the statues of Shakespeare and Charlie Chaplin in the middle of the square. Continue towards the bright lights of **Piccadilly Circus** (see p95) and the Shaftesbury Memorial Fountain, and then walk up Shaftesbury Avenue, centre of the city's theatre district. Turn off here into bustling **Chinatown** (see p95), with its colourful shops and great-value restaurants.

Lunch in Chinatown is obligatory. Enjoy dumplings and dan dan noodles at **Baozilnn** (25 Newport Court), or the calm of the excellent **Joy King Lau** (see p101) on Leicester Street, just off Lisle Street.

AFTERNOON

Spend the afternoon in colourful and lively **Soho**. Buy some fresh fruit from the stall in **Berwick Street Market**, then stroll up Wardour Street, and join in for the free ping-pong on Soho Square. Reward yourself with tea and a slice of cake at the delightful **Maison Bertaux** (see p100) in Greek Street.

See map on pp94–5 ←

Shopping

Hamleys
MAP J2 ■ 188–196 Regent St W1

London's largest toyshop *(see pp78–9)* is worth a visit just to see their fabulous window displays.

I Camisa & Son
MAP K2 ■ 61 Old Compton St W1

Established back in 1929, this authentic Italian deli is packed to the ceiling with an awesome selection of Italian foods.

Foyles
MAP L2 ■ 107 Charing Cross Rd WC2

In a street of bookshops, this grandmother of all bookshops is something of an institution.

Dover Street Market
MAP L4 ■ 18–22 Haymarket SW1Y

Find cutting-edge fashion at this chic retail space offering designer clothing – such as Comme des Garçons – as well as homeware. There is a café on the top floor.

Milroy's of Soho
MAP L2 ■ 3 Greek St W1

A West End whisky specialist, Milroy's of Soho has a small bar where malts can be sampled.

Liberty
MAP J2 ■ 210–220 Regent St W1

This is one of London's most appealing department stores *(see p79)*. Opened in 1875, the shop remains famous for its "Liberty Print" fabrics.

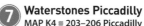 Waterstones Piccadilly
MAP K4 ■ 203–206 Piccadilly

Part of a chain of bookshops, the Piccadilly branch is housed in an Art Deco building with six floors containing over 200,000 books. The store has cafés as well as a cocktail bar.

Lina Stores
MAP K3 ■ 18 Brewer St W1F

Named after the Genovese woman who established it, this family-run Italian deli has been operating at this address since 1944. Quality Italian produce is imported and fresh pasta is made on the premises every day.

 Algerian Coffee Stores
MAP K3 ■ 52 Old Compton St W1

Opened in 1887, this is one of the oldest shops in Soho. It sells more than 80 kinds of coffee and exudes a wonderful aroma. Over 120 types of speciality teas and herbal infusions can also be bought here.

⑩ Goldsboro Books
MAP L3 ■ 23–27 Cecil Court WC2

Long-standing independent bookstore specializing in signed first editions, both fiction and non-fiction.

Liberty department store

Late Night Venues

 PizzaExpress Jazz Club
MAP K2 ■ 10 Dean St W1

This Soho branch of the PizzaExpress chain stays open until midnight, with its regular jazz nights proving an attractive draw.

 100 Wardour Street
MAP K3 ■ 100 Wardour St W1

An all-day restaurant serving modern European dishes with a twist. Live music and DJs play in the evening. There is also a lounge and bar.

 Soho Theatre Bar
MAP K2 ■ 21 Dean St W1

The buzzy bar at this hip comedy and theatre venue is open until 11pm (1am for members and those with a ticket for a performance).

4 Live at Zédel
MAP K3 ■ 20 Sherwood St W1

A Parisian-style brasserie, Zédel hosts comedy, jazz, blues, drag as well as late-night cabaret. The stylish American bar is also open until midnight or 1am.

5 Balans Café
MAP L2 ■ 34 Old Compton St W1

This lively bar is open 24 hours a day. Hot dishes and sandwiches accompany the wines and cocktails .The eggs Benedict here is to die for.

 Milk and Honey
MAP K2 ■ 61 Poland St W1
■ 020 7065 6800 ■ www.mlkhny.com

A cool Soho club spread over three floors with a great bar for cocktail enthusiasts. Open to non-members until 11pm by reservation only – and to members until 3am.

7 Ronnie Scott's
MAP L2 ■ 47 Frith St W1
■ 020 7439 0747

Opened in 1959 by saxophonist Ronnie Scott as a small basement club, this premier jazz venue *(see p72)* is buzzing every night of the week.

The impressive bar at Cahoots

8 Cahoots
MAP K3 ■ 13 Kingly Court W1
■ www.cahoots-london.com

Sporting a 1940s theme of a retro underground station, this basement bar hosts live music and mainly focuses on old tunes. Open until 3am Fridays and Saturdays. Book ahead.

9 Thirst Soho
MAP L2 ■ 53 Greek St W1

Offering an impressive cocktail menu along with early happy hours, Thirst Soho serves its visitors all day in its cosy bar. Open until 3am, it also features a late-night DJ with a dance floor downstairs.

10 El Camión Mexicano
MAP K3 ■ 25–27 Brewer St W1

As the pubs close, night owls head for El Camión, which serves a late-night Mexican menu from 11pm to 2:30am. The Pink Chihuahua cocktail bar downstairs stays open until 3am Monday to Saturday.

El Camión Mexicano restaurant

See map on pp94–5

Pubs and Cafés

Dog and Duck
MAP L2 ■ 18 Bateman St

Mahogany panelling, tiled walls and ornate mirrors make this tiny pub a wonderful slice of Victoriana. George Orwell celebrated the success of *Animal Farm* here and the upstairs dining room is named after the writer.

A taste of Paris at Maison Bertaux

2 Maison Bertaux
MAP L3 ■ 28 Greek St W1

Set in the heart of Soho, this little corner of Paris attracts a faithful clientele, who love its delicious coffee and heavenly cakes.

3 French House
MAP L3 ■ 49 Dean St W1

A small, one-bar establishment where conversation flows freely among strangers, this Soho pub was once the haunt of the artist Francis Bacon (1909–92).

4 Bar Italia
MAP L2 ■ 22 Frith St W1

Sit at the bar or out on the pavement and enjoy the old-school Soho vibe while having a cup of classic Italian coffee. A huge screen at the back of the bar shows Italian football matches. Open 7am to 5am daily and until midnight on Sundays.

5 My Place Soho
MAP K2 ■ 21 Berwick St W1

This cosy, intimate space has great value and is frequented by locals and visitors alike. You'll find top-class coffee, evening cocktails and an excellent diverse menu served from 8 in the morning until late every day.

6 The Admiral Duncan
MAP L3 ■ 54 Old Compton St W1

A small, lively bar in Old Compton Street – one of dozens in the area with a gay clientele.

7 The Breakfast Club
MAP K2 ■ 33 D'Arblay St W1 ■ 020 7434 2571

One of 12 branches across London, this is an excellent all-day breakfast spot. Go for the chorizo hash browns.

8 John Snow
MAP K3 ■ 39 Broadwick St W1

Always busy, this Victorian pub with cosy drinking compartments is delightfully atmospheric.

9 The Cork and Bottle
MAP L3 ■ 44–6 Cranbourn St WC2

This basement wine bar is a favourite with connoisseurs due to its exceptional wine list and excellent (if eclectic) food menu.

10 The Coach and Horses
MAP L3 ■ 29 Greek St W1

Long associated with writers and journalists, this pub is a Soho institution that became the first vegetarian and vegan pub in London in 2012.

Patrons at The Coach and Horses

Restaurants

PRICE CATEGORIES

For a three-course meal for one with half a bottle of wine (or equivalent meal), taxes and extra charges.

£ under £30   **££** £30–50   **£££** over £50

1 Ceviche
MAP L3 ■ 17 Frith St W1 ■ 020 7292 2040 ■ ££

Opened in 2012, this Peruvian restaurant has been a big hit. Named after its signature dish of citrus-cured fish, it has a laid-back atmosphere and the food is delicious.

2 Hoppers
MAP L2 ■ 49 Frith St W1 ■ ££

An inviting, down-to-earth Sri Lankan restaurant in Soho where diners mix and match small mouth-watering curries and sides with fermented rice and lentil pancakes.

3 Burger and Lobster Soho
MAP K2 ■ 36–8 Dean St W1 ■ 020 7432 4800 ■ ££

Offering perfectly cooked, meaty burgers, juicy steamed or char-grilled lobster and buttery lobster rolls with wasabi mayo. Service is friendly, quick and polished.

4 Joy King Lau
MAP L3 ■ 3 Leicester St WC2 ■ 020 7437 1132 ■ £

Experience a diverse selection of Cantonese dishes. At lunchtime there is an enormous choice of delicious dim sum served from trolleys.

5 Restaurant Yoshino
MAP K3 ■ 3 Piccadilly W1 ■ 020 7287 6622 ■ ££

Traditional favourites such as sushi, sashimi and tempura are served here. The extensive menu offers set three-course meals as well as à la carte. Try the mouthwatering Japanese barbecue dishes such as Wagyu beef or ox tongue.

6 Yauatcha
MAP K2 ■ 15–17 Broadwick St W1 ■ 020 7494 8888 ■ ££

Book ahead to enjoy steamed scallop *shu mai* or venison in puff pastry at this highly regarded dim sum spot.

7 J Sheekey
MAP L3 ■ 28–32 St Martin's Court WC2 ■ 020 7240 2565 ■ ££

The best fish restaurant in London in a charming setting, with dishes such as shellfish and Cornish fish stew.

The sleek interior of J Sheekey

8 Kricket
MAP K3 ■ 12 Denman St W1 ■ 020 7734 5612 ■ ££

This busy two-floor restaurant serves imaginative Indian sharing plates.

9 Busaba Eathai
MAP K2 ■ 106–110 Wardour St W1 ■ 020 7255 8686 ■ ££

A trendy Thai restaurant serving a terrific Pad Thai.

10 Barrafina
MAP K2 ■ 26–27 Dean St W1 ■ ££

Enjoy quality tapas at the counter in this stylish restaurant. It's extremely popular, so be prepared to queue.

See map on pp94–5

Covent Garden

One of London's most distinct squares and liveliest areas, Covent Garden is a popular destination for Londoners and tourists alike. At its heart is the capital's first planned square, laid out in the 17th century by Inigo Jones and completed by the addition of the Royal Opera House. While the Piazza is renowned for its luxury stores, nearby Neal Street and Neal's Yard are home to independent boutiques. To the south of Covent Garden is Somerset House, which is the setting for outdoor concerts in summer and a superb ice skating rink in winter, while its courtyard is often used for events. To get the full impact of the imposing riverside setting, enter from the Embankment side.

Column at the centre of Seven Dials

COVENT GARDEN

Previous pages Ballet at the Royal Opera House

1 Somerset House
MAP N3 ■ Strand WC2 ■ Open
8am–11pm daily (exhibitions and
galleries from 10am–6pm Sat–Tue,
11am–8pm Wed–Fri) ■ www.
somersethouse.org.uk

Once a riverside palace, and later
home to the Navy Board and Inland
Revenue, Somerset House's upper
floors are now occupied by over 100
organizations. Much of the building is
open to the public. Highlights include
the Embankment Galleries, with
diverse exhibitions.

2 Royal Opera House
MAP M2 ■ Bow St WC2
■ 020 7304 4000 ■ Backstage tours:
10:30am, 12:30pm & 2:30pm Mon–
Sat ■ Adm ■ www.roh.org.uk

London's impressive premier music
venue is home to both the Royal Opera

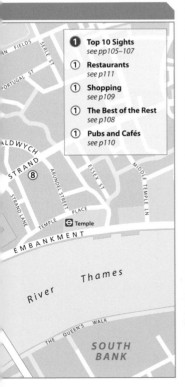

and Royal Ballet companies *(see p70)*.
The present Neo-Classical theatre
was designed in 1858 by E M Barry
and recycles a portico frieze recov-
ered from the previous building, which
was destroyed by fire. The Opera
House was expanded in the 1990s to
incorporate the old Victorian wrought-
iron floral hall, which now houses a
restaurant and champagne bar.

3 Seven Dials Market
MAP M2 ■ Earlham St WC2
■ Open 11am–11pm Mon–Sat, noon–
10:30pm Sun ■ www.sevendials
market.com

This food hall, tastefully transformed
from a 19th-century former banana
warehouse, is the perfect introduction to the city's latest culinary
trends. A row of food and wine stalls
upstairs and inventive street-food
vendors in the atrium, offer global
specialities. Don't miss the unique
cheese conveyer belt that offers
tasters the best of British cheeses.

4 The Piazza and Central Market
MAP M3 ■ WC2

For 300 years, Covent Garden was a
fruit, vegetable and flower market –
immortalized by Lerner and Loewe's
hit musical *My Fair Lady*. In the 1970s
the market moved and the lovely
iron and glass Victorian halls were
transformed into a vibrant, modern-
day shopping area, surrounded
by cafés and bars and enlivened by
regular street entertainment.

Apple Market, Covent Garden

5 Seven Dials
MAP E3 ■ WC2

"Covent Garden's hidden village", this unusual street layout was created by Thomas Neale (1641–99), as a way to increase rents, which were then charged by frontage size rather than interior space. The sundial at the central monument has only six faces. The seven streets leading off it contain a mixture of shops, offices, restaurants and theatres.

6 Floral Street
MAP M3 ■ Floral St WC2

With some of the best shops in the area, this cobbled street is home to stylish British designers such as Ted Baker and Paul Smith. The Floral Court, just off here, is filled with a profusion of foliage and connects the deli, restaurants, cellar and the giant shop at the high-end and elegant Petersham Nurseries.

7 London Transport Museum
MAP M3 ■ Covent Garden Piazza WC2 ■ Open 10am–6pm daily ■ Adm ■ www.ltmuseum.co.uk

This museum *(see p57)* explores London's transport, and its society and culture along the way, through some 450,000 objects. See vehicles that have served the city for over two centuries. You can

COVENT GARDEN ARCHITECT

Inigo Jones (1573–1652) designed Covent Garden **(below)** as London's first planned square. The low roofs and classical portico of St Paul's Church were influenced by the Italian architect Andrea Palladio (1518–80). As a set designer for royal masques, Jones was responsible for introducing the proscenium arch and moveable scenery to the London stage.

also try your hand at driving an iconic double-decker bus or an Underground train.

8 Neal's Yard
MAP M2 ■ Neal St WC2

This delightful enclave is full of colour, with painted shop fronts, flower-filled window boxes and oil drums, and cascades of plants tumbling down the walls. This was once alternative London, with wholefood cafés but is now a cluster of appealing restaurants and wine bars. Visit the now global Neal's Yard Remedies for

Buses on show at the London Transport Museum

Neal's Yard Remedies

natural cures and beauty products, or try a variety of British cheeses at Neal's Yard Dairy round the corner in Shorts Gardens. Seek out Homeslice for a pizza or try veggie delights at Food Café; either will set you up for an hour of shopping.

9 St Paul's Church
MAP M3 ▪ Bedford St WC2
▪ Open 8:30am–5pm Mon–Fri, 9am–1pm Sun ▪ www.actorschurch.org

Inigo Jones built this church (known as "the actors' church") with the main portico facing east, onto the Piazza, and the altar at the west end. Clerics objected to this unorthodox arrangement, so the altar was moved. The entrance is through the garden while the grand east door is essentially a fake.

10 Theatre Royal, Drury Lane
MAP M2 ▪ Catherine St WC2
▪ Guided tours

Drury Lane is synonymous with the London stage. This theatre has a splendid entrance, with magnificent stairways leading to the circle seats. The theatre has staged some of the biggest musical extravaganzas, including *South Pacific*, *My Fair Lady*, *The Producers*, *Hello, Dolly!*, *Miss Saigon* and – following refurbishment in 2020 – *Frozen*. The first theatre on this site was built in 1663 for Charles II, whose mistress Nell Gwynne trod the boards.

A WALK AROUND COVENT GARDEN

▶ MORNING

Take the Tube to Leicester Square and head up nearby Monmouth Street, where the delicious smell of coffee roasting will lead you to the **Monmouth Coffee Company** *(see p110)* for coffee and a pastry. Continue up Monmouth Street until you reach the small entrance to Neal's Yard. Buy some natural soap at Neal's Yard Remedies and check out the cheese in Neal's Yard Dairy round the corner in Short's Gardens, before exploring the shops in Earlham Street. Visit **Covent Garden Piazza** *(see p105)* for the street entertainers outside Inigo Jones's elegant **St Paul's Church**. Take a look inside before eating lunch at the hip Korean restaurant **On The Bab** *(see p111)*.

AFTERNOON

Pop into **Benjamin Pollock's Toyshop** *(see p109)* in the Piazza, then turn down Russell Street and Wellington Street to the Strand. Cross the road and turn left to **Somerset House** *(see p105)*, a palatial Neo-Classical building that is home to numerous organizations. Pause to relax in the café by the courtyard fountains. Next, check out the Embankment Galleries at riverside level, with exhibitions dedicated to the contemporary arts, including design, fashion, architecture and photography. For more contemporary art and design as well as fashion events, exit Somerset House and walk towards 180 The Strand, home to a maze of gallery spaces, studios and offices.

See map on pp104–5

The Best of the Rest

(1) London Film Museum
MAP M3 ▪ 45 Wellington St WC2
▪ Adm ▪ www.londonfilmmuseum.com

Home to the Bond in Motion exhibition, this is the biggest collection of James Bond vehicles and props ever staged.

(2) Donmar Warehouse
MAP P5 ▪ 41 Earlham St WC2
▪ 020 3282 3808 ▪ www.donmarware
house.com

This 251-seater venue (see p71) produces theatrical performances. As well as new plays, it also stages at least one classic per season.

(3) Backstage tours of the Royal Opera House
Book online in advance for backstage tours of the opera house (see p105). You might catch a dance rehearsal.

(4) London Coliseum
MAP L3 ▪ St Martin's Lane WC2
▪ 020 7845 9300 ▪ www.eno.org

Opened in 1904, the home of the English National Opera (see p70) has a distinct Edwardian flavour.

(5) River Cruises
MAP M4 ▪ Embankment WC2

Embankment Pier is the boarding point for a range of trips, from

Victoria Embankment Gardens

dining cruises to the Tate Boat linking both branches of the Tate (see pp28–31).

(6) Victoria Embankment Gardens
MAP M4 ▪ WC2

During the summer, outdoor concerts are held in these gardens by the river.

(7) Freemasons' Hall
MAP F3 ▪ 60 Great Queen St WC2 ▪ www.ugle.org.uk

Take a free tour of the Grand Temple and ceremonial areas. Be sure to visit the museum here.

(8) 180 The Strand
MAP N3 ▪ 180 Strand

Set in an iconic Brutalist building, it houses a mix of creative companies and the Store Studios, attracting thousands to its contemporary video exhibitions. London Fashion Week is held here. Check in advance for events.

(9) Benjamin Franklin House
MAP E4 ▪ 36 Craven St WC2 ▪ Adm

The only remaining home of this US founding father (see p66), offers an insight into his life and achievements.

(10) Cleopatra's Needle
MAP F4 ▪ Victoria Embankment WC2

This granite obelisk was originally erected in Heliopolis around 1450 BC and transported to London in 1878. Its inscriptions and hieroglyphics document the achievements of the pharaohs of ancient Egypt.

Riverboat cruising along the Thames

Shopping

1 **The Tintin Shop**
MAP M3 ▪ 34 Floral St WC2

Selling everything, from keyrings and Snowy toys to limited edition models, Tintin fans will love this shop.

2 **Whisky Exchange**
MAP M3 ▪ 2 Bedford St WC2E

The two floors are stacked with spirits from around the world. Fill your own bottle straight from the cask.

3 **Neal's Yard Remedies**
MAP M3 ▪ 15 Neal's Yard WC2H

Remedies, toiletries and make up, all made with purely natural ingredients, have been sold at this shop for more than 30 years.

4 **Stanfords**
MAP M3 ▪ 7 Mercer Walk WC2

With an extensive range of travel guides, literature, maps and gifts, this shop is a traveller's paradise. There is a small coffee shop, too.

5 **St Martin's Courtyard**
MAP L3 ▪ Long Acre WC2

London's latest shopping and dining destination is a stylish yet charming urban village enclave, with alfresco tables and top-name stores.

6 **Pylones**
MAP M2 ▪ 15 The Market WC2E

This French store is home to a kooky collection of colourful, eye-catching accessories and household goods. Ideal for unusual gifts for children and adults alike.

7 **Penhaligon's**
MAP M3 ▪ 41 Wellington St WC2E

In business since the 1870s, this eccentric British perfumery has a glorious range of fragrances and accessories for both men and women. Their luxury candles make elegant gifts.

BOW WOW London

8 **BOW WOW London**
MAP M2 ▪ 50A Earlham St WC2H

Setting a new standard for the dapper dog-around-town, this dog boutique stocks the finest designer dog products to spoil your pooch with.

9 **The Tea House**
MAP M2 ▪ 15a Neal St WC2

Over a hundred teas, ranging from Moroccan Minty to Mango & Maracuja, are on sale at this speciality shop in Neal Street. There are also novelty teapots and books on how to master the art of tea-making.

10 **Benjamin Pollock's Toyshop**
MAP M3 ▪ 44 The Market WC2E

The place to go for theatrical gifts and traditional toys such as puppets and musical boxes.

Inside Benjamin Pollock's Toyshop

See map on pp104–5

Pubs and Cafés

 LaduRée
MAP M3 ■ 1 Market Building WC2E

This Parisian-style tearoom is known for its delectable macarons, but it also serves other stunning cakes and pastries, as well as champagne.

2 Wild Food Café
MAP M2 ■ 14 Neal's Yard WC2

Long known as the Whole Food Café, this vegan and vegetarian eatery focuses on organic, wild foods that have been cooked as little as possible.

3 Freud
MAP L2 ■ 198 Shaftesbury Ave W1

With a choice of coffees, cocktails and bottled beers, this basement attracts a designer crowd in the evenings.

4 Covent Garden Grind
MAP M3 ■ 42 Maiden Lane

As the name suggests, the Grind group offers top-class coffee along with a brunch menu. They serve cocktails and sharing plates as well in the evening.

5 The Lamb and Flag
MAP M3 ■ 33 Rose St WC2

This traditional pub, serving cask bitter, is one of the oldest in the West End *(see p77)* and was frequented by Charles Dickens. Delicious roasts are served at Sunday lunchtimes.

6 Snog
MAP M3 ■ 5 Garrick St WC2

If you want some low-calorie indulgence then Snog's fat-free organic yogurts are well worth checking out. There are four flavours plus plenty of healthy and not-so-healthy things to dollop on top.

 Monmouth Coffee Company
MAP L2 ■ 27 Monmouth St WC2

One of the best places in London to buy and sample really good coffee *(see p92)*. There's also a wonderful small café that serves delicious French pastries.

8 Lowlander
MAP M2 ■ 36 Drury Lane WC2

Belgian beer and European cuisine served in a relaxed setting attract drinkers and diners alike to this popular spot.

9 Porterhouse
MAP M3 ■ 21–2 Maiden Lane WC2

There are excellent beers and a great atmosphere to be enjoyed in this pub with bars over 12 levels.

10 Gordon's Wine Bar
MAP M4 ■ 47 Villiers St WC2

An ancient and atmospheric candle-lit cellar, where wine, port and Madeira are served from the barrel in schooners or beakers.

The cavernous interior of Gordon's Wine Bar

Restaurants

> **PRICE CATEGORIES**
> For a three-course meal for one with half a bottle of wine (or equivalent meal), taxes and extra charges.
>
> £ under £30   ££ £30–50   £££ over £50

1 The Ivy
MAP L2 ▪ 1–5 West St WC2
▪ 020 7836 4751 ▪ £££

Mere mortals need to book several months ahead in order to get a table in London's most star-struck restaurant. However, it's worth waiting for the delicious brasserie-style food and lively atmosphere.

2 The Barbary
MAP M2 ▪ 16 Neal's Yard, WC2
▪ 020 7324 7722 ▪ ££

Sit at the bar of this award-winning restaurant (see p74) while watching the chefs at work. The menu offers dishes with Middle Eastern and North African influences.

3 Mon Plaisir
MAP L2 ▪ 19–21 Monmouth St WC2 ▪ 020 7836 7243 ▪ ££

One of the oldest French restaurants in London, this place has four rooms, each of a different size and feel. Daily specials keep the menu fresh. Set lunch and pre-theatre menus offer better value for money.

4 Rock and Sole Plaice
MAP M2 ▪ 47 Endell St WC2
▪ 020 7836 3785 ▪ ££

A popular place in central London, Rock and Sole Plaice serves excellent traditional English fish and chips.

5 The Delaunay
MAP N2 ▪ 55 Aldwych WC2B
▪ 020 7499 8558 ▪ £££

Open from breakfast until late, seven days a week. this elegant restaurant offers an extensive à la carte menu inspired by the grand cafés of Europe. Patrons can also enjoy breakfast or brunch, and even afternoon tea.

Vibrant interior of the Cora Pearl

6 Cora Pearl
MAP M3 ▪ Henrietta St WC2E
▪ 020 7324 7722 ▪ ££

Occupying two floors, this smart restaurant with elegant interiors and vintage lighting, is a delightful addition to Covent Garden. The food menu reflects British and French influences.

7 On The Bab
MAP M3 ▪ 36 Wellington St WC2 ▪ 020 7240 5568 ▪ ££

Bustling with a lively crowd, this restaurant serves finger-licking Korean street food.

8 Opera Tavern
MAP M3 ▪ 23 Catherine St WC2
▪ 020 7836 3680 ▪ £££

Enjoy scrumptious Italian and Spanish tapas complemented by a terrific wine list at this tavern.

9 Rules
MAP M3 ▪ 35 Maiden Lane WC2 ▪ 020 7836 5314 ▪ £££

London's oldest restaurant (see p74) has been famed since 1798 for its "oysters, pies and game".

10 Souk
MAP L2 ▪ 27 Litchfield St WC2
▪ 020 7240 1796 ▪ £

From mint tea to tagines and belly dancing to Arabic music, this place offers a real taste of Marrakech.

See map on pp104–5

TOP10 Bloomsbury and Fitzrovia

Literary, legal and scholarly, this is the brainy quarter of London. Dominated by two towering institutions, the British Museum and the University of London,

Charles Dickens

and bolstered by the nearby Inns of Court, it is an area of elegant squares and Georgian façades, of libraries, bookshops and publishing houses. Most famously, the Bloomsbury Group, known for novelist Virginia Woolf, lived here during the early decades of the 20th century. Fitzrovia's reputation as a raffish place was enhanced by the characters who drank at the Fitzroy Tavern, such as Welsh poet Dylan Thomas (1914–53) and the painter Augustus John (1878–1961).

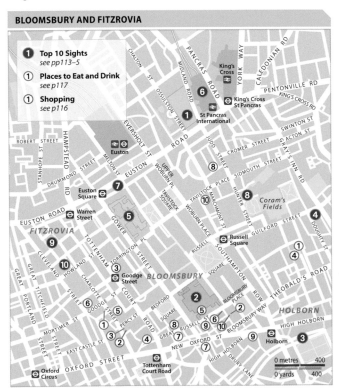

The red-brick exterior of the British Library

1 British Library

MAP L1 ■ 96 Euston Rd NW1
■ Library: open 9:30am–8pm Mon–
Thu (until 6pm Fri & 5pm Sat), 11am–
5pm Sun & public holidays ■ Treasures
Gallery: open 9:30am–6pm Mon &
Wed–Fri (until 8pm Tue & 5pm Sat),
11am–5pm Sun ■ Adm for temporary
exhibitions ■ www.bl.uk

The British Library holds copies of
everything published in the UK and
Ireland, as well as many historical
publications from around the world.
"Readers" have free access to these,
while everyone else can enjoy the
space and the regular exhibitions.
A permanent display in the Sir John
Ritblat Treasures Gallery includes two
out of the four existing editions of
Magna Carta (1215), a Gutenberg
Bible (1455), Shakespeare's first folio
(1623) and many breathtaking illuminated manuscripts. The glass walls
in the core of the building reveal
the huge leather volumes from the
King's Library, donated by George III.
There are regular talks and events,
a café and a restaurant.

2 British Museum

See pp12–15.

3 Sir John Soane's Museum

MAP N1 ■ 13 Lincoln's Inn Fields
WC2 ■ Open 10am–5pm Wed–Sun
■ Closed public hols ■ www.soane.org

A particular pleasure of this unique
museum is watching visitors' faces
as they turn a corner and encounter
yet another unexpected gem. Sir John
Soane, one of Britain's leading 19th-
century architects, crammed three
adjoining houses with antiques and
various other treasures, displayed in
the most ingenious of ways. The basement crypt, which he designed to
resemble a Roman catacomb, is particularly original. *The Rake's Progress*
(1753), a series of eight paintings by
Hogarth, is another highlight. Be sure
to ask about the free tours of the
upstairs private apartments. Tickets
can be booked online in advance
too. The houses are situated on the
northern side of Lincoln's Inn Fields,
the heart of legal London. Lincoln's
Inn, located on the east side of the
square, is one of the best-preserved
Inns of Court, with part of it dating
from the 15th century.

Interior of Sir John Soane's Museum

4 Charles Dickens Museum

MAP F2 ■ 48 Doughty St WC1 ■ Open 10am–5pm Tue–Sun ■ Adm ■ www. dickensmuseum.com

Home to Charles Dickens from 1837 to 1839, during which time he completed some of his best work (including *The Pickwick Papers*, *Oliver Twist* and *Nicholas Nickleby*), this five-storey house offers a fascinating glimpse into the life and times of the great Victorian author and social reformer. The rooms are laid out just as they might have been in Dickens' time. Nearby Doughty Mews provides another step back to Victorian times.

5 University College London

MAP E2 ■ Gower St WC1 ■ Museums: open 1–5pm Mon–Sat; www.ucl.ac. uk/culture

Founded in 1826, UCL is one of the world's leading multidisci-plinary universities and has a couple of fascinating collections of international importance, includ-ing the Petrie Museum of Egyptian Archaeology and the intriguing Grant Museum of Zoology. The university also hosts public lectures. Visitors can see the well-preserved body of Jeremy Bentham, the philosopher, enclosed in a case at the main building.

THE BLOOMSBURY GROUP

The Bloomsbury Group was an informal set of writers, artists and intellectuals who lived in and around Bloomsbury at the beginning of the 20th century. The group, with its modern attitudes towards feminism and politics, first gathered at the home of the Stephen sisters, Virginia, later famous as Virginia Woolf (**below**) and Vanessa, later known as Vanessa Bell.

6 St Pancras International Station

MAP E1 ■ Euston Rd NW1

One of the glories of Victorian Gothic architecture, this railway terminus, opened in 1868, was designed by Sir George Gilbert Scott. Eurostar trains depart from here, although most of the frontage is in fact the St Pancras Renaissance Hotel.

St Pancras International Station

7 Wellcome Collection
MAP E2 ■ 183 Euston Rd NW1 ■ Open 10am–6pm Tue, Wed & Fri–Sun (until 10pm Thu) ■ www.wellcomecollection.org

The medical collection of businessman and philanthropist Sir Henry Wellcome (1853–1936), founder of one of the world's leading pharmaceutical companies, explores connections between medicine, life and art in the past, present and future, and houses regular temporary exhibitions. The top floor feaures a creatively designed reading room where visitors can relax and read. There is a café and an excellent bookshop as well.

8 Foundling Museum
MAP E2 ■ 40 Brunswick Sq WC1 ■ Open 10am–5pm Tue–Sat, 11am–5pm Sun ■ Adm ■ www.foundlingmuseum.org.uk

Established in 1739 by Thomas Coram, the Foundling Hospital provided a refuge for abandoned children until it closed in 1954. The original interiors from the hospital are on display, while the exhibits tell the stories of the thousands of children who were cared for here. Also on display are artworks donated by 18th- and 19th-century artists, including Gainsborough, Reynolds and Hogarth.

9 Fitzroy Square
MAP D2 ■ Fitzroy Sq W1

Much of this square, completed in 1798, was designed by Scottish architect Robert Adam. Its many residents have included Victorian prime minister Lord Salisbury, who lived at No 21, the playwright George Bernard Shaw and the novelist Virginia Woolf.

10 BT Tower
MAP D2

At 190 m (620 ft), this was the tallest building in London when it opened in 1965. It is now used as a media and telecommunications hub and is closed to the public.

BT Tower

BLOOMSBURY AND FITZROVIA ON FOOT

Brunswick Centre
Bloomsbury Coffee House
Curzon Bloomsbury
Bloomsbury Square
Fitzroy Tavern
British Museum
Roka
Bedford Square
Jarndyce

▶ **MORNING**

Arrive at the **British Museum** (see pp12–15) at 10am (opening time) so that you can enjoy the Great Court in peace. View Norman Foster's glass dome while having coffee at the café here, then wander the museum's extraordinary galleries. Don't miss the great Assyrian bas-reliefs on your way out.

Browse the antiquarian book and print shops, such as **Jarndyce** (see p116), along Great Russell and Museum streets. Turn left up Little Russell Street, noticing the fine Hawksmoor church of St George's. Loop around Bloomsbury Square and check out the list of Bloomsbury group literary figures posted here. Head west to Bedford Square with its Georgian houses. Cross Tottenham Court Road and carry on to Charlotte Street.

AFTERNOON

See the photos of literary figures such as Dylan Thomas in the basement bar of **Fitzroy Tavern** (see p117) at No 16 Charlotte Street, while enjoying a pre-lunch drink. If you fancy something more exotic than pub grub, try some barbecued Japanese food at **Roka** (see p117) a little further along Charlotte Street.

After lunch, head to the **Brunswick Centre** (1 Byng Place) for shopping, from food to fashion. This awesome concrete-and-glass megastructure was a 1960s housing and retail complex. Catch a film at arthouse cinema **Curzon Bloomsbury** (Brunswick Centre), or have a coffee at **the Bloomsbury Coffee House** (see p117).

See map on p112

Shopping

 La Fromagerie
MAP F2 ■ 52 Lamb's Conduit St WC1N

Head to the Cheese Room for the best Beaufort Chalet d'Alpage, La Fromagerie's signature cheese.

2 Hobgoblin Music
MAP K1 ■ 24 Rathbone Place WC1

If you're looking for a Chinese flute, mandolin, Irish drum or any other folk instrument, then this wonderful shop has an endlessly fascinating range from every part of the world.

3 Heals
MAP E2 ■ 196 Tottenham Court Rd W1

London's leading furniture store is a showcase for the best of British design. There is also a good café.

 Maggie Owen
MAP F2 ■ 13 Rugby St WC1

This former dairy in the heart of Bloomsbury sells chic, contemporary costume jewellery and accessories from across Europe.

5 British Museum Shop
MAP L1 ■ 22 Great Russell St WC1

Find a wide range of exquisite crafts and jewellery in this museum shop. Everything from a pair of earrings modelled on those of ancient Egypt to contemporary crafts can be found.

 Contemporary Ceramics Centre
MAP L1 ■ 63 Great Russell St WC1

An outstanding gallery that showcases the very best in contemporary studio ceramics, particularly work by British potters.

7 James Smith & Sons
MAP L1 ■ 53 New Oxford St WC1

Established in 1830, James Smith & Sons is a beautiful shop that will meet all your umbrella, parasol, cane and walking-stick needs.

8 L. Cornelissen & Son
MAP M1 ■ 105a Great Russell St WC1

This specialist art supplies shop has wood panelling and rows of glass jars full of pigments.

9 Jarndyce
MAP L1 ■ 46 Great Russell St WC1

This handsome antiquarian bookshop specializes in 18th- and 19th-century British literature.

10 London Review Bookshop
MAP M1 ■ 14 Bury Place WC1

Opened by the literary magazine the *London Review of Books*, this shop is a favourite among readers for its informed staff and richly varied stock. It also regularly hosts readings by a wide range of authors.

Patrons at London Review Bookshop

Places to Eat and Drink

PRICE CATEGORIES

For a three-course meal for one with half a bottle of wine (or equivalent meal), taxes and extra charges.

£ under £30 ■ ££ £30–50 ■ £££ over £50

1 Roka

MAP K1 ■ 37 Charlotte St W1 ■ 020 7580 6464 ■ £££

Japanese robatayaki cuisine involves slow-cooking the food on skewers over a charcoal grill. At Roka, this is done at the centrally placed grill, in full view of the customers.

2 Truckles of Pied Bull Yard

MAP M1 ■ Off Bury Place WC1 ■ 020 7404 5338 ■ ££

This wine bar really comes to life in the summertime, when the outdoor terrace is filled with people enjoying chilled rosé and Pimm's on comfortable sofas.

3 House of Ho

MAP K1 ■ 1 Percy St W1 ■ 020 7434 0194 ■ ££

Set in a lovely four-storey Georgian townhouse and decorated with modern flair, this Vietnamese restaurant serves traditional meals with a contemporary twist. Enjoy a bowl of pho, Vietnamese noodle soup.

4 Hakkasan

MAP K1 ■ 8 Hanway Place W1 ■ 020 7927 7000 ■ £££

Its location may not be salubrious but this Michelin-starred Chinese restaurant and cocktail bar is superb.

5 Fitzroy Tavern

MAP K1 ■ 16 Charlotte St W1 ■ £

The pub that gave its name to the surrounding area (Fitzrovia), was once a haunt of London luminaries including George Orwell, Dylan Thomas and Tommy Cooper.

6 Salt Yard

MAP K1 ■ 54 Goodge St W1 ■ 020 7637 0657 ■ ££

Top-notch modern Spanish tapas are served at Salt Yard. Diverse menu ranges from Old Spot pork belly with cannellini beans to chargrilled squid.

Outdoor seating at Dalloway Terrace

7 Dalloway Terrace

MAP L1 ■ 16–22 Great Russell St WC1B ■ 020 7347 1221 ■ ££

Pop in for the pre-theatre menu and afternoon tea at this secret garden with beautiful walls (heated in winter).

8 Norfolk Arms

MAP E2 ■ 28 Leigh St WC1 ■ 020 7388 3937 ■ ££

This gastropub serves tapas-style portions of Mediterranean food. It's a local favourite.

9 Princess Louise

MAP M1 ■ 20 High Holborn WC1

A beautifully restored Victorian pub with carved mahogany partitions separating the drinking areas.

10 Bloomsbury Coffee House

MAP E2 ■ 20 Tavistock Place WC1 ■ 020 7837 2877 ■ ££

This basement café is a perfect pitstop for cakes and light lunches.

See map on p112

🔟 Mayfair and St James's

Home to some of London's historical buildings and wealthiest individuals, many of the wonderful shops around here were established to serve the royal court. Piccadilly – named after the fancy collars called "picadils" that were sold at a shop here in the 18th century – divides St James's to the south from Mayfair to the north, where shops continue up Bond Street, Cork Street and Savile Row to Oxford Street. With the Royal Academy of Arts here since 1868, Mayfair has long been one of the best addresses in town. Today most of London's top commercial art galleries are here.

Guard at Buckingham Palace

MAYFAIR AND ST JAMES'S

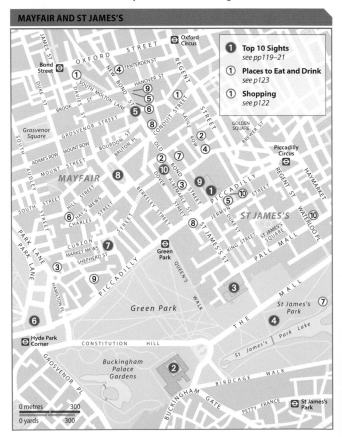

❶	**Top 10 Sights** see pp119–21
①	**Places to Eat and Drink** see p123
①	**Shopping** see p122

0 metres 300
0 yards 300

Taddei Tondo, and J M W Turner's atmospheric and bleak *Dolbadern Castle, North Wales* (1800). In the Royal Academy's popular annual summer exhibition *(see p59)*, new works by both established and unknown artists are displayed.

The Royal Academy of Arts

1 Royal Academy of Arts
MAP J4 ■ Burlington House, Piccadilly W1 ■ Open 10am–6pm daily (until 10pm Fri) ■ Adm for temporary exhibitions ■ www.royalacademy.org.uk

Major temporary art exhibitions are staged at Burlington House, home of Britain's most prestigious fine arts institution. The building is one of Piccadilly's few surviving 17th-century mansions. New permanent galleries opened to the public in 2018 marking the gallery's 250th anniversary. Displays include Michelangleo's *Virgin and Child with the Infant St John*, known as the

2 Buckingham Palace
See pp24–5.

3 St James's Palace
MAP K5 ■ The Mall SW1
■ Closed to public

Built by Henry VIII *(see p52)*, on the site of the former Hospital of St James, the palace's redbrick Tudor gatehouse is a familiar landmark.

4 St James's Park
MAP K5–L5 ■ SW1
■ Open 5am–midnight daily

This is undoubtedly London's most elegant park, with dazzling flower beds, exotic wildfowl on the lake, the lovely view from St James's Café *(see p123)* next to the lake and music on the bandstand *(see p54)* in summer. The bridge over the lake has a good view of Buckingham Palace to the west and, to the east, of the Foreign Office from where civil servants once governed the British Empire that covered one fifth of the world.

Buckingham Palace as seen from St James's Park

5 Bond Street
MAP J3–J4

London's most exclusive shopping street, Bond Street (which is known as New Bond Street to the north and Old Bond Street to the south) has long been the place for high society to promenade: many of its establishments have been here for over 100 years. The street is home to top fashion houses, elegant galleries such as Halcyon, Sotheby's auction rooms and jewellers such as Tiffany and Asprey. Where Old and New Bond Street meet, there is a delightful sculpture of wartime leaders Franklin D Roosevelt and Winston Churchill on a bench – it's well worth a photograph.

6 Apsley House
MAP D5 ▪ 149 Piccadilly, Hyde Park Corner W1 ▪ Open Jan–Mar: 10am–4pm Sat & Sun; Apr–Oct: 11am–5pm Wed–Sun; Nov & Dec: 10am–4pm Wed–Sun ▪ Adm

Designed by Robert Adam in the 1770s as the home of the Duke of Wellington (see p63), Apsley House is given over to the paintings and memorabilia of the great military leader, and is still partly occupied by the family. The paintings include *The Waterseller of Seville* by Diego Velázquez. The nude statue of Napoleon by Antonio Canova has special poignancy.

HANDEL IN MAYFAIR

The great composer *(see p63)*, George Frideric Handel (**below**) arrived in London in 1710 to have his operas staged at the capital's reputed venues. In 1723, he was appointed Composer to the Chapel Royal and moved to Mayfair. He lived there until his death in 1759. By the end of his life, he had written 31 operas for London audiences.

7 Shepherd Market
MAP D4

This square was named after Edward Shepherd who developed the area in around 1735. Today, this pedestrianized area in the heart of Mayfair, between Piccadilly and Curzon Street is a good place to visit on a summer evening for a drink or dinner. Ye Grapes, dating from 1882, is the principal pub, while local restaurants include Titu, Misto, Le Boudin Blanc and Iran.

The imposing façade of Apsley House

Ye Grapes in Shepherd Market

In the 17th century, an annual May Fair was held here, giving the wider area its name.

8 Berkeley Square
MAP D4

This pocket of green in the middle of Mayfair was planted in 1789 and its 30 huge plane trees may be the oldest in London. Famous residents include Clive of India at No. 45 and Winston Churchill, who lived at No. 48 as a child. Memorial benches in the square bear moving inscriptions, many from Americans billeted here during World War II. It was the London base of P G Wodehouse's Bertie Wooster and Jeeves.

9 Burlington Arcade
MAP J4 ■ 51 Piccadilly W1
■ www.burlingtonarcade.com

This arcade of bijou shops was built in 1819 for Lord George Cavendish of Burlington House (see p119) to prevent people from throwing rubbish into his garden. The arcade of luxury stores is patrolled by uniformed beadles who control unseemly behaviour.

10 Royal Institution
MAP J3 ■ 21 Albemarle St W1
■ Museum: open 9am–5pm Mon–Fri
■ www.rigb.org

The Royal Institution was founded in 1799 to encourage the practical application of scientific knowledge. Its most influential member was Michael Faraday (1791–1867), a pioneer of electro-technology. The three floors of the Faraday Museum explore science, the highlight being Faraday's 1850s magnetic laboratory.

EXPLORING ST JAMES'S

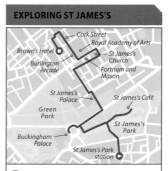

▶ MORNING

Starting from St James's Park Tube, walk up through Queen Anne's Gate, noting the lovely 18th-century houses. Pass through the alley in the corner into Birdcage Walk, then **St James's Park** (see p119). Get a coffee from **St James's Café** (see p123) and watch the pelicans before heading to **Buckingham Palace** (see pp24–5) for the Changing of the Guard at 11am. Afterwards, head up The Mall past **St James's Palace** (see p119) into St James's Street. Turn into Jermyn Street, and check out such shops as perfumery Floris and cheeseseller Paxton and Whitfield. Walk through St James's Church, leaving by the north exit onto Piccadilly, where a craft market is held from Wednesday to Saturday, and a food market on Mondays and Tuesdays. Head west down Piccadilly to Fortnum & Mason.

AFTERNOON

Fortnum & Mason (see p78) is the perfect place to have lunch at one of the store's several restaurants, where the dieter's choice is caviar and half a bottle of champagne. Cross Piccadilly to the **Royal Academy of Arts** (see p119) and enjoy their permanent collection, including Michelangelo's *Taddei Tondo*. Window-shop along Burlington Arcade and the **Cork Street** galleries (see p122). Turn into Bond Street, heading for **Brown's Hotel** (see p174) to relax over afternoon tea.

See map on p118 ←

Shopping

1 Browns
MAP D3 ▪ 23–27 South Molton St W1

London's most famous designer clothing store stocks pieces by Burberry, Balenciaga, Alexander McQueen and Stella McCartney among many others.

2 Asprey
MAP J3 ▪ 167 New Bond St W1

The UK royal family have bought their jewels here for more than a century. Other luxury items to be found here include exquisite vases, handbags and silver gifts.

3 Charbonnel et Walker
MAP J4 ▪ 1 The Royal Arcade, 28 Old Bond St W1

One of the best chocolate shops in town with a tempting array of hand-made goodies. Fill one of the pretty boxes with your choice of treats.

4 Gieves and Hawkes
MAP J3 ▪ 1 Savile Row W1

Purveyors of fine, handmade suits and shirts to the gentry since 1785, this shop is one of the best known in a street of expert tailors. Off-the-rack clothes are also available.

5 Fortnum & Mason
MAP J4 ▪ 181 Piccadilly W1

Famous for its food hall and restaurants, this elegant department store *(see p78)* still has male staff who wear coat-tails.

Try the extravagant ice creams in the Parlour restaurant or enjoy their afternoon tea.

6 Mulberry

MAP J3 ▪ 50 New Bond St W1

Come here for must-have leather handbags, purses and other luxurious accessories and shoes.

7 Cork Street Galleries

MAP J3

Cork Street is famous for its art galleries. You can view or purchase works by the best artists here, from Picasso and Rothko to Damien Hirst.

8 Sotheby's
MAP J3 ▪ 34–35 New Bond St W1

View everything from pop star memorabilia to Old Master paintings at this fine arts auction house founded in 1744.

9 Fenwick
MAP J3 ▪ 63 New Bond St W1

A small, upmarket department store with designer labels, accessories and expensive lingerie.

10 Hatchards
MAP K4 ▪ 187 Piccadilly W1

Established in 1797 and now owned by Waterstones, this bookshop is the oldest in the UK. It is the official supplier of books to the Queen and other royals.

Fortnum & Mason, the iconic department store on Piccadilly

Places to Eat and Drink

PRICE CATEGORIES

For a three-course meal for one with half a bottle of wine (or equivalent meal), taxes and extra charges.

£ under £30 ££ £30–50 £££ over £50

 Sketch
MAP J3 ▪ 9 Conduit St W1
▪ 020 7659 4500 ▪ £££

Culinary genius is to be found in the arty surroundings at Sketch. The Gallery is informal and features British artist David Shrigley's work. The pricier Lecture Room attracts fashionable and famous people.

 Momo
MAP J3 ▪ 25 Heddon St W1
▪ 020 7434 4040 ▪ £££

Brilliantly decorated in a kasbah style, this North African restaurant serves *tajines* and couscous. The Mo Café next door serves tea and snacks.

3 Galvin at Windows
MAP D4 ▪ 22 Park Lane W1
▪ 020 7208 4021 ▪ £££

At the top of the Hilton, this restaurant has fine London views and superb French-influenced cuisine.

4 Rasa W1
MAP D3 ▪ Dering St W1 ▪ 020 7629 1346 ▪ £

Serving dosas, vegetarian curries and seafood, Rasa mirrors the true flavours of South Indian cuisine.

5 Bond Street Kitchen
MAP J3 ▪ Fenwick, 63 New Bond St W1 ▪ ££

The modern British cuisine upstages the department store setting. A variety of mains, salads and some interesting sharing platters are offered here.

6 The Greenhouse
MAP D4 ▪ 27a Hay's Mews W1
▪ 020 7499 3331 ▪ £££

Exquisite two-Michelin-starred modern European cuisine in a serene Mayfair location.

Verandah seating at St James's Café

7 St James's Café
MAP L5 ▪ St James's Park SW1
▪ 020 839 1149 ▪ £

This café is a simple watering hole in the leafy surroundings of St James's Park. Customers can watch the world go by through the café's large glass windows.

8 The Wolseley
MAP J4 ▪ 160 Piccadilly W1
▪ 020 7499 6996 ▪ £££

The Art Deco interior gives this famous brasserie *(see p75)* an air of glamour. You need to book ahead for the formal restaurant.

9 El Pirata
MAP D4 ▪ 5–6 Down St W1
▪ 020 7491 3810 ▪ Closed Sun ▪ ££

A lively, casual and enticing tapas restaurant which excels at the Spanish classics.

10 Wild Honey
MAP K4 ▪ 8 Pall Mall W1
▪ 020 7389 7820 ▪ ££

Wonderful, largely French-influenced food with the finest seasonal produce is on offer at this beautifully designed restaurant. It is located within the Sofitel Hotel.

See map on p118 ←

TOP 10 Kensington and Knightsbridge

The heart of affluent and cultural London life, this is where wealthy visitors come to shop, not least because it's home to Harrods. It's also the location of Kensington Palace, its place in history once intertwined with the life of Princess Diana, and the great Victorian museums of South Kensington. Some of the best antique shops can be found on Kensington Church Street but for a better bargain try Portobello Road – a lively place to be on a Saturday.

Gate detail, Kensington Palace

KENSINGTON AND KNIGHTSBRIDGE

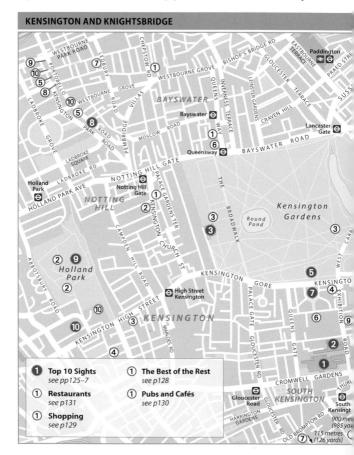

1	Top 10 Sights *see pp125–7*	1	The Best of the Rest *see p128*
1	Restaurants *see p131*	1	Pubs and Cafés *see p130*
1	Shopping *see p129*		

Natural History Museum
From earthquakes to blue whales, the natural world is exhibited in this museum *(see pp20–21)*.

 Science Museum
The scientific achievements on show at this museum *(see pp22–3)* are truly awe inspiring.

3 Kensington Palace
MAP A4 ■ Kensington Palace Gardens W8 ■ Open 10am–4pm daily (Mar–Oct: until 6pm) ■ Adm ■ www.hrp.org.uk

This delightful royal residence, which used to be the residence of Diana,

The elegant Kensington Palace

Princess of Wales *(see p52)* as well as Princess Margaret, the Queen's sister, is still in use by members of the royal family. Tours and exhibits offer glimpses into both the public and the private lives of some of the palace's most illustrious former residents, including the exhibits on Queen Victoria, who lived here as a child, as well as the grand State Apartments of George II.

4 Victoria and Albert Museum
MAP B5–C5 ■ Cromwell Rd SW7 ■ Open 10am–5:45pm daily (until 10pm every Fri) ■ www.vam.ac.uk

A cornucopia of treasures is housed in this museum named after the devoted royal couple and affectionately known as the V&A. Fine and applied arts from all over the world, from ancient China to contemporary Britain are on display here. Highlights include The Great Bed of Ware (1590s), mentioned in Shakespeare's first folio of 1623. In total, there are seven floors of galleries. The stunning British Galleries display more than 3,000 objects illustrating the best of British art and design since 1500.

5 Albert Memorial
MAP B4 ■ Kensington Gardens SW7

This edifice is a fitting tribute to Prince Albert, Queen Victoria's beloved consort, who played a large part in establishing the South Kensington museums. Located opposite the Royal Albert Hall, the memorial was designed by George Gilbert Scott and completed in 1876. At its four corners are statues representing the Empire, which was at its height during Victoria's reign.

6 Harrods
MAP C4 ■ **87–135 Brompton Rd SW1**

No backpacks, no torn jeans – the doormen at Harrods ensure that even people in the store are dressed tastefully. This famous emporium *(see p78)* began life in 1849 as a small, impeccable grocer's, and the present terracotta building was built in 1905. It is most striking at night, when it is illuminated by 12,000 lights. The store has more than 300 departments and you should not miss the wonderfully tiled and decorated food halls *(see p129)*, which are great for picnic foods as much as for exotic specialities.

7 Royal Albert Hall
MAP B5 ■ **Kensington Gore SW7** ■ **Open for performances and tours** ■ **www.royalalberthall.com**

When Queen Victoria laid the foundation stone for The Hall of Arts and Sciences, to everyone's astonishment she put the words "Royal Albert" before its name, and today it is usually just referred to as the Albert Hall. This huge, nearly circular building, modelled on Roman amphitheatres *(see p71)*, seats 5,000. Circuses, sport, dance and all manner of musical entertainments are held here, notably the Sir Henry Wood Promenade Concerts, familiarly known as the Proms.

PRINCE ALBERT

Queen Victoria and her first cousin Prince Albert of Saxe-Coburg-Gotha **(below)** were both 20 when they married in 1840. Albert was a Victorian in every sense, and his interest in the arts and sciences led to the founding of the great institutions of South Kensington. He died at the age of 41, and the queen mourned him for the rest of her life. They had nine children.

8 Portobello Road
MAP A3–A4

Running through the centre of the decidedly fashionable Notting Hill, Portobello Road, with its extensive selection of antique shops, is a great place to spend some time. With its main day on Saturday, the famous market *(see p79)* starts just beyond Westbourne Grove and offers antiques, fruit and vege-tables, sausages, bread and cheeses, then music, clothes and bric-à-brac. Under the railway bridge at Portobello Green, there is a young designers' clothes market on Fridays

The red brick and terracotta exterior of the Royal Albert Hall

and Saturdays. Take a seat by the window at GAIL's Artisan Bakery (No. 138) and enjoy coffee and cake or a sandwich while watching the world go by. Street food is also widely available.

A formal garden in Holland Park

⑨ Holland Park
MAP A4–A5 ▪ Ilchester Place W8

There is a great deal of charm about Holland Park, where enclosed gardens are laid out like rooms in an open-air house. At its centre is Holland House, a beautiful Jacobean mansion, which was largely destroyed in a bombing raid in 1941. What remains is used as a wedding venue and the backdrop for summer concerts. Peacocks roam in the woods and in the gardens, including the Dutch Garden, where dahlias were first planted in England.

⑩ Leighton House Museum
MAP A5 ▪ 12 Holland Park Rd W14 ▪ Open 10am–5:30pm Wed–Mon ▪ Adm

All the themes of the Victorian Aesthetic movement can be found in the extraordinary Leighton House. It was designed by Lord Leighton (see p62) and his friend George Aitchison in the 1860s. Its high point is the fabulous Arab Hall, with a fountain and stained-glass cupola. Some of the oil paintings in the collection are from Leighton himself, such as *The Death of Brunelleschi* (1852). Other artists such as Tintoretto and Edward Burne-Jones are also represented.

KENSINGTON ON FOOT

▶ MORNING

Start at the South Kensington Tube station, and follow the signs to the **Victoria & Albert Museum,** (see p125). Spend a delightful hour wandering in the Medieval and Renaissance Galleries. Pause for coffee at the beautiful museum café that has rooms adorned with original Victorian decor. Then, follow Old Brompton Road to the **Brompton Oratory** (see p51), and take a look at its grand Italianate interior, with 12 marble Apostles.

Cross the road and turn right into Beauchamp Place, where shops display creations by English designers such as Bruce Oldfield and Caroline Charles. Continue down into Pont Street, and turn left up Sloane Street. Check out Hermès, Chanel and Dolce & Gabbana before walking up towards Knightsbridge Tube, turning left into Brompton Road for **Harrods**.

It has 19 bars and restaurants, including the Champagne Terrace and the Harrods Tea Rooms on the fourth floor.

AFTERNOON

Five minutes north of Harrods, **Hyde Park** (see p54) offers a peaceful walk along the south bank of the Serpentine. Heading for **Kensington Palace** (see p125), you pass the famous statue of JM Barrie's *Peter Pan* and the Round Pond. West of here, view the Kings Apartments, then visit the Sunken Garden opposite, where The **Kensington Palace Pavilion** (see p130) provides traditional afternoon tea.

See map on pp124–5 ←

The Best of the Rest

1 Queens Ice and Bowl
MAP A3 ■ 17 Queensway W2 ■ Bowling: 10am–11pm Sun–Thu (until midnight Fri & Sat); skating day and evening sessions daily ■ Adm ■ www.queens.london

Enjoy ten-pin bowling and ice-skating all year round here – but try to avoid the after-school crowd.

2 Holland Park Opera
MAP A4–A5 ■ Abbotsbury Rd W14 ■ Adm ■ www.operaholland park.com

The open-air theatre (see p127) hosts an annual summer season of opera, against the stunning backdrop of Holland House.

3 Serpentine Galleries
MAP B4 ■ Kensington Gardens W2 ■ Open 10am–6pm daily ■ www.serpentinegalleries.org

In the southeast corner of the gardens, these galleries (see p59) host short-term contemporary art exhibitions.

4 Royal Geographical Society
MAP B4 ■ 1 Kensington Gore ■ Open 9am–5pm Mon–Fri ■ www.rgs.org

Founded in 1830, this learned society hosts exhibitions of maps, photographs and much more in its Pavilion.

5 Electric Cinema
MAP A3 ■ 191 Portobello Rd W11 ■ www.electriccinema.co.uk

London's oldest purpose-built movie theatre is also one of its prettiest.

It offers 3D technology and luxury seats including sofas and double beds. There is also a bar and restaurant here.

Exterior of the Royal College of Music

6 Royal College of Music
MAP B5 ■ Prince Consort Rd SW7 ■ Open 8am–10pm daily ■ www.rcm.ac.uk

This beautiful 1894 building, houses UK's leading music college, which stages musical events throughout the year. During term-time there are student-led tours each Wednesday.

7 Royal Court Theatre
MAP C5 ■ Sloane Sq SW1 ■ www.royalcourttheatre.com

Pre-eminent since the 1960s, this theatre produces work by both established and emerging playwrights.

8 The Lookout
MAP C4 ■ Hyde Park W2

Escape the crowds and connect with nature in this eco-friendly space.

9 Speakers' Corner
MAP C3 ■ Hyde Park W2

This corner of Hyde Park attracts public speakers, especially on Sundays.

10 Design Museum
MAP A5 ■ 224–238 Kensington High St W8 ■ Open 10am–6pm daily ■ Adm for temporary exhibitions ■ www.designmuseum.org

Spectacular building displaying finest contemporary design, including architecture, fashion and furniture.

Swanky interior of Electric Cinema

Shopping

 1 Rigby & Peller
2 Hans Rd SW3 ■ 020 7225 4760 ■ Tube Knightsbridge

This company is famous for its high-quality lingerie, swimwear and corsetry, and superb fitting service. Lady Gaga, Gwyneth Paltrow and Princesses Beatrice and Eugenie are among those who have shopped here.

2 Harvey Nichols
MAP C4 ■ 109–125 Knightsbridge SW1

This is another top London store (see p78). There are seven glorious floors of fashion, beauty and home collections alongside one floor dedicated to high-quality food.

 3 Burberry
MAP C5 ■ 2 Brompton Rd SW1

Iconic British brand Burberry sells all its latest must-have seasonal collection items here, as well as its timeless trenchcoats, checked clothing and distinctive luggage.

The Burberry store in Knightsbridge

4 Sloane Street
MAP C5

A dazzling concentration of luxury and designer shops extends along the street south of the vast Harvey Nichols department store.

 5 Artisan du Chocolat
MAP C5 ■ 89 Lower Sloane St SW1

Combining extraordinary craftsmanship and artistry, this store creates some of London's most innovative chocolates.

The iconic Harrods building

 6 Harrods
London's most famous store (see p78) is full of the finest goods that money can buy. Specialities here (see p126) include food, fashion, china, glass and kitchenware.

7 Designers Guild
MAP B6 ■ 267–277 King's Rd SW3

Designers Guild's fabrics and wallcoverings have a fresh, vibrant style all of their own. The variety on show is stunning.

8 Cutler and Gross
MAP C5 ■ 16 Knightsbridge Green SW1

Treat yourself to the latest eyewear and browse the superb collection of retro classics.

9 John Sandoe Books
MAP C5 ■ 10 Blacklands Terrace SW3

An unmissable experience for the discerning bibliophile, this bookshop is crammed to the rafters with a wonderful selection of volumes.

10 Ceramica Blue
10 Blenheim Crescent W11 ■ Tube Ladbroke Grove

This delightful little Notting Hill shop stocks a unique, highly eclectic range of ceramics, glassware, fabrics and other household accessories.

See map on pp124–5

Pubs and Cafés

1 Redemption
MAP A3 ▪ 6 Chepstow Rd W2

Providing a healthy alternative, this alcohol-free bar offers wholesome vegan food which is also sugar-free and wheat-free. Enjoy the delicious mocktails that are served in vintage glasses.

Flower-bedecked exterior of Churchill Arms

2 Churchill Arms
MAP A4 ▪ 119 Kensington Church St W8

Filled with intriguing bric-à-brac and Churchill memorabilia, this is a large, friendly Victorian pub. Inexpensive Thai food is served in the conservatory at lunchtime and for dinner until 9pm.

3 Kensington Palace Pavilion
MAP A4 ▪ Kensington Palace W8

With views overlooking the Sunken Garden, the elegant restaurants and tearooms here *(see p127)* are open for breakfast and lunch. This is the only place in London that allows you to enjoy afternoon tea inside a royal palace.

4 The Scarsdale Tavern
MAP A5 ▪ 23a Edwardes Sq W8

Just a couple of blocks from Kensington High Street, this cosy and popular neighbourhood pub serves decent food with a variety of good ales.

5 Nags Head
MAP C4 ▪ 53 Kinnerton St SW1

A short walk from Hyde Park is this little gem serving Adnams beer. The low ceilings and wood panelling add to the cosy, village-like atmosphere here. Mobile phones are not allowed.

6 The Castle
MAP A3 ▪ 225 Portobello Rd W11

This busy gastropub is a great spot for craft beer as well as for people-watching.

7 The Anglesea Arms
MAP B6 ▪ 15 Selwood Terrace SW7

Lovely, traditional local pub with a worn yet handsome darkwood interior. It offers excellent seasonal dishes, pub classics and a top selection of ales.

8 Trailer Happiness
MAP A3 ▪ 177 Portobello Rd W11

The bar's kitsch but cosy decor is the perfect place to enjoy some of the liveliest cocktails in town.

9 Paxtons Head
MAP C4 ▪ 153 Knightsbridge SW1

A popular watering-hole for both locals and visitors, this old pub caters for all tastes, with cocktails and flavoured vodkas as well as real ales. Traditional pub fare is also served.

10 Portobello Stalls
MAP A3 ▪ Portobello Rd W11 ▪ Tube Westbourne Park

Lined along the market here are stalls offering delicious portions of ethnic food of every kind. Visit the Acklam Village Market for live music and delicious street food.

Restaurants

PRICE CATEGORIES

For a three-course meal for one with half a bottle of wine (or equivalent meal), taxes and extra charges.

£ under £30   ££ £30–50   £££ over £50

1 Clarke's
MAP A5 ■ 124 Kensington Church St W8 ■ 020 7221 9225 ■ £££

The menu consists of whatever chef Sally Clarke decides to cook for the evening meal. No matter what it is, it will be excellent.

2 Belvedere
MAP A4 ■ Holland Park W8 ■ 020 7602 1238 ■ £££

The restaurant's charming setting in Holland Park is enhanced by its good European food. From the patio in summer, you may hear distant opera from the park's open-air theatre.

3 Kitchen W8
MAP A5 ■ 11–13 Abingdon Rd W8 ■ 020 7937 0120 ■ £££

A satisfying blend of British and French cuisine characterizes this chic but comfortable restaurant, perfect for a romantic dinner.

4 Amaya
MAP C5 ■ Halkin Arcade, Lowndes St SW1 ■ 020 7823 1166 ■ £££

Amaya's dishes take modern Indian cuisine to a new level. Flash-grilled scallops, spinach and fig tikkis, and tapas-style Indian food are served up in a stylish rosewood-panelled dining room.

5 Core by Clare Smyth
MAP A3 ■ 92 Kensington Park Rd W11 ■ 020 3937 5086 ■ £££

With extraordinary attention to detail and a dedication to UK produce, this restaurant is run by Michelin-starred chef Clare Smyth and her team. You have a great choice of tasting menus or à la carte.

6 Royal China
MAP A3 ■ 13 Queensway W2 ■ 020 7221 2535 ■ ££

A tempting variety of dim sum, including delicious sweet lotus seed buns, are the main attraction here.

7 The Ledbury
MAP A3 ■ 127 Ledbury Rd W11 ■ 020 7792 9090 ■ £££

Praise has been heaped on chef Brett Graham's food, which mixes global influences with *haute cuisine*.

8 Claude Bosi at Bibendum
MAP C5 ■ 81 Fulham Rd SW3 ■ 020 7581 5817 ■ £££

Once a Michelin tyre factory, this restaurant is adorned with tiles and stained glass.

Interior of Claude Bosi at Bibendum

9 Ognisko
MAP B5 ■ 55 Prince's Gate, Exhibition Rd SW7 ■ 020 7589 0101 ■ ££

Polish cuisine is served in an elegant dining room. There's an alfresco terrace for warmer nights.

10 Dinner by Heston Blumenthal
MAP C4 ■ 66 Knightsbridge ■ 020 7201 3833 ■ £££

This restaurant serves imaginative dishes inspired from historic Tudor feasts. Try their 'meat fruit'.

See map on pp124–5 ➡

TOP 10 Regent's Park and Marylebone

Ceramic plate, Wallace Collection

Once a medieval village surrounded by fields and a pleasure garden, Marylebone is now an elegant area. In the 19th century, the area's grand mansion blocks were used by doctors to see wealthy clients. The medical connection continues today in the discreet Harley Street consulting rooms of private medical specialists. Encircled by John Nash's magnificent terraces is Regent's Park, where office workers, kids and dog walkers enjoy the inviting lawns and fabulous flowers.

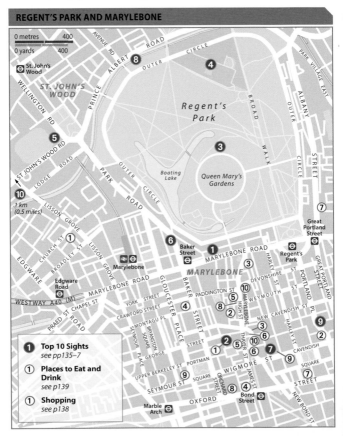

REGENT'S PARK AND MARYLEBONE

1	**Top 10 Sights** see pp135–7
①	**Places to Eat and Drink** see p139
①	**Shopping** see p138

1 Madame Tussauds

MAP C2 ■ Marylebone Rd NW1
■ Opening times vary, check website
■ Adm ■ www.madametussauds.com

This, the very first museum of waxwork models of the famous, has long been one of London's major attractions (see p68). The Star Wars Experience allows you to walk inside ten sets from the movies, including the flight deck of the Millenium Falcon. Book online in advance for slightly cheaper tickets.

2 Wallace Collection

MAP D3 ■ Manchester Sq W1 ■ Open 10am–5pm daily ■ www.wallacecollection.org

"The finest private collection of art ever assembled by one family," is the claim of the Wallace Collection, and it is hard to disagree. Sir Richard Wallace, who left this collection to the nation in 1897 (see p58), was not only outrageously rich but a man of great taste. As well as many galleries of fine Sèvres porcelain and an unrivalled collection of armour and furniture, there are a number of exceptional old master paintings by English, French and Dutch artists, including Frans Hals' The Laughing Cavalier.

3 Regent's Park

MAP C1–D2 ■ NW1
■ Open 5am–dusk daily

The best part of Regent's Park (see p54) is the Inner Circle. Here are Queen Mary's Gardens, with beds of nearly 12,000 wonderfully fragrant roses, the Open Air Theatre with its summer Shakespeare plays, and the

Fountain in Regent's Park

Regent's Bar & Café, which is one of the best of the park's six cafés. Boats, tennis courts and deck chairs can be rented and in summer musical performances take place on the bandstand.

4 London Zoo

MAP C1 ■ Regent's Park NW1
■ Open Apr–Aug: 10am–6pm; Sep, Oct & Mar: 10am–5pm; Nov–Feb: 10am–4pm ■ Adm ■ www.zsl.org

Lying on the northern side of Regent's Park, London Zoo (see p68) is home to over 750 different animal species. One of the most breathtaking enclosures is the imaginative Land of the Lions, where Asiatic lions roam around a recreation of the Gir Forest, skirted by a miniature Indian village. The Rainforest Life and In with the Lemurs walk-through exhibits, let you get close to some adorable creatures.

A tigress and her cub taking an afternoon nap at London Zoo

5 Marylebone Cricket Club Museum

MAP B2 ■ St John's Wood NW8 ■ Open Mon–Fri (book a tour in advance) ■ Adm ■ www.lords.org

Founded in 1787, the MCC is the governing body of the game, and its home ground, Lord's, is a venue for Test matches. The world's oldest sporting museum is only accessible via a daily guided tour of the ground. Its star exhibit is the tiny trophy known as The Ashes. Booking is essential, and note that the only way to visit on match days is with a match ticket.

6 Sherlock Holmes Museum

MAP C2 ■ 221b Baker St NW1 ■ Open 9:30am–6pm daily ■ Adm ■ www.sherlock-holmes.co.uk

This museum is small but great fun. Take a camera when you visit and get your picture taken sitting by the fire in the great detective's front room, wearing a deerstalker hat and smoking a pipe. A Victorian policeman stands guard outside and upstairs, wax dummies re-enact moments from Holmes's most famous cases.

7 Wigmore Hall

MAP D3 ■ 36 Wigmore St W1 ■ www.wigmore-hall.org.uk

One of the world's most renowned recital venues presents more than 460 events a year, featuring song,

REGENCY LONDON

Regent's Park was named after the Prince Regent (the future George IV), who employed John Nash in 1812 to lay out the park on the royal estate of Marylebone Farm. Nash was given a free hand and the result is a delight. Encircling the park are sumptuous Neo-Classical terraces, including Cumberland Terrace (**above**), named after the Duke of Cumberland.

early music, chamber music and new commissions as well as a diverse education programme. This hall, built in 1901, reputedly has one of the best acoustics in the world.

8 Regent's Canal

MAP C1

John Nash wanted the canal to go through the centre of his new Regent's Park, but objections from neighbours, who were concerned about smelly canal boats and foul-mouthed crews, resulted in it being sited on the northern side of the

Canal boats moored along Regent's Canal

park. In 1874, a cargo of explosives demolished the Macclesfield Bridge beside London Zoo.

(9) BBC Broadcasting House

MAP J1 ■ Portland Place W1
■ www.bbc.co.uk/showsandtours

The first radio broadcast was made from here in 1932, two months before the Art Deco building was officially opened. Redevelopment has now turned it into a state-of-the-art digital centre for BBC Radio, TV and BBC News and online services. The only way to visit "the Beeb" beyond the handsome Art Deco foyer is to apply for audience-member tickets, available for a range of radio and TV shows. Tours of the grounds have been prohibited for security reasons.

BBC Broadcasting House

(10) Abbey Road Studios

MAP B1 ■ 3 Abbey Rd NW8
■ www.abbeyroad.com

An iconic landmark in the capital, these studios are a must for The Beatles aficionados, as is the nearby zebra crossing shown on the *Abbey Road* (1969) album cover. Have a picture taken as you re-enact the "fab four" crossing the road. The studios are not open to the public, other than the occasional event, but there is a gift shop where you can buy souvenirs.

EXPLORING MARYLEBONE

Sherlock Holmes Museum
Madame Tussauds
St Marylebone Parish Church
Natural Kitchen
Reubens
Marylebone High Street
Marylebone Lane
St Christopher's Place
Sofra
Bond Street station

▶ MORNING

Before setting out for the day, reserve a ticket for **Madame Tussauds** *(see p135)* for the afternoon. Start at **Bond Street Tube**, exiting on Oxford Street. Opposite is St Christopher's Place, a narrow lane with charming shops, which opens into a pedestrian square. Stop for a coffee at one of the pavement tables at **Sofra** *(1 St Christopher's Place)*.

Continue into Marylebone Lane, a pleasant side street of small shops, which leads to **Marylebone High Street** *(see p138)* and its wide choice of designer shops. Stop for a bit in the peaceful memorial garden of **St Marylebone Parish Church**, planted with various exotic trees. Methodist minister and hymn-writer Charles Wesley (1707–88) has a memorial here.

AFTERNOON

For lunch, buy some delicious fish and chips from the Golden Hind *(see p139)*. For a lighter snack, try **Natural Kitchen** *(77–8 Marylebone High Street)*.

After lunch, bypass the infamous lines of people outside **Madame Tussauds** with your booking and spend an hour and a half checking out the celebrity wax figures.

Cross Marylebone Road to Baker Street, for tea and a sandwich at **Reubens** *(see p139)*, before heading for the charming **Sherlock Holmes Museum** at No. 221b, a faithful reconstruction of the fictional detective's home.

See map on p134

Shopping

 Alfie's Antiques Market
MAP C2 ▪ 13–25 Church St NW8

Vintage jewellery, fashion, Middle Eastern antiques, art and furniture are all under one roof, plus there is a café for when you're all shopped out.

 Marylebone Farmers' Market
MAP D3 ▪ Aybrook, St Vincent St & Moxon St W1 ▪ Open 10am–2pm Sun

With over 40 producers, this is London's biggest farmers' market.

③ **The Conran Shop**
MAP D3 ▪ 55 Marylebone High St W1

Set in an old stable building, Conran sells the best of modern British and classic mainland European designs in homeware and furniture, such as a Mies van der Rohe reclining chair.

 Dr. Martens
MAP C3 ▪ 386 Oxford St W1C5

Showcasing distinctive shoes and boots, this shop is continually favoured by Britain's youth subcultures.

 Daunt Books
MAP D3 ▪ 83–84 Marylebone High St W1

All kinds of travel books and literature are arranged along oak galleries in this atmospheric Edwardian travel bookshop.

⑥ **Marylebone Lane**
MAP D3 ▪ Off Marylebone High St W1

This charming lane off Marylebone High Street still has plenty of quirky gems to tempt the shopper.

⑦ **John Lewis**
MAP D3 ▪ 300 Oxford St W1

There isn't anything that you can't buy from this sophisticated department store. The vast collection of John Lewis ranges from clothes and furniture to electronics and stationery. It also has a gifts department, and the staff are both helpful and knowledgeable.

 Selfridges & Co
MAP D3 ▪ 400 Oxford St W1

Opened in 1909, this store has a handsome Neo-Classical façade. A London institution, Selfridges is great for designer fashion for women. Its award-winning food hall is wonderful.

⑨ **Margaret Howell**
MAP D3 ▪ 34 Wigmore St W1

Classic elegance for both men and women from one of Britain's top designers at her flagship store.

⑩ **Le Labo**
MAP D2 ▪ 28A Devonshire St W1

A luxury perfumery where the fragrances can be made to order with a personalized label.

Long oak galleries in the Edwardian interiors of Daunt Books

Places to Eat and Drink

PRICE CATEGORIES

For a three-course meal for one with half a bottle of wine (or equivalent meal), taxes and extra charges.

£ under £30   ££ £30–50   £££ over £50

The Wallace Restaurant
MAP D3 ■ Hertford House, Manchester Sq W1 ■ 020 7563 9505 ■ ££

Located in the courtyard of the Wallace Collection *(see p135)*, this smart café serves delicious lunches and afternoon teas. The menu changes regularly.

2 Artesian
MAP J1 ■ 1C Portland Place W1 ■ 020 7636 1000 ■ £££

A sophisticated bar, Artesian serves an upmarket tapas-style menu and cocktails to die for.

3 Caffè Caldesi
MAP D3 ■ 118 Marylebone Lane W1 ■ 020 7487 0754 ■ £££

This light and airy Italian eaterie offers classic dishes and a good wine list. The upstairs restaurant is slightly more formal.

4 Reubens
MAP C3 ■ 79 Baker St W1 ■ 020 7486 0035 ■ ££

One of the best kosher restaurants in London, Ruebens offers classic deli sandwiches such as salt beef.

5 Pachamama
MAP D3 ■ 18 Thayer St W1 ■ 020 7935 9393 ■ £££

This lively spot is one of the city's most popular Peruvian restaurants. It offers pisco-heavy cocktails and tapas with distinctive flavours.

6 Golden Hind
MAP D3 ■ 73 Marylebone Lane W1 ■ 020 7486 3644 ■ ££

Serving Londoners since 1914, this no-nonsense little place is popular with locals, and offers customers fish cakes and calamari as well as traditional English fish and chips.

7 Queen's Head & Artichoke
MAP D2 ■ 30–32 Albany St NW1 ■ 020 7916 6206 ■ ££

A snug upstairs dining room and bustling bar downstairs offer a wide range of good international food.

A range of cheeses at La Fromagerie

8 La Fromagerie
MAP D3 ■ 2–6 Moxon St W1 ■ 020 7935 0341 ■ ££

Sample the fine cheese and charcuterie plates here, along with delicious seasonal dishes.

9 Locanda Locatelli
MAP C3 ■ 8 Seymour St W1 ■ 020 7935 9088 ■ £££

Georgio Locatelli is one of the finest Italian chefs in the UK. Dishes are presented with great skill and care.

10 The Ivy Café
MAP D3 ■ 96 Marylebone High Lane ■ 020 3301 0400 ■ ££

A more casual spin-off from the well-known Ivy restaurant, this bistro offers an appetizing all-day menu that includes brunches, sandwiches, as well as classic mains.

See map on p134

🔟 The City

The ancient square mile of London, defined roughly by the walls of the Roman city, is a curious mixture of streets and lanes with medieval names, state-of-the-art finance houses and no fewer than 38 churches, many of them, including St Paul's Cathedral, designed by Sir Christopher Wren. Don't miss the City's old markets: Smithfield still operates as a meat market, Leadenhall is in many ways more attractive than Covent Garden, while the former fish market of Billingsgate offers a great view of the once busy Pool of London.

Bust of William Shakespeare, Guildhall Art Gallery

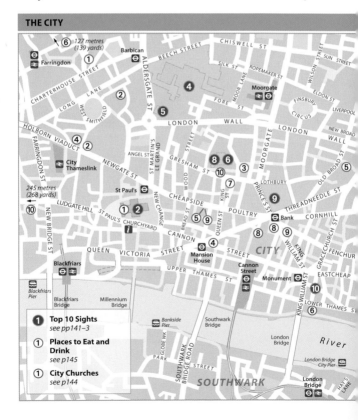

THE CITY

- **1** Top 10 Sights
  see pp141–3
- **①** Places to Eat and Drink
  see p145
- **①** City Churches
  see p144

① Tower of London
See pp38–41.

② St Paul's Cathedral
See pp42–5.

③ Tower Bridge
MAP H4 ▪ 020 7403 3761
▪ **Open 9:30am–5pm daily** ▪ **Adm**
▪ **www.towerbridge.org.uk**

When the Pool of London (the stretch of the Thames between Limehouse and Tower Bridge) was the gateway to the city, this bridge *(see p65)* was constantly being raised and lowered for sail and steam ships bringing their cargoes from all corners of the Empire. Pedestrians who needed to cross the river when the bridge was open had to climb up the

The majestic Tower Bridge

200 steps of the towers to the walkway. Today, visitors on the 90-minute Tower Bridge Exhibition tour enjoy panoramic views from the 42-m (140-ft) high glass-floored walkways. The entrance is at the northwest tower. It ends with a hands-on experience in the massive engine room and exits via a shop on the south bank.

④ Barbican Centre
MAP R1 ▪ **Silk St EC2** ▪ **Box office: 020 7638 8891** ▪ **www. barbican.org.uk**

This centre *(see p70)* plays host to music, dance, theatre, film and art events with top visiting performers and artists. There is also an excellent library, cafés and restaurants. Opened in 1982, the centre is part of the Barbican Estate, which houses over 4,000 people and also contains the Guildhall School of Music. There is also the Conservatory with tropical fish and over 20,000 species of plants and trees. The centre looks across a lake to St Giles Cripplegate church.

The Brutalist-style Barbican Centre

5 Museum of London

MAP R1 ■ 150 London Wall
EC2 ■ Open 10am–6pm daily
■ www.museumoflondon.org.uk

The world's largest urban history museum (see p56) reveals insights into prehistoric, Roman and medieval London, and its social development up to the present day, through the "War, Plague and Fire" and "World City" galleries. Visitors can also observe a re-creation of a Victorian Street.

6 Guildhall

MAP G3 ■ Great Hall: Guildhall Yard, Gresham St EC2; 020 7332 1313; open 10am–5pm Mon–Sat, noon–4pm Sun; closed for events, call ahead ■ www.guildhall.city oflondon.gov.uk

For around 900 years the Guildhall has been the administrative centre of London. The magnificent 15th-century Great Hall hosts important ceremonies, while the Guildhall Library houses rotating displays of historic manuscripts.

7 St Katharine Docks

MAP H4 ■ E1 ■ www.sk docks.co.uk

Located near Tower Bridge and the Tower of London, this is the place (see p65) to come and relax, to watch the rich on their yachts and the working sailors on the Thames barges, and enjoy the unique experience of

DICK WHITTINGTON

A stained-glass window (**below**) in St Michael, Paternoster Royal, depicts Dick Whittington (and his cat) – the hero of a well-known London rags-to-riches fairy tale. In fact, Richard Whittington, who was Lord Mayor of London four times between 1397 and 1420, was a wealthy merchant and the City's first major benefactor. He pioneered public lavatories, building them to overhang the Thames.

sailing up the river. There are several cafés as well as a number of popular bars and restaurants.

8 Guildhall Art Gallery and London's Roman Amphitheatre

MAP G3 ■ Gresham St EC2 ■ Open 10am–5pm Mon–Sat, noon–4pm Sun

On the east side of Guildhall Yard is the Guildhall Art Gallery, containing two floors of paintings that cover more than 400 years of art. Many works of art are associated with the City, and there are a number of romantic 19th-century paintings, including some pre-Raphaelite works. Combine the visit with a look at the remains of London's only Roman amphitheatre, discovered in 1988 by Museum of London archaeologists.

Boats docked in St Katharine Docks

⑨ Bank of England Museum

MAP G3 ▪ Bartholomew Lane EC2
▪ 020 7601 5545 ▪ Open 10am–5pm
Mon–Fri ▪ www.bankofengland.co.uk

This fascinating museum, located within the impressive walls of the Bank of England, tells the history of the bank from its foundation in 1694 to the present day. Its unique collections of coins, banknotes and artifacts are supplemented by interactive displays. Visitors can even handle a real gold bar.

⑩ Monument

MAP H4 ▪ Monument St EC3
▪ Open 9:30am–6pm daily ▪ Adm
▪ www.themonument.org.uk

Standing at 61.5 m (202 ft), this monument by Sir Christopher Wren offers panoramic views of the City of London. Commemorating the Great Fire of London, the height of this free-standing stone column is equal to its distance from the baker's shop in Pudding Lane where the fire started in 1666. Inside, 311 stairs spiral up to a viewing platform; when you return to the entrance, you will receive a certificate to say that you have made the climb.

The Monument, completed in 1677

THE CITY ON FOOT

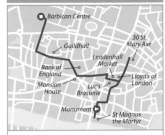

▶ MORNING

Start with a brisk trot up the 311 steps of the **Monument** and see how the surrounding narrow streets all slope down towards the Thames. Descend and carry on down Fish Street Hill across Lower Thames Street to the historic church of **St Magnus the Martyr** (see p144), where a model of the former London Bridge shows the city's great landmark as it was until the 18th century.

Return up Fish Street Hill and Philpot Lane to Lime Street to check out the Lloyd's of London building and "The Gherkin", 30 St Mary Axe. Enter the ornate, 1881 **Leadenhall Market** building (see p66) for trendy shops, restaurants and bars, and a delicious lunch at **Luc's Brasserie** (22 Leadenhall Market) in the market.

AFTERNOON

After lunch, see the City's historic financial buildings along Cornhill. Notice the Royal Exchange's grand Corinthian portico, behind which is a high-end shopping centre. Opposite is the Mansion House, official residence of London's Lord Mayor. To the north, across Threadneedle Street, is the **Bank of England**. Continue into Lothbury and along Gresham Street to **Guildhall** to admire the medieval Great Hall.

Head up Wood Street to the **Barbican Centre** (see p141) for a cocktail or the pre-theatre menu at the Osteria overlooking the lake. Check the programme for the day's events and attend a performance.

See map on pp140–41 ←

City Churches

1 St Paul's Cathedral
See pp42–5.

2 St Bartholomew-the-Great
MAP R1 ■ West Smithfield EC1
■ Open 8:30am–4pm Mon–Fri
(until 5pm in summer), 10:30am–
4pm Sat, 8:30am–8pm Sun ■ Adm

This is one of London's oldest churches *(see p51)*, built in the 12th century. Some Norman architectural details may be seen.

3 St Katharine Cree
MAP H3 ■ Leadenhall St EC3
■ Open 9:30am–4pm Mon–Fri

One of eight churches to survive the Great Fire of London in 1666, this building dates from about 1630. Both Purcell and Handel played its organ.

4 St Sepulchre-without-Newgate
MAP Q1 ■ Holborn Viaduct EC1
■ Open noon–2pm Tue & Thu,
11am–3pm Wed

The City's largest post-Fire church after St Paul's, St Sepulchre is famous for its peal of 12 bells. Recitals are held throughout the week.

5 St Mary-le-Bow
MAP G3 ■ Cheapside EC2 ■ Open 7am–6pm Mon–Fri

St Mary-le-Bow was rebuilt by Christopher Wren after its destruction in the 1666 Great Fire of London.

St Mary-le-Bow

6 St Magnus the Martyr
MAP H4 ■ Lower Thames St EC3 ■ Open 10am–4pm Tue–Fri

Designed by Wren in the 1670s, the splendid church retains its elegant pulpit. Celebrated choral recitals take place throughout the year.

7 All Hallows by the Tower
MAP H3 ■ Byward St EC3
■ Open 8am–6pm Mon–Fri (Nov–Mar: until 5pm), 10am–5pm Sat & Sun, except during services

Take a guided tour of this church, which dates from Saxon times.

The dome of St Stephen Walbrook

8 St Stephen Walbrook
MAP G3 ■ 39 Walbrook EC4
■ Open 10am–4pm Mon–Tue & Thu,
11am–3pm Wed, 10am–3:30pm Fri

Christopher Wren's parish church is considered to be one of his finest.

9 St Mary Woolnoth
MAP G3 ■ Lombard St EC3
■ Open 7:30am–5:15pm Mon–Fri

One of Nicolas Hawksmoor's six surviving London churches, this was built in his typically bold Baroque style and completed in 1727.

10 St Lawrence Jewry
MAP R2 ■ Guildhall EC2
■ Open 9am–5pm Mon–Fri

Beautiful stained-glass windows of historic figures are the highlight here.

Places to Eat and Drink

PRICE CATEGORIES

For a three-course meal for one with half a bottle of wine (or equivalent meal), taxes and extra charges.

£ under £30   ££ £30–50   £££ over £50

The bar at Jerusalem Tavern

1 St John Smithfield
MAP F2 ▪ 26 St John St EC1
▪ 020 7251 0848 ▪ £££

Sister restaurant of St John Bread & Wine *(see p163)*, this delightful British place is famous for "nose-to-tail" dining with bold flavours and a focus on offal. Delicious light bar meals available.

2 Viaduct Tavern
MAP Q1 ▪ 126 Newgate St EC1
▪ 020 7600 1863 ▪ Closed Sat & Sun ▪ £

Built on the site of a former jail, this former Victorian gin palace has a unique period atmosphere thanks to its ornate wall paintings and other original fittings. Sandwiches and snacks are served all week.

3 Hawksmoor
MAP G3 ▪ 10 Basinghall St EC2
▪ 020 7397 8120 ▪ £££

Huge and bustling, Hawksmoor has revived the old London tradition of the steakhouse, with a variety of cuts, all cooked perfectly to order. One of several branches around the city.

4 Sweetings
MAP R2 ▪ 39 Queen Victoria St EC4 ▪ Open 11:30am–3pm Mon–Fri
▪ No reservations ▪ ££

This is a weekday lunchtime haven for fish lovers. Starters such as potted shrimp are followed by plaice and Dover sole.

5 Vertigo 42
MAP H3 ▪ Tower 42, 25 Old Broad St EC2 ▪ 020 7877 7842
▪ Reservations required ▪ ££

Make sure to visit this ostentatious, sky-scraping champagne bar on the 42nd floor.

6 Jerusalem Tavern
MAP G2 ▪ 55 Britton St EC1

Snug and rustic, with delft tiles and box pews, this tiny pub oozes charm.

7 City Càphê
MAP G3 ▪ 17 Ironmonger Lane EC2 ▪ Open 11:30am–4:30pm Mon–Fri ▪ £

Pork *banh mi* is the speciality at this small Vietnamese café in the heart of the City. It gets pretty busy so you may need to queue, but it's well worth the wait.

8 1 Lombard Street
MAP G3 ▪ 1 Lombard St EC3
▪ 020 7929 6611 ▪ Closed Sat & Sun ▪ £££

Enjoy modern European fare served in a former banking hall. This is one of the most striking dining locations.

9 Café Below
MAP G3 ▪ Cheapside EC2
▪ 020 7329 0789 ▪ £

This popular café in the crypt of St Mary-le-Bow church serves breakfast and lunch on weekdays.

10 Ye Olde Cheshire Cheese
MAP Q2 ▪ 145 Fleet St EC4

One of London's most famous pubs, this 17th-century establishment has served luminaries such as Samuel Johnson and Charles Dickens.

See map on pp140–41

TOP 10 North London

Beyond Regent's Park, London drifts up into areas that were once distant villages where the rich built their country mansions. Parts of their extensive grounds now make up the wild and lofty expanse of Hampstead Heath. Some of the "villages", such as

Karl Marx's tombstone, Highgate Cemetery

Hampstead and Highgate, are still distinct from the urban sprawl that surrounds them, with attractive streets full of well-preserved architecture. Other parts of north London have different flavours – from bustling Camden, with its canalside market and lively pubs, to fashionable Islington, with its clothes and antique shops and smart bars.

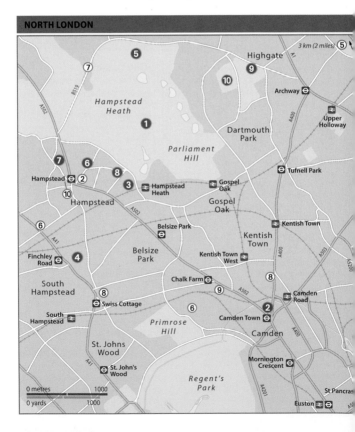

NORTH LONDON

1. Hampstead Heath and Parliament Hill

Heath Information Centre: Staff Yard, Highgate Rd NW5; 020 7332 3773 ■ Tube Hampstead

A welcome retreat from the city, this large, open area is one of the best places in London for walking. Covering miles of country-side, it contains ancient woodlands and ponds for swimming and fishing. The top of Parliament Hill has great city views and is a popular place for kite-flying.

2. Camden Markets

Camden High St and Chalk Farm Rd NW1 ■ Tube Camden Town ■ Open 10am–6pm daily

The most exciting north London markets are linked by the busy and colourful Camden High Street. Camden Market *(see p79)*, near the Tube station, has stalls selling clothes, shoes and jewellery. Further up the road, by the canal, both Camden Lock Market and Stables Market sell an eclectic mix of arts and crafts, vintage and street fashions. There are plenty of bars and cafés, plus street food stalls.

The 19th-century Keats House

3. Keats House

10 Keats Grove NW3 ■ Train to Hampstead Heath, Tube Hampstead or Belsize Park ■ 020 7332 3868 ■ Open 11am–5pm Wed–Sun ■ Adm ■ www.cityoflondon.gov.uk/keats

Keats Grove, off Downshire Hill, is one of the loveliest areas of Hampstead. The house where the poet John Keats *(see p62)* wrote much of his work contains facsimiles of his fragile manuscripts and letters, and personal possessions. It also hosts poetry readings and talks.

4. Freud Museum

20 Maresfield Gardens NW3 ■ Tube Finchley Rd ■ 020 7435 2002 ■ Open noon–5pm Wed–Sun ■ Adm ■ www.freud.org.uk

Sigmund Freud, the founder of psychoanalysis, came to live here when his family fled Nazi-occupied Vienna. The house *(see p62)* contains Freud's collection of antiques, his library, including first editions of his own works, and the couch on which his patients related their dreams.

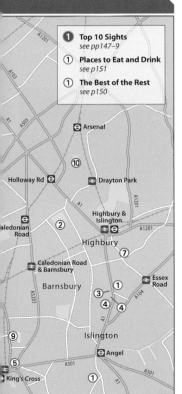

Arsenal

(10)

Holloway Rd — Drayton Park

Highbury & Islington

(2)

aledonian Road

Highbury

(7)

Caledonian Road & Barnsbury

Barnsbury

Essex Road

(1)

(3)

(4) (4)

Islington

(9)

Angel

(5)

King's Cross

(1)

Eighteenth-century Kenwood House, Hampstead Heath

⑤ Kenwood House
Hampstead Lane NW3 ▪ Tube Golders Green or Archway then bus 210 ▪ 020 8348 1286 ▪ Open 10am–5pm daily (Nov–Mar: until 4pm) ▪ Tours available ▪ www.english-heritage.org.uk/visit/places/kenwood

This mansion *(see p59)*, filled with Old Masters, is set in an estate on the edge of Hampstead Heath. Vermeer's *The Guitar Player* and a self-portrait by Rembrandt are among the star attractions. Summer concerts are often held when audiences picnic in the grassy bowl – and there is a shop and café.

⑥ Burgh House
New End Sq NW3 ▪ Tube Hampstead ▪ 020 7431 0144 ▪ Open noon–4pm Wed–Fri & Sun ▪ www.burghhouse.org.uk

Built in 1704 and housing Hampstead Museum, this grand house has a good selection of local books and a map of the famous people who have lived in this area. The panelled music room is used for concerts and meetings, the Peggy Jay Gallery has contemporary art exhibitions, and the café has a terrace and a cosy indoor space.

⑦ Fenton House
Hampstead Grove NW3 ▪ Tube Hampstead ▪ 020 7435 3471 ▪ Open Mar–Oct: 11am–5pm Wed–Sun ▪ Adm ▪ www.nationaltrust.org.uk/fenton-house-and-garden

This 17th-century mansion is the oldest in Hampstead. Its exceptional

HAMPSTEAD WELLS

Hampstead's heyday began in the early 18th century, when a spring in Well Walk (**below**) was recognized as having medicinal properties. This brought Londoners flocking to take the waters from the Pump Room within the Great Room at Well Walk, which also housed an Assembly Room for dances and concerts. The spa gradually fell into disrepute, but Hampstead retained its fashionable status.

collection of Chinese and European porcelain, furniture and needlework was bequeathed to the National Trust with the house in 1952. A formal walled garden contains an orchard.

⑧ 2 Willow Road
2 Willow Rd NW3 ▪ Train to Hampstead Heath ▪ 020 7435 6166 ▪ Open Mar–Oct: 11am–5pm Wed–Sun ▪ Adm ▪ www.nationaltrust.org.uk/2-willow-road

Designed in 1939 by the architect Ernö Goldfinger for himself and his wife, artist Ursula Blackwell, this is a fine example of modern architecture in the UK. Goldfinger designed all the furniture and collected works by Henry Moore, Max Ernst and Marcel Duchamp. Admission from 11am–2pm is strictly limited to hourly tours.

9 Lauderdale House

Highgate Hill, Waterlow Park N6 ■ Tube Archway ■ 020 8348 8716 ■ Open 11am–4pm Mon–Thu (timings vary Fri–Sun) ■ www.lauderdale house.org.uk

Dating from the late 16th century, Lauderdale House was once associated with Charles II and his mistress Nell Gwynne. It now houses a popular arts and cultural centre, with regular concerts and exhibitions.

10 Highgate Cemetery

Swain's Lane N6 ■ Tube Archway ■ 020 8340 1834 ■ East Cemetery: open 10am–5pm (Nov–Feb: until 4pm), last adm 30 min prior to closing ■ Closed for funerals (phone to check) ■ West Cemetery: guided tours only, usually 11am, 1:45pm Mon–Fri, 10:30am–4pm Sat & Sun (Nov–Feb: until 3pm) ■ Adm for both ■ www.highgatecemetery.org

Across the heath from Hampstead, Highgate developed as a healthy, countrified place for the nobility, who built large mansions here in the 18th and 19th centuries. Many of these famous people are buried in Highgate Cemetery. Opened in 1839, its Victorian architecture and fine views soon made it a very popular outing for Londoners. Karl Marx and novelist George Eliot are buried in the less glamorous East Cemetery.

Grave markers in Highgate Cemetery

EXPLORING NORTH LONDON

▶ MORNING

Starting at **Hampstead Tube station**, head left down pretty Flask Walk (the Flask pub once sold spa water) to the local museum in **Burgh House** for some background on the area. Then spend some time exploring the many attractive back streets, most of which are lined with expensive Georgian houses and mansions. Visit **Well Walk**, fashionable in the days of the Hampstead spa (a fountain in Well Passage on the left still remains).

Stop for a coffee at one of the many cafés along Hampstead High Street and then make your way to **Keats House** *(see p147)*, spending half an hour looking around. Afterwards, a stroll across **Hampstead Heath** to **Kenwood House** will prepare you for lunch.

AFTERNOON

The Brew House at Kenwood serves excellent light meals and has a fine position beside the house, overlooking the lake. After lunch, visit the house itself.

Leave the Heath by the nearby East Lodge and catch a No. 210 bus back towards Hampstead. The bus passes the **Spaniards Inn** *(see p76)* and Whitestone Pond, the Heath's highest point. Alight at the pond and walk to the Tube station, taking a train to Camden Town. Spend the rest of the afternoon in lively Camden Lock Market *(see p147)*, ending the day on the Lockside terrace.

See map on pp146–7 ←

The Best of the Rest

1 Sadler's Wells
MAP F2 ▪ Rosebery Ave EC1
▪ 020 7863 8000 ▪ www.sadlers
wells.com
London's premier venue *(see p71)*
for dance attracts internationally
renowned artists and companies
from around the world.

2 Freightliners Farm
Sheringham Rd N7
▪ Tube Highbury & Islington,
Caledonian Rd ▪ 020 7609 0467
▪ www.freightlinersfarm.org.uk
A little bit of the countryside in the
city with animals, produce, gardens
and a vegetarian café.

3 Almeida Theatre
Almeida St N1 ▪ Tube Angel
or Highbury & Islington ▪ 020 7359
4404 ▪ www.almeida.co.uk
This famous local theatre attracts
top actors and directors from the
UK and the US.

4 King's Head Theatre Pub
MAP F1 ▪ 115 Upper St N1
▪ 020 7226 8561 ▪ www.kingshead
theatrepub.co.uk
A busy, delightful Victorian pub with
a 110-seat theatre hosting opera
performances and new plays at the
back. There's also a wide selection
of wines and ale.

5 Alexandra Palace
Alexandra Palace Way N22
▪ Tube Wood Green ▪ 020 8365 2121
▪ www.alexandrapalace.com
Set in the 196 acres of Alexandra
Park, this restored 1873
exhibition centre is
principally used as
an ice-skating rink
and concert venue.

6 Camden Arts Centre
Arkwright Rd NW3 ▪ Train
or tube to Finchley Rd ▪ www.
camdenartscentre.org
This place is known for its fascinating
contemporary art exhibitions and
excellent art book shop.

7 Estorick Collection
39A Canonbury Sq N1
▪ Tube Highbury and Islington
▪ www.estorickcollection.com
Elegant Georgian house with a
superb collection of 20th-century
Italian art, including works
by Amedeo Modigliani and
Emilio Greco.

8 Hampstead Theatre
Eton Ave NW3 ▪ Tube Swiss
Cottage (exit 2) ▪ 020 7722 9301
▪ www.hampsteadtheatre.com
This important fringe theatre is a
venue for ambitious new writing,
and has produced plays by innovative
English writers such as Harold Pinter,
Michael Frayn and Mike Leigh.

9 Roundhouse
Chalk Farm Rd NW1
▪ Tube Chalk Farm ▪ 0300 678
9222 ▪ www.roundhouse.org.uk
This former Victorian railway shed
is now an exciting venue for both
theatre and music.

10 Emirates Stadium Tours
Hornsey Rd, Highbury N7
▪ Tube Arsenal ▪ 020 7619 5003
▪ arsenaldirect.arsenal.com
The tour of the stadium – home to
Arsenal Football Club – covers
the directors' box, home
changing room,
players' tunnel and
the Arsenal Museum.

**Alexandra
Palace**

Places to Eat and Drink

PRICE CATEGORIES
For a three-course meal for one with
half a bottle of wine (or equivalent meal),
taxes and extra charges.
....
£ under £30   **££** £30–50   **£££** over £50

1 Ottolenghi
MAP G1 ▪ 287 Upper St N1
▪ 020 7288 1454 ▪ ££

Yotam Ottolenghi has revitalized
London's approach to Middle Eastern
food with his flavourful dishes based
on the finest – and sometimes
unusual – ingredients.

2 The Flask
14 Flask Walk NW3 ▪ Tube
Hampstead ▪ 020 7435 4580 ▪ ££

Dating from 1700, this pub has a
country atmosphere, good cask
beer and homemade pub food.

3 Dishoom
MAP E1 ▪ 5 Stable St N1 ▪ 020
7420 9321 ▪ ££

With decor inspired from colonial-era
Bombay, Dishoom offers a stylish
take on Indian cuisine. Don't miss the
signature black daal, or the cocktails.

4 Gallipoli Again
MAP G1 ▪ 120 Upper St N1
▪ 020 7359 1578 ▪ ££

Good quality Turkish cuisine with an
emphasis on mezze in a busy, bois-
terous and friendly bistro. The walls
are adorned with small portraits.

5 Camino
MAP E1 ▪ 3 Varnisher's Yard N1
▪ 020 7841 7330 ▪ ££

Enjoy tapas and great cocktails as well
as Spanish wines, sherries and traditional cider in a relaxed atmosphere.

6 Lemonia
89 Regent's Park Rd NW1
▪ Tube Chalk Farm ▪ 020 7586 7454
▪ ££

Traditional and modern Greek dishes
served in a brasserie-style setting.
There is an attractive conservatory.

Spaniards Inn, Hampstead Heath

7 Spaniards Inn
Spaniards Rd NW3 ▪ 020 8731
8406 ▪ Tube Hampstead or East
Finchley ▪ ££

One of London's most famous old
pubs, this offers traditional English
pub food and great Sunday roasts.

8 Arancini Brothers
115A Kentish Town Rd
NW1 ▪ Tube Camden Town ▪ 020
3583 2242 ▪ £

A characterful café whose speciality
is arancini, risotto rice balls stuffed
with a mix of vegetables coated with
flour and fried. There are plenty of
options, all made on the premises
and all delicious.

9 Rotunda
MAP E1 ▪ 90 York Way N1
▪ 020 7014 2840 ▪ ££

A classy restaurant with fine views
of the Battlebridge Basin. The menu
changes regularly and uses seasonal
ingredients; the meat is sourced
from the restaurant's own farm.

10 28 Church Row
28 Church Row ▪ 020 7993
2062 ▪ ££

Quality ingredients go into simple
Spanish and Italian cuisine served
here in small, shareable plates.
The restaurant is located in a
Georgian building on one of the
prettiest streets in the area.

See map on pp146–7

🔟 South and West London

The palaces that once graced London's river to the south and west of the city centre were built in places that remain popular today, from Hampton Court and Richmond in the west, downriver to Greenwich. There, on a deep meander in the Thames, a vast Tudor palace was the dramatic first sight of the city for anyone arriving by ship. It has been replaced by Wren's handsome Old Royal Naval College, a stunning building that is the high point of this UNESCO World Heritage Site and the start of the many delights of Greenwich, home of Greenwich Mean Time and *Cutty Sark*, the world's last surviving tea clipper.

Richmond's palace has also disappeared, but opposite the Park lies Kew Palace in the grounds of the incomparable Kew Gardens. Chiswick House, Ham House and Syon House are the best of a number of palatial mansions near Richmond, while culture is catered for in the Dulwich Picture Gallery and the Horniman Museum.

Shepherd Gate Clock, Greenwich

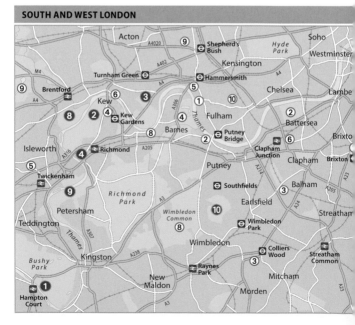

SOUTH AND WEST LONDON

1 Hampton Court

East Molesey, Surrey KT8
■ Train Hampton Court ■ 0844 482
7777 ■ Open Apr–Oct: 10am–6pm
daily; Nov–Mar: 10am–4:30pm daily
(last adm 1 hour before closing)
■ Adm ■ www.hrp.org.uk

Originally leased and substantially
enlarged by Cardinal Wolsey in 1514,
Hampton Court *(see p52)* was handed
over to Henry VIII in 1528. Visiting
this historic Tudor palace and its
extensive grounds is a popular day
out from London. As well as family
trails and special exhibitions, audio
tours are available and costumed
interpreters bring the Tudor world
to life. Events held through the year
include a week-long music festival
in June, which regularly attracts
big-name performers. In July, the
grounds are filled by the world's
largest flower show, organized by
the Royal Horticultural Society. Trains
from Waterloo take about half an
hour but for a delightfully leisurely
trip, catch a boat from Westminster
Pier, which takes about four hours.

Palm House, Kew Gardens

2 Kew Gardens

Kew TW9 ■ Train & Tube Kew
Gardens ■ 020 8332 5655 ■ Open
10am daily (closing times vary
between 3:30–6pm in winter
and 6–9pm in summer); check
website ■ Adm ■ www.kew.org

This former royal garden holds the
world's largest plant collection of
around 30,000 species. Temperate
House, the world's largest Victorian
glasshouse, reopened post restoration
in 2018. Kew Palace and Queen
Charlotte's Cottage *(see p52)* were
used as residences by George III,
whose parents, Prince Frederick
and Princess Augusta, laid the first
garden here. Take a Kew Explorer
Land train tour of the gardens – you
can get on and off it any time.

3 Chiswick House & Gardens

Burlington Lane, Chiswick W4
■ Tube Turnham Green ■ 020 3141
3350 ■ House: open Apr–Oct:
10am–5pm Wed–Mon; adm
■ Gardens: open 7am–dusk
all year ■ www.chiswickhouseand
gardens.org.uk

This piece of Italy in London is a
high spot of English 18th-century
architecture. This fine example
of a Palladian villa, with its dome,
portico and painted interiors,
was built for Lord Burlington by
architect William Kent. The house
is packed with references to ancient
Rome and Renaissance Italy. The
Italianate gardens are complemented with temples, statues
and a lake.

Georgian buildings lining the bank of the Thames, Richmond

4 Richmond
Train to Richmond

This attractive, wealthy riverside suburb, with its quaint shops, pubs and pretty lanes, is worth visiting for its delightful riverside walks, which you can follow to Ham House. Its vast royal park *(see p55)* is home to red and fallow deer. There is also a spacious Green, where cricket is played in summer, which is overlooked by the lovely restored Richmond Theatre and the early 18th-century Maids of Honour Row, which stands next to the last vestiges of an enormous Tudor palace.

5 Dulwich Picture Gallery
Gallery Rd SE21 ■ Train to North or West Dulwich ■ 020 8693 5254 ■ Open 10am–5pm Tue–Sun ■ Adm ■ www.dulwichpicturegallery. org.uk

The oldest purpose-built public art space in England, this gallery *(see p58)* is located opposite the main entrance to Dulwich Park and is well worth the journey from central London. Apart from the stunning collection, including the exquisite *Girl at a Window* by Rembrandt (1645) and fine portraits by Gainsborough, there are regular exhibitions, lectures and other events, as well as over 12,000 sq m (130,000 sq ft) of lawns on which to relax.

6 Greenwich
Greenwich SE10 ■ Train to Greenwich; DLR Cutty Sark, Greenwich ■ Royal Observatory, Maritime Museum & Queen's House: open 10am–5pm daily; adm ■ www.visit greenwich.org.uk ■ www.rmg.co.uk

The World Heritage Site of Greenwich includes Sir Christopher Wren's Old Royal Naval College, Greenwich Park *(see p55)*, the Planetarium and the Royal Observatory Greenwich where the Prime Meridian was established. Bordering the park are the Queen's House *(see p53)* and the National Maritime Museum *(see p56)*. The Greenwich Market and the nearby *Cutty Sark (see p65)* are must-sees.

7 Horniman Museum
100 London Rd SE23 ■ Train to Forest Hill ■ 020 8699 1872 ■ Open 10am–5:30pm daily ■ Aquarium: adm ■ www.horniman.ac.uk

Built in 1901 by Frederick Horniman, this museum appeals to both adults

GREENWICH PALACE

The ruins of this enormous royal riverside palace lie beneath the Old Royal Naval College. Many of the Tudor monarchs lived here, including Henry VII and Henry VIII who was born here. Abandoned under the Commonwealth in 1652, it was eventually demolished for Wren's present buildings.

and children. It has a superb anthropological collection, along with galleries on natural history. There is also an aquarium, a café overlooking the gardens and a small petting zoo.

8 Syon House and Park

Brentford, Middlesex ■ Train to Syon Lane ■ 020 8560 0882 ■ House: open mid-Mar–Oct: 11am–5pm Wed, Thu & Sun ■ Gardens: open 10:30am–5pm daily ■ Adm ■ www.syonpark.co.uk

This Neo-Classical villa is home to the Duke of Northumberland. It has fine Robert Adam interiors and a 0.4-sq-km (0.2-sq-mile) garden landscaped by Capability Brown.

9 Ham House and Garden

Ham Street, Richmond, Surrey ■ Train to Richmond ■ 020 8940 1950 ■ House: open noon–4pm daily; ■ Adm ■ www.nationaltrust.org.uk/ham-house-and-garden

This 17th-century house and garden was at the centre of court intrigue during Charles II's reign. It is richly furnished and there is a fine picture collection. The Orangery serves dishes made from its garden produce.

The façade of Ham House

10 Wimbledon Lawn Tennis Museum

Church Road, Wimbledon SW19 ■ Tube Southfields ■ 020 8946 6131 ■ Open 10am–5pm daily ■ Adm ■ www.wimbledon.com

With a view of the famous Centre Court, the museum tells the story of tennis, from its gentle, amateur beginnings to its professional status today. The first tennis championships were held in Wimbledon in 1877.

A DAY EXPLORING MARITIME GREENWICH

MORNING

Start the day from **Westminster Pier**, because the best way to arrive at **Greenwich** (see p153) is by boat. The journey takes 50–60 minutes and there are terrific river sights on the way (see pp64–5). Visit the historic tea clipper **Cutty Sark** (see p65) where you can walk beneath the impressive copper hull.

Behind is Greenwich Market, liveliest on weekends. Grab a coffee here, and then explore the surrounding streets, full of antique and other charming shops. Turn into **Wren's Old Royal Naval College** (see p153), visit the magnificent Painted Hall and admire its murals, then walk around the Grand Square and down to the river. Stop for some lunch and a pint at the old **Trafalgar Tavern** (on the far side of the Naval College) overlooking the river.

AFTERNOON

After lunch, make your way to the **National Maritime Museum** (see p56), **Queen's House** (see p53) and the **Royal Observatory Greenwich** (see p153), which is on the hill behind. Explore the fascinating museum, the largest of its kind in the world, then make your way to the observatory. This is the home of world time, and stands on the 0° longitude Prime Meridian. You can be photographed with one foot in the eastern hemisphere and one in the west. Return to Central London by boat, DLR or rail from Greenwich.

See map on pp152–3

The Best of the Rest

 Brixton Market
Electric Avenue to Brixton Station Rd SW9 ■ Tube Brixton ■ www.brixtonmarket.net

This lively market lies at the heart of London's Caribbean community. Shop for fresh produce and bargain fabrics, and enjoy street food in nearby Brixton Village and Market Row.

 Battersea Park
The park (see p69) includes a boating lake, a children's zoo, sports facilities, and a gallery. There is also a woodland walk, the Peace Pagoda, as well as sculptures by Henry Moore and Barbara Hepworth.

The Peace Pagoda, Battersea Park

 Merton Abbey Mills
Watermill Way SW19 ■ Tube Colliers Wood ■ www.mertonabbey mills.org.uk

An arts and crafts village on the River Wandle, with a working Victorian watermill, a children's theatre and weekend craft market.

④ WWT London Wetland Centre
Queen Elizabeth Walk SW13 ■ Train to Barnes ■ Open 9:30am–4:30pm daily (summer until 5:30pm); last adm 1 hour before closing ■ Adm ■ www.wwt.org.uk

Managed by the Wildfowl & Wetlands Trust, this haven for

wild birds and animals is one of the best urban wildlife sites in Europe.

⑤ World Rugby Museum
Rugby Rd ■ Train to Twickenham ■ 020 8892 8877 ■ Open 10am–5pm Tue–Sat, 11am–5pm Sun ■ Adm (no tours on match days) ■ www.worldrugbymuseum.com

Tour this impressive national home of rugby before visiting the museum.

⑥ Battersea Arts Centre
Lavender Hill SW11 ■ Train to Clapham Junction ■ 020 7223 2223 ■ www.bac.org.uk

One of the main fringe theatre venues, with a huge programme of activities.

⑦ Peckham
Train to Peckham Rye

Peckham is emerging as London's next cultural hot spot with Caribbean grocery stalls and pawnbroker shops. Peckham Levels is a multi-storey car park turned into a cultural and creative space.

⑧ Wimbledon Common
Wimbledon Common SW19 ■ Train to Wimbledon ■ www.wpcc.org.uk

Visit the windmill then enjoy a walk. Head for southside pubs the Crooked Billet and the Hand in Hand.

⑨ Osterley Park and House
■ **Jersey Rd** ■ Train to Isleworth ■ 020 8232 5050 ■ Adm ■ www.nationaltrust.org.uk/osterley-park-and-house

A large Georgian mansion on a country estate on the outskirts of west London.

⑩ Emirates Air Line
27 Western Gateway Royal Docks E16 and Greenwich Peninsula SE10 ■ Opening times vary, check website ■ Adm ■ www.emiratesairline.co.uk

This cable car links Docklands with Greenwich Peninsula, offering great views of the city and river.

Places to Eat and Drink

PRICE CATEGORIES

For a three-course meal for one with half a bottle of wine (or equivalent meal), taxes and extra charges.

£ under £25   ££ £25–50   £££ over £50

The City Barge pub at Chiswick

1 ### The River Café
Thames Wharf, Rainville Rd W6 ■ Tube Hammersmith ■ 020 7386 4200 ■ £££

This imaginative Hammersmith restaurant, housed in a converted warehouse with a river terrace is considered to be the "one of the best Italian restaurants outside Italy" by many.

2 ### Thai Square Putney Bridge
2–4 Lower Richmond Rd SW15 ■ Tube Putney Bridge ■ 020 8780 1811 ■ ££

A brilliant view of the river from this smart, innovative glass restaurant makes it a good spot year-round, and the Thai menu is excellent.

3 ### Chez Bruce
2 Bellevue Rd SW17 ■ Train to Wandsworth Common ■ 020 8672 0114 ■ £££

Stylish yet relaxed, Michelin-starred Chez Bruce serves excellent modern French and Mediterranean food next to leafy Wandsworth Common. Service is impeccable and booking is essential.

4 ### The Glasshouse
14 Station Parade, Kew, TW9 ■ Tube Kew Gardens ■ 020 8940 6777 ■ £££

Exciting, modern European food is served at this relaxed restaurant.

5 ### The Gate
51 Queen Caroline St W6 ■ Tube Hammersmith ■ 020 7833 0401 ■ ££

Probably the best vegetarian restaurant in London, The Gate is worth hunting out. The gourmet menu changes regularly, and the meals are hearty and inventive.

6 ### The City Barge
27 Strand-on-the-Green W6 ■ Train to Kew Bridge ■ 020 8994 2148 ■ ££

Set in a delightful enclave of 18th-century Thames-side London, this appealing pub serves hearty food.

7 ### Peckham Bazaar
119 Consort Rd, SE15 ■ 020 7732 2525 ■ ££

This restaurant serves pan-Balkan food cooked on the outdoor grill. Marinated octopus and quail often make an appearance on the rotating menu.

8 ### The Brown Dog
28 Cross St SW13 ■ Train Barnes Bridge ■ 020 8392 2200 ■ ££

With its warm atmosphere, this gastropub feels like a real discovery. Beer is sourced locally and in the summer you can eat in the garden.

9 ### Esarn Kheaw
314 Uxbridge Rd W12 ■ Tube Shepherd's Bush ■ 020 8743 8930 ■ ££

Authentic Thai food, with all the usual favourites as well as more unusual dishes such as mud fish sweet-and-sour soup.

10 ### The Harwood Arms
Walham Grove SW6 ■ Tube Fulham Broadway ■ 020 7386 1847 ■ £££

The first gastropub to be awarded a Michelin star, the Harwood Arms offers delicious Sunday roasts and an inventive British menu.

See map on pp152–3

☷ East London

Always a vibrant, working-class area, the East End has also prided itself on providing a refuge for successive generations of immigrants, from French silk weavers to Jewish and Bangladeshi garment workers. Today, the media and finance worlds occupy stylish developments in the Docklands, galleries and restaurants have sprouted in Hoxton and trendy markets draw visitors who marvel at the area's unspoiled 18th- and 19th-century architecture.

Rugs, Spitalfields Market

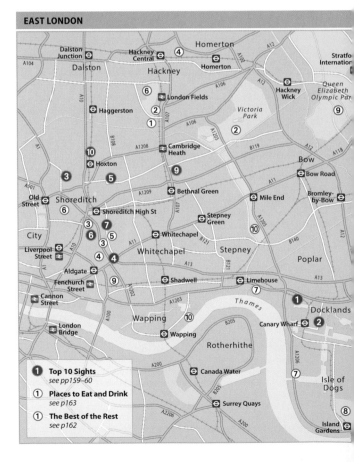

EAST LONDON

Dalston Junction · Hackney Central · Homerton · ④ · Homerton · Stratford International

Dalston · Hackney · Queen Elizabeth Olympic Park · ⑨

⑥ · ▣ London Fields · Hackney Wick

⑥ Haggerston · ② · ① · Victoria Park · ②

⑩ · ▣ Cambridge Heath · Bow · ▣ Bow Road

⑥ Hoxton · ⑨ · Bromley-by-Bow

❸ Shoreditch · ❸ · ❺ · ▣ Bethnal Green · ▣ Mile End

Old Street · ⑥ · ▣ Shoreditch High St · Stepney Green · ⑩

City · ❸ ❼ · ❸ ❺ ❸ · ▣ Whitechapel · Stepney

Liverpool Street · ④ · ❹ ❹ · Whitechapel · Poplar

Aldgate · ⑨ · ▣ Shadwell · ▣ Limehouse · ⑦

Fenchurch Street · ❶ Docklands

Cannon Street · *Thames*

London Bridge · Wapping · ⑩ · Canary Wharf · ❷

▣ Wapping · Rotherhithe · Isle of Dogs

❶ **Top 10 Sights**
see pp159–60

① **Places to Eat and Drink**
see p163

① **The Best of the Rest**
see p162

▣ Canada Water · ⑦

▣ Surrey Quays · ⑧ · Island Gardens

1 Museum of London Docklands

West India Quay E14 ■ **Tube & DLR Canary Wharf, DLR West India Quay, Thames Clippers Canary Wharf Pier** ■ **020 7001 9844** ■ **Open 10am–6pm daily** ■ **www.museumoflondon.org.uk**

Set in a historic warehouse, this museum explores the history of London's river, port and people with a wealth of objects on display. Don't miss Mudlarks, an interactive area for kids; Sailortown, an atmospheric recreation of 19th-century riverside Wapping; and London, Sugar & Slavery, which reveals the city's involvement in the slave trade.

The iconic towers of Canary Wharf

2 Canary Wharf
Tube & DLR Canary Wharf

The centrepiece of the Docklands development is Canary Wharf and the 240-m (800-ft) One Canada Square designed by the US architect Cesar Pelli. The tower is not open to the public but the complex includes a mall with shops, restaurants and bars. The area's exciting architecture includes the stunning Canary Wharf tube station, designed by Norman Foster, and an enclosed rooftop garden above at Crossrail Place.

3 Hoxton and Shoreditch
Tube Old St or train Hoxton

Once renowned as a hub for British contemporary art (thanks in large part to the now-closed White Cube art gallery on Hoxton Square), this trendy area is now home to a growing tech community around the junction of Old Street and City Road, dubbed 'Silicon Roundabout'. Lively at night, bars, pubs and restaurants here include The Three Crowns, The Fox and the Queen of Hoxton.

4 Whitechapel Gallery
MAP H3 ■ **77–82 Whitechapel High St E1** ■ **020 7522 7888** ■ **Open 11am–6pm Tue–Sun (until 9pm Thu)** ■ **www.whitechapelgallery.org**

This excellent gallery has a reputation for showing cutting-edge contemporary art from around the world. The gallery has launched the careers of David Hockney, Gilbert and George and Anthony Caro. Behind the distinctive 1901 Arts and Crafts façade there is a bookshop, café and restaurant.

THE HUGUENOTS IN LONDON

Driven from France in 1685, the Huguenots were Protestants fleeing religious persecution by Catholics. They were mostly silk weavers, whose masters and merchants settled in Spitalfields and built the beautiful Georgian houses (**below**) around Fournier, Princelet and Elder streets. Spitalfields silk was famous for its fine quality, but by the mid-19th century the industry had declined.

⑤ Columbia Road Market
Columbia Rd E2 ▪ Tube Old St
▪ Open 8am–3pm Sun

A ten-minute walk from the north end of Brick Lane, Columbia Road comes alive on Sunday mornings, as it fills with stalls teeming with plants and flowers. It is a delightful cornucopia of all things horticultural at wholesale prices. The street is also home to some charming restaurants, bars and stores selling, among other things, homemade bread and farmhouse cheeses through the week.

⑥ Spitalfields
MAP H2 ▪ Commercial St E1
▪ Opening times vary ▪ www.old spitalfieldsmarket.com

Streets such as Fournier Street, lined with 18th-century Huguenot silk weavers' houses remind that this area, just east of the City, has provided a refuge for immigrant populations for centuries. London's oldest market, Old Spitalfields Market has traditional food stalls, cafés and a large shopping complex. The market draws many browsers and shoppers, eager to find a bargain among the fashion, vintage clothing, and crafts stalls here. There are also free events such as lunchtime concerts. Thursdays are good for antiques and collectibles. Opposite is one of Europe's great Baroque churches. Christ Church, built between 1714 and 1729, was designed by Nicholas Hawksmoor.

⑦ Brick Lane
Brick Lane E1 ▪ Tube Aldgate East, train to Shoreditch

Once the centre of London's Jewish population, this street is now the heart of London's Bangladeshi community. Some of the city's best bagels are available from the 24-hour Brick Lane Beigel Bake, a famous dawn haunt for late-night revellers. There are inexpensive restaurants, vintage and designer shops and a lively flea market on Sundays.

Crowds exploring Brick Lane

The silver fins of the Thames Barrier

⑧ Thames Barrier
Information Centre ■ 1 Unity Way SE18 ■ Train to Charlton or Woolwich Dockyard ■ 020 8305 4188 ■ Visitor Centre: open 10:30am–4pm Thu–Sun (summer daily) ■ Adm

With its 10 curved gates rising like shark fins from the river, this barrier (see p65) is a magnificent sight. There is a small visitor centre on the south side.

⑨ V&A Museum of Childhood
Cambridge Heath Rd E2 ■ Tube Bethnal Green ■ 020 8983 5200 ■ Open 10am–5:45pm daily ■ www.vam.ac.uk/moc

Everyone will find something to delight them here: from dolls and teddy bears to train sets and games through the ages. There are activities for children of all ages every day, plus special events at weekends and in school holidays, some linked to current exhibitions.

⑩ Museum of the Home
MAP H2 ■ 136 Kingsland Rd E2 ■ Train to Hoxton ■ 020 7739 989 ■ Opening times vary ■ www.museumofthehome.org.uk

Set in a beautiful 18th-century almshouse, this fascinating museum explores the evolution of the home and home life from 1600 to the present day. A series of rooms and gardens are decorated in distinct period style, reflecting changes in society, behaviour, style and taste. One of the restored almshouses remains open for tours all year round.

A DAY AROUND THE EAST END

▶ MORNING

Start at **Old Spitalfields Market**, where a mixture of stalls selling clothes, food and collectibles, fill the floor daily. Have a delicious breakfast at **St John Bread & Wine** (see p163) opposite the market at 96 Commercial Street.

Walk around the corner into Fournier Street, where the gallery at No. 5 retains the panelling of the 18th-century silk weavers' houses. Stroll along Princelet and Elder streets, just off Fournier, for a taste of historic London.

Head into **Brick Lane** to browse among the numerous sari and Bangladeshi gift shops and then stop for lunch at one of the many curry houses.

AFTERNOON

After lunch head to Whitechapel Road. Notice the Arts and Crafts façade of the **Whitechapel Gallery** (see p159). Pop into the gallery's stunning two-floor exhibition space dedicated to contemporary and modern art.

Finally, take a ride on the driverless Docklands Light Railway from Tower Gateway, for some of the best views of East London. Emerge at **Canary Wharf** (see p159) to see some impressive architecture around Cabot Square, and end the day with a drink at **The Gun** (see p163) on Cold Harbour.

Canary Wharf clock

The Best of the Rest

1 Theatre Royal Stratford East

Gerry Raffles Sq E15 ▪ Train, Tube & DLR Stratford ▪ 020 8534 0310 ▪ www.stratfordeast.com

This local theatre with an international reputation was established by the director Joan Littlewood in 1953.

2 Victoria Park

Bow E9 ▪ Tube Bethnal Green

One of East London's largest parks, with a boating lake and pretty garden.

3 Dennis Severs' House

MAP H2 ▪ 18 Folgate St E1 ▪ 020 7247 4013 ▪ Open noon–4pm Sun, noon–2pm & 5–9pm Mon, Wed & Fri ▪ Adm ▪ dennissevershouse.co.uk

Created by artist Dennis Severs, this is an 18th-century silk-weaver's home (see p160). Each room appears as if the inhabitants have just left it – dinner is half-eaten and cooking smells emanate from the kitchen.

4 Sutton House

2–4 Homerton High St E9 ▪ Train Hackney Central ▪ 020 8986 2264 ▪ Check website for timings ▪ Adm ▪ www.nationaltrust.org.uk/sutton-house

This Tudor merchant's house dates from 1535 and is one of the oldest in the East End.

5 House Mill

Three Mill Lane E3 ▪ Tube Bromley-by-Bow ▪ 020 8980 4626 ▪ Open May–Oct: 11am–4pm Sun (1st Sun in Mar, Apr & Dec) ▪ Guided tours only ▪ Adm ▪ www.housemill.org.uk

Built in 1776, this tidal mill was once the country's largest. Today it is a working museum.

6 London Fields Lido

London Fields Westside E8 ▪ Train Hackney Central ▪ 020 7254 9038 ▪ Adm

Amidst the greenery of London Fields is an Olympic-sized, Art Deco heated outdoor swimming pool.

7 Docklands Sailing & Watersports Centre

Millwall Dock, 235a Westferry Rd E14 ▪ DLR Crossharbour ▪ 020 7537 2626 ▪ www.dswc.org

Enjoy sailing, kayaking and windsurfing facilities here.

8 Mudchute Farm

Pier St E14 ▪ Open 9am–5pm daily ▪ DLR Mudchute ▪ 020 7515 5901 ▪ www.mudchute.org

Britain's largest city farm has livestock and a riding school.

The futuristic ArcelorMittal Orbit

9 ArcelorMittal Orbit

3 Thornton St E20 ▪ Train, Tube & DLR Stratford ▪ Open 11am–5pm Mon–Fri, 10am–7pm Sat & Sun ▪ Adm ▪ www.arcelormittalorbit.com

Designed for the 2012 London Olympics, this 114-m-(374-ft)-tall sculpture offers great views of the city and the world's highest tunnel slide. Advance booking is advised.

10 Mile End Park

Mile End Rd E3 ▪ Tube Mile End ▪ 020 7364 5227

One of London's most unusual parks with an Art Pavilion, Ecology Pavilion, sports centre and a go-kart track.

Places to Eat and Drink

PRICE CATEGORIES
For a three-course meal for one with half a bottle of wine (or equivalent meal), taxes and extra charges.

£ under £30   ££ £30–50   £££ over £50

1 Buen Ayre
50 Broadway Market E8
020 7275 9900 ■ ££

Located in Hackney, this restaurant specializes in authentic Argentinian food and steaks.

2 Bright
Netil House, 1 Westgate St E8
020 3095 9407 ■ ££

It's all about the food at this cool, stripped-back restaurant, where diners sit at scrubbed-oak tables. Menu comprises of a mix of classic Italian and modern European dishes.

3 St John Bread & Wine
MAP H2 ■ 94–96 Commercial St E1 ■ 020 7251 0848 ■ ££

This sister restaurant of St John (see p145) is a much-loved local haunt. It has a great wine list, and the bakery sells amazing bread and cakes to go.

4 Som Saa
MAP H3 ■ 43a Commercial St, E1 ■ 020 7324 7790 ■ ££

Originally a 'pop-up' eatery, Som Saa has grown into a stylish Thai restaurant. It offers innovative Thai dishes including deep-fried whole seabass, as well as curries and salads.

Façade of Prospect of Whitby

5 Sheba
MAP H3 ■ 136 Brick Lane E1
0207 247 7824 ■ £

There's plenty of competition to be found in Brick Lane, but Sheba has maintained an impressively consistent record when it comes to producing delicious curries.

6 The Fox
MAP H2 ■ 28 Paul St EC2
020 7729 5708 ■ ££

The menu here celebrates fried chicken. Food can be had upstairs in this lovely refurbished pub, which is frequented by City types looking for decent ales and wines.

7 The Grapes
76 Narrow St E14 ■ DLR West Ferry ■ 020 7987 4396

It is said that Charles Dickens danced on the tables at this pub. The heated terrace and upstairs dining room have Thames views.

8 The Gun
27 Coldharbour E14 ■ DLR South Quay/Blackwell ■ 020 7519 0075 ■ ££

This swish Docklands operation overlooking the Thames serves up quality gastropub food.

9 Café Spice Namaste
16 Prescot St E1 ■ Tube Tower Hill & Aldgate ■ 020 7488 9242
■ Closed Sun ■ ££

A long-established Indian restaurant, serving pan-Indian food with Asian and European influences.

10 Prospect of Whitby
57 Wapping Wall E1
■ Tube Wapping
■ 020 7481 1095 ■ ££

East London's oldest riverside pub dates to 1520, and has old beams, a pewter bar and great river views.

See map on pp158–9

Streetsmart

Modern interior of St Pancras
International Station

Getting Around

Arriving by Air

Heathrow, Gatwick, Stansted, Luton and City. airports serve London.

Heathrow, London's main airport, is 24 km (15 miles) west of central London. The Heathrow Express to Paddington is a quick but pricey way into the centre, taking 15 minutes. Trains run from 5:12am until 11:42pm daily. The rail service on the Elizabeth Line is due to open in late 2021, and will be a cheaper alternative. Cheaper still is the Tube, which takes an hour from all terminals to King's Cross. National Express runs a coach service from Heathrow's bus station to Victoria Coach Station.

Gatwick airport, is 45 km (28 miles) south of London. The Gatwick Express train leaves the South Terminal every 15 minutes for Victoria railway station, taking 30 minutes. The National Express coach takes an hour longer, leaving for Victoria every 1.5–2 hours.

Stansted, London's third busiest airport, is 56 km (35 miles) northeast of London. The Stansted Express train to Liverpool Street takes 45 minutes and runs every 15 minutes. National Express provides 24-hour coaches to Victoria and Stratford, taking between 1 and 2 hours. From **Luton Airport**, 50 km (31 miles) north of the city, a shuttle bus takes passengers to Luton Airport Parkway station, from which trains go to St Pancras, taking 20 minutes. **London City Airport** is 14 km (9 miles) from the centre. The airport is served by Docklands Light Railway (DLR) from Bank station.

International Train Travel

St Pancras International is the London terminus for **Eurostar**, the high-speed train linking the UK with the Continent.

You can buy tickets and passes for multiple international journeys via **Eurail** or **Interrail**; advance reservations are usually not required but always check that your pass is valid on the service on which you wish to travel before attempting to board.

Eurostar runs regular services from Paris, Brussels and Amsterdam (via Brussels) to London via the Channel Tunnel. **Eurotunnel** operates a drive-on-drive-off train service between Calais and Folkestone, in southeast England.

Domestic Train Travel

The UK's railway system is complicated and can be confusing. Lines are run by several different companies, but they are coordinated by **National Rail**, which operates a joint information service.

London has eight main railway termini serving different parts of Britain (Charing Cross, Euston, King's Cross, London Bridge, St Pancras, Paddington, Waterloo and Victoria). There are also over 300 smaller London stations.

Each main terminus is the starting point for local and suburban lines that cover the whole of southeast England.

London's local and suburban train lines are used by commuters every day. For visitors, rail services are most useful for trips to the outskirts of London and areas of the city without nearby Underground connections (especially in south London). If you are planning to travel outside of the capital, always try to book rail tickets in advance.

Long-Distance Bus Travel

Coaches from European and UK destinations arrive at Victoria Coach Station. The biggest operator in the UK is **National Express**. **Eurolines** is its European arm, offering a variety of coach routes to London from other European cities. Fares start from around £17 and vary depending on distance. Book in advance.

Public Transport

Transport for London (**TFL**) is London's main public transport authority. Safety and hygiene measures, timetables, ticket information, transport maps and more can be found on their website.

TFL divides the city into six charging zones for Underground, Overground and National Rail services, radiating out from Zone 1 in the centre. On buses, there is a flat fare for each trip, no matter how far you travel.

Tickets

Tube and rail fares are expensive, especially individual tickets. If you expect to make multiple trips around the city in a short space of time, you can buy a one-day off-peak Travelcard, which gives unlimited travel on all systems after 9:30am on weekdays (or any time on Saturday, Sunday and public holidays) until 4:30am the next morning within Zones 1–4 or 1–6 for a flat fee.

If you wish to travel more freely, purchase a pay-as-you-go Oyster card or Visitor Oyster card (valid for all London zones, as well as Heathrow and Gatwick Express), which you can preload and top up with credit (note that a £5 deposit is required when buying an Oyster card and you will need one card per person). You can also use contactless credit or debit cards in the same way as the Oyster card. It is cheaper to pay as you go using contactless or Oyster as fares are subject to daily and weekly caps.

When using public transport, you "touch in" with your card on a yellow card reader, and the corresponding amount is deducted. On Underground, DLR and Overground trains, you must also remember to "touch out" where you finish your journey, or you will be charged a maximum fare, though the excess can usually be reclaimed via

the website if you forget. Prices rise during peak times: 6:30–9:30am and 4–7pm Mon–Fri.

Buy Travelcards and Oyster cards at Underground and local rail stations, or any shop that has the TFL "Ticket Stop" sticker in the window. Many smaller stations just have self-service machines. You can also purchase them from overseas agents in around 30 countries.

The Underground and DLR

The London Underground (commonly referred to as "the Tube") has 11 lines, all named and colour-coded, which intersect at various stations. The construction of an additional line, the Elizabeth line, is currently underway. Following setbacks, this will open in late 2021 at the earliest.

Some lines, like the Jubilee, have a single branch; others, like the Northern, have more than one, so it is important to check the digital boards on the platform and the destination on the front of the train.

Trains run every few minutes 7:30–9:30am and 4–7pm, and every 5–10 minutes at all other times. The Jubilee, Northern, Central, Victoria and Piccadilly lines offer a 24-hour service on selected routes on Fridays and Saturdays. All other lines operate roughly 5am–12:40am Mon–Sat, with reduced hours on Sun.

The DLR (Docklands Light Railway) is a mostly overground network of

trains that run from the City to stops in east and southeast London, including City Airport and Greenwich. It operates roughly 5:30–12:30am Mon–Sat, 7am–11:30pm Sun, with trains departing every 3 minutes.

Stations with step-free access are marked on Tube maps, which are located on all trains and at every station.

DIRECTORY

ARRIVING BY AIR

Gatwick
w gatwickairport.com

Heathrow
w heathrow.com

London City Airport
w londoncityairport.com

Luton Airport
w london-luton.co.uk

Stansted
w stanstedairport.com

INTERNATIONAL TRAIN TRAVEL

Eurail
w eurorail.com

Eurostar
w eurostar.com

Eurotunnel
w eurotunnel.com

Interrail
w interrail.eu

DOMESTIC TRAIN TRAVEL

National Rail
w nationalrail.co.uk

LONG-DISTANCE BUS TRAVEL

Eurolines
w eurolines.eu

National Express
w nationalexpress.com

PUBLIC TRANSPORT

TFL
w tfl.gov.uk

The Overground

Marked on Tube maps by an orange line, the Overground connects with the Underground and main railway stations at various points across the city. It operates in much the same way as the Underground, and covers most areas of the city without nearby Underground connections. The line between Highbury & Islington and New Cross Gate runs 24 hours Friday and Saturday.

Bus

Slower but cheaper than the Tube, buses are also a good way of seeing the city as you travel.

Bus routes are displayed on the TFL website and on maps at bus stops. The destination and route number is indicated on the front of the bus and the stops are announced on board.

Buses do not accept cash so a ticket, Oyster card or contactless payment is required.

A single fare costs £1.50, while unlimited bus travel caps out at £4.50 – just use the same card each time you use the bus to reach the daily cap.

The hopper fare allows you to make unlimited bus journeys for free within an hour of travel. Travel is free on buses for under-16s as long as they carry a Zip Oyster photocard. Apply for one on the TFL website at least four weeks before you are due to arrive.

The Night buses (indicated by the letter "N" added before the route number) run on many popular routes from 11pm until 6am, generally 3–4 times per hour up to 2 or 3am.

Taxis

London's iconic black cabs can be hailed on the street, booked online or over the phone, or picked up at taxi ranks throughout the city. The yellow "Taxi" sign is lit up when the taxi is free. The driver's cab licence number should be displayed in the back of the taxi.

All taxis are metered, and fares start from £3. Taxi apps such as Uber also operate in London. **Dial-a-Cab** and **Licensed London Taxi** services can be booked by phone or online.

Driving

Holders of non-UK licences, including EU citizens, may need to apply for an International Driving Permit. Check with your local automobile association before you travel, or consult the UK Driver and Vehicle Licensing Agency (**DVLA**).

Driving in London

EEA citizens can drive in the UK, so long as they carry their full and valid licence, registration and insurance documents. Check the UK government's website to see the latest developments and changes related to Brexit. Other foreign nationals can drive a car or motor-cycle for 12 months, on the same terms. Inform your insurer before travelling.

However, driving in London is not recom-mended. Traffic is slow-moving, parking is scarce and expensive, and in central London there is the added cost of the **Congestion Charge** – a £15 daily charge for driving in central London 7am–10pm daily.

In the event of an accident, contact the **AA** for roadside assistance.

Parking

Parking is prohibited at all times wherever the street is marked with double yellow or red lines by the kerb.

If there is a single yellow line, parking is normally allowed from 6:30pm–8am Mon–Sat and all day Sun, but exact hours vary, so always check the signs along each street before leaving your vehicle. Where there is no line at all, parking is free at all times, but this is rare in central London. Rental car drivers are still liable for parking fines.

Car Rental

To rent a car in the UK you must be 21 or over (or in some cases, 25) and have held a valid driver's licence for at least a year.

Driving out of central London will take about an hour in any direction, more during rush hours; if you want to tour the countryside, it can be easier to take a train to a town or city outside London and rent a car from there. Airports tend to offer cheaper car rental.

Rules of the Road

Drive on the left. Seat belts must be worn at all times by the driver and all passengers. Children up to 135 cm tall or the age of 12 or under must travel with the correct child seat for their weight and size.

Mobile phones may not be used while driving except with a "hands-free" system. Third-party insurance is required by law.

Overtake on the outside or right-hand lane. When approaching a round-about, give priority to traffic approaching from the right, unless indicated otherwise. All vehicles must give way to emergency services vehicles.

It is illegal to drive in bus lanes during certain hours. See roadside signs for restrictions.

The drink-driving legal limit (p170) is strictly enforced and penalities upon conviction can be severe.

Cycling

You need a strong nerve to cycle in London's traffic, but it can be a great way to see the city. For a traffic-free route, head to the Thames Path, which runs along the banks of the river.

Santander Cycles, London's self-service cycle hire, has docking stations in central London. Bikes can also be rented from the **London Bicycle Tour Company** and other rental companies throughout the city.

Be aware that drink-drive limits (p170) also apply to cyclists.

Walking

Walking is a rewarding way to get around in London. The centre is not large, and you will be surprised at how short the distance is between places that seem far apart on the Tube.

Guided walking tours abound, with themes including Jack the Ripper, ghosts and hauntings and Shakespeare's London. The longest established operator, **London Walks**, offers a wide choice.

Boats and Ferries

Car ferries departing from Calais and Dunkirk arrive in Dover or Folkestone, around 2 hours' drive from London.

Passenger and car-ferry services also sail from other ports in northern France to the south of England, as well as from Bilbao and Santander in Spain to Portsmouth or Plymouth.

Ferry services also run to other ports around the country from the Netherlands and the Republic of Ireland.

London by Boat

Some of London's most spectacular views can be seen from the Thames.

MBNA Thames Clippers runs river services every 20 minutes on catamarans between Westminster and North Greenwich in both directions, via the London Eye, Bankside and Tower Bridge. Running between Battersea Power Station and London Bridge, the Tate Boat, or RB2, is also operated by MBNA Thames Clippers and connects the Tate Britain and Tate Modern museums.

Standard tickets cost £9 in the central zone, but discounted fares apply if bought online, via the Thames Clippers app or when using a Travelcard, contactless or Oyster card (pay as you go).

A number of providers offer **river tours** and experiences on the Thames, with numerous options available, from dining experiences to hop-on-hop-off services.

DIRECTORY

TAXIS

Dial-a-Cab
w dialacab.co.uk

Licensed London Taxi
w licensedlondontaxi.co.uk

DRIVING

DVLA
w gov.uk/driving-nongb-licence

DRIVING IN LONDON

AA
w theaa.com

Congestion Charge
w tfl.gov.uk/modes/driving/congestion-charge

CYCLING

Santander Cycles
w tfl.gov.uk/modes/cycling/santander-cycles

London Bicycle Tour Company
w londonbicycle.com

LONDON BY BOAT

MBNA Thames Clippers
w thamesclippers.com

River Tours
w tfl.gov.uk/modes/river/about-river-tours

Practical Information

Passports and Visas

For entry requirements, including visas, consult your nearest British embassy or check the **UK Government** website. For a stay of up to six months for the purpose of tourism, citizens of the US, Canada, Australia and New Zealand do not need a visa to enter the country. Post-Brexit arrangements for citizens from EEA countries will vary depending on the terms agreed; the rights of Irish citizens will not change.

Government Advice

Now more than ever, it is important to consult both your and the UK government's advice before travelling. The **UK Foreign and Commonwealth Office**, the **US Department of State**, and the **Australian Department of Foreign Affairs and Trade** offer the latest information on security, health and regulations.

Customs Information

You can find information on the laws relating to goods and currency taken in or out of the UK on the **UK Government** website.

Insurance

We recommend that you take out a comprehensive insurance policy covering theft, loss of belongings, medical care, cancellations and delays, and read the small print carefully. Emergency treatment is usually free from the National Health Service, and there are reciprocal arrangements with Australia, New Zealand and some others (check the **NHS** website for details). Healthcare arrangements for EEA citizens – currently covered by the **EHIC** (European Health Insurance Card)– are likely to change in 2021. Check the NHS website for the most up-to-date information.

Health

The UK has a world-class healthcare system. Emergency medical care in the UK is generally free. It is important to arrange comprehensive medical insurance before travelling. If you have an EHIC card, be sure to present this as soon as possible. You may have to pay after treatment and reclaim the money later. Those without an EHIC may have to pay upfront for medical treatment and reclaim on insurance at a later date; check the NHS website for details of reciprocal agreements in place for treatment between your home country and the UK.

No vaccinations are needed before visiting the UK. Tap water in the UK is safe to drink, unless otherwise stated.

For minor ailments go to a pharmacy or chemist. These are plentiful throughout the city; chains such as Boots and Superdrug have branches in almost every shopping district. If you have an accident or medical problem requiring non-urgent medical attention, you can find details of your nearest non-emergency medical service on the NHS website. Alternatively, you can contact **NHS 111** (the NHS emergency care service) at any hour online or by calling 111, or go to your nearest Accident and Emergency (A&E) department.

You may need a doctor's prescription to obtain certain pharmaceuticals; the pharmacist can inform you of the closest doctor's surgery or medical centre where you can be seen by a GP (general practitioner).

Smoking, Alcohol and Drugs

The UK has a smoking ban in all public places, including bars, cafés, restaurants, public transport, train stations and hotels.

The UK legal limit for drivers is 80 mg of alcohol per 100 ml of blood, or 0.08 per cent BAC (blood alcohol content). This is roughly equivalent to one small glass of wine or a pint of regular-strength lager; however, it is best to avoid drinking altogether if you plan to drive. The possession of illegal drugs is prohibited and could result in a prison sentence.

ID

There is no requirement for visitors to carry ID, but in the case of a routine check you may be asked to show your passport and visa documentation. Anyone who looks under 18 may be asked for photo ID to prove their age when buying alcohol.

Personal Security

London is a relatively safe city to visit. Pick-pocketing is less of a problem than in many other European capitals. Keep your belongings in a safe place and with you at all times, use your common sense and be alert to your surroundings. Use only licensed black cabs displaying an identification disc.

Make sure possessions are insured, and if possible leave passports and tickets in the hotel safe. If you have anything stolen, report the crime as soon as possible to the nearest police station. Get a copy of the crime report in order to claim on your insurance

Contact your embassy if you have your passport stolen, or in the event of a serious crime or accident

For emergency **police**, **fire** or **ambulance** services dial 999 or 112 – the operator will ask which service you require; If you need urgent medical help, dial the NHS 111 service instead.

Anything found on the Tube, buses, trains or black cabs is sent to the **TFL Lost Property Office**. Allow three to five days for items to get there; property is held for three months.

As a rule, Londoners are very accepting of all people, regardless of their race, gender or sexuality. Homosexuality was legalized in England in 1967 and in 2004, the UK recognized the right to legally change your gender. If you do feel unsafe, the **Safe Space Alliance** pinpoints your nearest place of refuge.

Travellers with Specific Requirements

Accessibility information, braille maps, apps and audio guides for public transport are available from the TFL website. The Tube has many stations with step-free access. The city's bus fleet is wheelchair-accessible.

In the City, Westminster, Camden and Kensington and Chelsea, a disabled-driver badge allows you to park in Blue Badge bays only. The Visit London website offers handy tips on the city's accessibility provisions. **AccessAble** has a useful searchable online directory.

Most large hotels and attractions have wheelchair access and disabled toilets, but make sure you check before booking.

Even if a restaurant has wheelchair access, the dining area and toilet may be on different floors, so check when booking.

Museums and galleries offer audio tours, which are useful to those with impaired vision. **Action on Hearing Loss** and the **RNIB** (Royal National Institute of Blind People) can also offer useful information and advice. Call theatres and cinemas in advance to ask about disabled seating. Many theatres have a sign-language interpreter at some performances.

DIRECTORY

PASSPORTS AND VISAS
UK Government
w gov.uk/check-uk-visa
w gov.uk/guidance/visiting-the-uk-after-brexit

GOVERNMENT ADVICE
Australian Department of Foreign Affairs and Trade
w smartraveller.gov.au

UK Foreign and Commonwealth Office
w gov.uk/foreign-travel-advice

US Department of State
w travel.state.gov

CUSTOMS INFORMATION
UK Government
w gov.uk/duty-free-goods

INSURANCE
EHIC
w gov.uk/european-health-insurance-card

NHS
w nhs.uk

HEALTH
NHS 111
w 111.nhs.uk

PERSONAL SECURITY
Police, Fire, Ambulance
(999 or 112

Safe Space Alliance
w safespacealliance.com

TFL Lost Property Office
MAP C2
■ 63–81 Pelham St SW7
(0343 222 1234

TRAVELLERS WITH SPECIFIC REQUIREMENTS
AccessAble
w accessable.co.uk

Action on Hearing Loss
w actiononhearingloss.org.uk

RNIB
w rnib.org.uk

Time Zone

London operates on Greenwich Mean Time, which is one hour behind Continental European Time and five hours ahead of US Eastern Seaboard Time. The clock advances one hour during "British Summer Time", spanning the last Sunday in March until the last Sunday in October. At anytime of year you can check the correct time by dialling 123 on a BT landline to contact the 24-hour automated Speaking Clock service (note there is a charge for this service).

Money

The UK's currency is the pound sterling. One pound sterling (£1) is divided into 100 pence (100p). Paper notes are in denominations of £5, £10, £20 and £50. Coins are £2, £1, 50p, 20p, 10p, 5p, 2p and 1p. Major credit and debit cards are accepted in most shops and restaurants, while prepaid currency cards are accepted in some. Contactless payments are widely accepted in London, including on public transport. However, it is always worth carrying some cash, as some smaller businesses and markets still operate a cash-only policy. Cash machines are conveniently located at banks, train stations, shopping areas and main streets.

Tipping in London is discretionary. In restaurants it's customary to tip 10–12.5 per cent for good service. It is usual to tip taxi drivers 10 per cent and hotel porters, concierge and housekeeping £1–2 per bag or day.

Electrical Appliances

The electricity supply is 240 volts AC. Plugs are of a three-square-pin type. Most hotels have shaver sockets in the bathrooms.

Mobile Phones and Wi-Fi

Check before leaving home whether your mobile phone will work in the UK. Visitors travelling to the UK with EU tariffs should check whether they are affected by data roaming charges.

Internet access is very easy to find in London. Free Wi-Fi hotspots are widely available in the city centre. Cafés and restaurants will usually give you their Wi-Fi password, though you should make a purchase beforehand. Wi-Fi is also available in most hotels, often for free, and in many public places. Both O2 (*www.o2.co.uk/connectivity*) and Virgin Media (on the Under-ground; *https://my.virginmedia.com/wifi*) offer Wi-Fi across central London, though you will need to register to access their hotspots; note that only their customers can avail Virgin hotspots.

Postal Services

Standard post in the UK is handled by the **Royal Mail**. There are post office branches throughout London, generally open 9am–5:30pm Monday to Friday and until 12:30pm on Saturday.

You can buy 1st-class, 2nd-class and international stamps in post offices, shops and supermarkets. Distinctive red post boxes are located on main streets throughout the city.

Weather

London's weather is very unpredictable: an umbrella and raincoat are advisable all year round. To check ahead, visit the **Met Office** website, which carries detailed forecasts for the next five days.

Opening Hours

Shops generally open from about 9am–6pm Monday to Saturday, with late-night shopping until at least 8pm on Thursdays. Sunday has limited trading hours: these vary but many stores open from 10am–4pm.

Museum and gallery times vary widely: it's better to check before starting out. Some museums and attractions are closed on Mondays. Last admission to many attractions is 30 minutes before closing.

On public holidays, public services are closed and some shops, museums and attractions either close or operate shorter hours.

COVID-19 The pandemic continues to affect London. Some museums, tourist attractions and hospitality venues are operating on reduced or temporary opening hours, and require visitors to make advance bookings for a specific date and time. Always check ahead before visiting.

Visitor Information

Visit London is the official tourist organization for London; its services include a what's on guide, maps, event calendars, offers on theatre tickets and an accommodation booking scheme. Major visitor centres include the **City Information Centre**, right by St Paul's from where the walking tours of the city depart, and **Greenwich Tourist Information**, which offers advice on places to stay, guided tours, day trips and much more. Visitor Centres run by TFL are also located in major transport hubs such as Piccadilly Circus and Victoria and Kings Cross St Pancras stations, as well as Gatwick and Heathrow airports.

London can be an expensive city, but there are a number of ways in which costs can be reduced, and many museums are free. Students and under-18s pay lower admission to many exhibitions, and holders of an ISIC (International Student Identity Card) or IYTC (International Youth Travel Card) are eligible for a range of other discounts.

A number of visitor passes and discount cards are available online and from participating tourist offices. These cards are not free, so consider carefully how many of the offers you are likely to take advantage of before buying one. For a full list of the options available, consult the Visit London website.

One such card is the **London Pass**, which offers free entry to more than 80 of the city's top attractions, fast-track entry to some busier sights, money off selected tours and discounts in participating shops and restaurants, with the option of adding unlimited travel.

Local Customs

Always stand to the right on escalators or stairwells. Allow passengers to exit before you board public transport. On the Tube, it is customary to offer your seat to passengers who are less able-bodied, pregnant or elderly.

Language

English is the official language spoken in London. However, it is a multicultural city, in which you will hear many languages spoken. Numerous attractions and tour companies offer foreign language tours.

Taxes and Refunds

VAT (Value Added Tax) is charged at 20 per cent and almost always included in the marked price. Stores offering tax-free shopping display a distinctive sign and will provide you with a VAT 407 form to validate when you leave the country. EU residents should check www.gov.uk for the lastest advice.

Accommodation

London offers a huge variety of accommodation to suit any budget, including luxury five-star hotels, family-run B&Bs and budget hostels.

Lodgings can fill up and prices become inflated during the summer, so it's worth booking well in advance. London hotels usually quote room rates rather than prices per person and include VAT in their published rates. Look for special offer deals: prices can be lower if you book a minimum of two nights, for example. The best deals at budget hotel chains are to be had online and well in advance. But do consider calling to request last-minute deals, too.

A comprehensive list of accommodation to suit all needs can be found via Visit London.

DIRECTORY

POSTAL SERVICES
W postoffice.co.uk
W postoffice.co.uk/mail/poste-restante

Royal Mail
📞 0345 774 0740
W royalmail.com

WEATHER

Met Office
W metoffice.gov.uk

VISITOR INFORMATION

City Information Centre
MAP R2 ■ St Paul's Churchyard EC4
📞 020 7332 1456

Greenwich Tourist Information
Old Royal Navy College, SE10
📞 020 8305 5235

London Pass
W londonpass.com

Visit London
W visitlondon.com

Places to Stay

PRICE CATEGORIES
For a standard, double room per night (with breakfast
if included), taxes and extra charges.

£ under £125   ££ £125–250   £££ over £250

Luxury Hotels

Brown's Hotel
MAP J4 ▪ Albemarle St W1
▪ 020 7493 6020 ▪ www.
roccofortehotels.com ▪ £££
Founded in 1837 by
James Brown, valet to
Lord Byron, this Mayfair
hotel accommodates
country society staying in
London. With 115 rooms
set across 11 Georgian
townhouses, it is deco-
rated with contemporary
as well as antique art,
while retaining its inti-
macy and charm. It is
renowned for its after-
noon teas in the English
Tea Room.

Claridge's
MAP D3 ▪ 49 Brook St W1
▪ 020 7629 8860 ▪ www.
claridges.co.uk ▪ £££
This historic hotel
established a reputation
for glamour and style
following its Art Deco
makeover in 1929 and
has maintained it ever
since. Favoured by A-list
celebrities, a stay here
is guaranteed to make
you feel pampered.

The Connaught
MAP D3 ▪ 1 Carlos Place
W1 ▪ 020 7499 7070
▪ www.the-connaught.
co.uk ▪ £££
Tucked away in a quiet
corner of Mayfair, the
Connaught is more dis-
creet than other grand
hotels in London. With
two Michelin stars, this
hotel has one of the
finest restaurants, as
well as a small spa with
a black granite pool.

The Lanesborough
MAP D4 ▪ 1 Hyde Park
Corner SW1 ▪ 020 7259
5599 ▪ www.oetker
collection.com/hotels/
the-lanesborough ▪ £££
Since its reopening
after an extensive reno-
vation, this opulent hotel
has maintained its repu-
tation as one of London's
most decadent hotels.
The rooms are adorned
with chandeliers, and its
Michelin-starred restau-
rant, Céleste, offers a
fine dining experience.

Mandarin Oriental
MAP C4 ▪ 66 Knightsbridge
SW1 ▪ 020 7235 2000
▪ www.mandarinoriental.
com ▪ £££
The Edwardian-style
Mandarin Oriental is home
to world-renowned res-
taurants. From the rooms
to the lobby, every part
of this hotel is stunning.
Following a fire in 2018,
the hotel had undergone
a multi-million pound
renovation, that included
a spa in the lower level.

ME London
MAP N3 ▪ 336–37 The
Strand WC2 ▪ 020 7395
3400 ▪ www.melia.com
▪ £££
With its black-and-white,
classy decor and stunning
pyramid-shaped reception,
a visit to ME London
is like stepping into a
sci-fi film. The futuristic
feel continues with the
ground-floor restaurants,
atrium champagne bar
and the Radio Rooftop
Bar, which has panoramic
views of the city skyline.

The Ritz
MAP K3 ▪ 150 Piccadilly
W1 ▪ 020 7300 2222
▪ www.theritzlondon.
com ▪ £££
One of London's most
glamorous hotels, the Ritz
is decorated in Louis XVI
style, with shades of blue,
yellow, pink and peach,
gold and silk trimmings,
chandeliers and period
furniture. Afternoon tea
in the Palm Court is
popular and the swanky
restaurant has a gar-
den terrace.

The Savoy
MAP M4 ▪ Strand WC2
▪ 020 7836 4343 ▪ www.
thesavoylondon.com/
savoy ▪ £££
In a lovely riverside setting,
the Savoy is London's top
traditional hotel and has
been restored to its ori-
ginal Art Deco splendour.
Leisure facilities include
a private pool and gym.

Shangri-La at
The Shard
MAP H4 ▪ 31 St Thomas
St SE1 ▪ 020 7234 8000
▪ www.shangri-la.com/
london/shangrila ▪ £££
Occupying floors 34
to 52 of the city's highest
skyscraper, The Shard,
this is one of Asia's top
hotel chains. The rooms
here are spacious and
the service attentive but it
is the views that make
the stay a memorable
experience. The

swimming pool on the 52nd floor is also one of the highest in London.

The Waldorf Hilton
MAP N3 ■ Aldwych WC2 ■ 020 7836 2400 ■ www. hilton.com ■ £££
This is one of London's great Edwardian hotels, located a stone's throw from theatres and shopping districts. The leisure facilities are excellent.

Character Hotels

Durrants Hotel
MAP D3 ■ George St W1 ■ 020 7935 8131 ■ www. durrantshotel.co.uk ■ ££
Set close to Marylebone High Street and Bond Street, this Georgian hotel has been in business since 1790. It has a comfortable, old-fashioned style, with antique furniture and modern bathrooms.

Portobello Hotel
MAP A4 ■ 22 Stanley Gardens W11 ■ 020 7727 2777 ■ www.portobello hotel.com ■ ££
Brimming with character, each of the 21 rooms in this boutique hotel is individually decorated – some with wall-to-wall murals – and tastefully furnished. This is exactly the kind of hotel you would hope to find near London's great antiques market. A light snack menu accompanies an honesty bar, which stocks a fantastic selection of wine, beer and spirits.

The Rookery
MAP Q1 ■ 12 Peter's Lane, Cowcross St EC1 ■ 020 7336 0931 ■ www. rookeryhotel.com ■ ££
Located at a short distance from St Paul's Cathedral,

the hotel takes its name from the gang of thieves who once operated in this area near the famous Smithfield market. An atmospheric warren of rooms has been linked together to create a brilliant hotel that evokes Victorian London, with a touch of the Gothic.

York and Albany
MAP D1 ■ 127–29 Parkway, NW1 ■ 020 7387 5700 ■ www.gordonram sayrestaurants.com/york-and-albany ■ ££
Situated between Regent's Park and Camden, this is the Gordon Ramsay organization's version of a gastropub, with deliciously inventive cuisine. Above it is the surprisingly secluded townhouse, with eight beautiful, luxurious rooms and suites combining period fittings and cutting-edge electronics.

Blakes Hotel
MAP B6 ■ 33 Roland Gardens SW7 ■ 020 7370 6701 ■ www.blakes hotels. com ■ £££
This hotel is a Victorian delight filled with sumptuous cushions and drapes as well as bamboo and bird cages. Each room is individually styled with exotica from all over the world. The grand Blakes Below bar in the basement, designed by Anouska Hempel, takes the theme forward.

The Chesterfield
MAP D4 ■ 35 Charles St W1 ■ 020 7491 2622 ■ www.chesterfield mayfair.com ■ £££
Set in the heart of Mayfair, just off Berkeley Square, this 4-star luxury hotel is full of British old-world charm. The honey served at

breakfast comes directly from the beehives, found at the hotel's rooftop. The fine dining restaurant serves excellent British food.

The Gore
MAP B5 ■ 190 Queen's Gate SW7 ■ 020 7584 6601 ■ www.starhotels collezione.com ■ £££
Built in 1892 under the patronage of Prince Albert, consort of Queen Victoria, this hotel retains a relaxed, fin-de-siècle feel. Its Persian rugs, potted palms and paintings are in keeping with the elegance of the building, and rooms are furnished with antiques. The restaurant, 190 Queen's Gate, is recommended as well.

Hazlitt's
MAP L2 ■ 6 Frith St W1 ■ 020 7434 1771 ■ www. hazlittshotel.com ■ £££
A literary event as much as a hotel, Hazlitt's is located in the former townhouse of the essayist William Hazlitt (1778–1830). The hotel's literary feel is enhanced by its library of books signed by the many authors who have stayed as guests at the hotel.

Designer Hotels

Eccleston Square Hotel
MAP D5 ■ 37 Eccleston Sq SW1 ■ 020 3503 0750 ■ www.ecclestonsquare hotel.com ■ ££
Overlooking the lush gardens of Eccleston Square, this luxury boutique hotel is aimed at the ultra-sophisticated and offers high-tech facilities, including massage beds.

Hoxton Hotel
MAP H2 ▪ 81 Great Eastern St EC2 ▪ 020 7550 1000 ▪ www.thehoxton.com ▪ ££
Set in the trendy area of Shoreditch, and with branches in Holborn and Southwark, the Hoxton offers small but cool individual rooms at reasonable prices. An "urban breakfast bag" is delivered to your room each morning.

The Zetter Hotel
MAP F2 ▪ 86–88 Clerkenwell Rd EC1 ▪ 020 7324 4567 ▪ www.thezetter.com ▪ ££
Modern with retro touches, this laid-back option offers luxuries such as the latest in-room entertainment, walk-in rain showers and free espresso machines. The rooftop studios feature private terraces and outdoor bathtubs. Different artists in residence display their work in the atrium every six weeks.

Charlotte Street Hotel
MAP K1 ▪ 15–17 Charlotte St W1 ▪ 020 7806 2000 ▪ www.firmdalehotels.com ▪ £££
Tasteful and comfortable, with padded armchairs, antiques and log fires in the drawing room and library. The "Bloomsbury Group" theme that adorns the entire hotel features original artworks and a mural in the bustling Oscar bar and restaurant.

COMO Metropolitan
MAP D4 ▪ Old Park Lane W1 ▪ 020 7447 1000 ▪ www.comohotels.com/metropolitanlondon ▪ £££
Contemporary and stylish, this was one of the first of the classy modern hotels in London, with black-clad staff, cool interiors and bright, airy bedrooms and suites. Go celebrity-spotting in Nobu, the hotel's fashionable Japanese-Peruvian restaurant.

COMO The Halkin
MAP D4 ▪ Halkin St SW1 ▪ 020 7333 1000 ▪ www.comohotels.com/thehalkin ▪ £££
A startlingly beautiful hotel in a Georgian townhouse, which has been given a thoroughly modern overhaul with luxurious marble, glass and dark wood details. The Basque restaurant is chic and the rooms are equipped for modern communication.

No. 5 Maddox Street
MAP J3 ▪ 5 Maddox St W1 ▪ 020 7647 0200 ▪ www.living-rooms.co.uk/hotel/no-5-maddox-st ▪ £££
Glass, steel and bamboo feature in the decor of these high-quality Japanese-style serviced apartments, with a restaurant delivery service, complimentary Artisan du Chocolat goodies, yoga mats, in-room spa treatments and full internet facilities.

Sanderson
MAP K1 ▪ 50 Berners St W1 ▪ 020 7300 1400 ▪ www.sbe.com/hotels/originals/sanderson ▪ £££
Designed by Phillipe Starck, this is one of London's most stylish hotels. Behind a 1950s office-block exterior, its plain decor is enlivened by Dalí-lips and Louis XV sofas, while the sparsely decorated bedrooms retain their sense of whimsy. Facilities include a gym, a spa and complimentary use of bicycles. Make sure to book a table for the themed Mad Hatter's afternoon tea.

St Martins Lane
MAP L3 ▪ 45 St Martin's Lane WC2 ▪ 020 7300 5500 ▪ www.sbe.com/hotels/originals/st-martins-lane ▪ £££
In the heart of the West End, the Sanderson's sister hotel has a lobby of theatrical proportions. The rooms have floor-to-ceiling windows and even the bathrooms (all of which have big tubs) are 50 per cent glass.

W London
MAP L3 ▪ 10 Wardour St, Leicester Sq W1 ▪ 020 7758 1000 ▪ www.marriott.co.uk/hotels/travel/lonhw-w-london-leicester-square ▪ £££
This glamorous West End hotel will have you feeling like the star of the show. The rooms feature designer beds and spa products. They offer good in-room dining options, while cocktail-lovers will enjoy the extensive menu at the bar. There is also an on-site fitness centre and a spa with a variety of relaxing treatments.

Business Hotels

Holiday Inn Express London City
MAP H2 ▪ 275 Old St EC1 ▪ 020 7300 4300 ▪ www.ihg.com/holidayinnexpress ▪ £
One among a chain of value-for-money London

hotels, the Holiday Inn Express London City is not actually in the City, but backs onto fashionable Hoxton Square *(see p159)*, an area known more for art than for business. The hotel offers complimentary breakfast and free Wi-Fi. There are several branches across London.

Andaz Liverpool Street

MAP H3 ▪ 40 Liverpool St EC2 ▪ 020 7961 1234 ▪ www.hyatt.com ▪ ££
Built in 1884 as the railway hotel serving Liverpool Street station, Andaz (meaning "personal style" in Hindi), fuses a 5-star hotel with boutique design flair. Set in a redbrick building with stylish, minimalist rooms, it has six restaurants and bars offering a great range of eating and drinking options.

London Bridge Hotel

MAP H4 ▪ 8–18 London Bridge St SE1 ▪ 020 7855 2200 ▪ www.london bridgehotel.com ▪ ££
Situated just over the river from the City, this handsome, modern, independently owned hotel is well equipped for business guests, with modern conference facilities. The Londinium restaurant serves modern British food.

The Tower Hotel

MAP H4 ▪ St Katharine's Way E1 ▪ 020 7523 5063 ▪ www.guoman. com ▪ ££
Many of the 800-plus rooms in this vast block close to Tower Bridge and St Katharine Docks boast spectacular river views.

The Bloomsbury Hotel

MAP L1 ▪ 16–22 Great Russell St WC1 ▪ 020 7347 1000 ▪ www.doyle collection.com ▪ £££
This Neo-Georgian building was designed by Edwin Lutyens for the YWCA in the 1930s. The Queen Mary Hall is now a conference centre and the former chapel a quiet meeting room. The rooms cater well to a business clientele, with internet facilities and work desks.

Canary Riverside Plaza

46 Westferry Circus E14 ▪ DLR Westferry ▪ 020 7510 1999 ▪ www.canary river sideplaza.com ▪ £££
As smart and stylish as you would expect from a Canary Wharf hotel, this is a straight-forward, well-equipped, contemporary-looking affair. Some rooms have window seats with river views, there's a spa, a fitness centre and indoor pool. The restaurant opens onto a terrace during summer.

Marble Arch Marriott

MAP D3 ▪ 134 George St W1 ▪ 020 7723 1277 ▪ www.marriott.co.uk ▪ £££
A modern hotel near the western end of Oxford Street. Facilities include a bar and restaurant, gym, health club and swimming pool.

There are also complete business facilities in the executive lounge.

The Park Tower Knightsbridge

MAP C4 ▪ 101 Knightsbridge SW1 ▪ 020 7235 8050 ▪ www. marriott.co.uk ▪ £££
With a circular building, this plush hotel, is a Knightsbridge landmark. The rooms and suites, with chaise lounges and window-side desks, offer views over Hyde Park and the city's skyline. Business guests are well catered for.

St Pancras Renaissance Hotel

MAP E1 ▪ Euston Rd NW1 ▪ 020 7841 3540 ▪ www.marriott.co.uk ▪ £££
Located in front of St Pancras International Station, home of the Eurostar, this is the perfect hotel for those who commute regularly from Europe. It also happens to be one of London's grandest and most palatial Victorian buildings, designed by Sir George Gilbert Scott.

Mid-Priced Hotels

Langham Court Hotel

MAP J1 ▪ 31–5 Langham St W1 ▪ 020 7436 6622 ▪ www.gemhotels.com ▪ £
Located in a side street close to Oxford Circus, this hotel, with its attractive façade, is as friendly inside as its exterior promises. The terrific Langham Brasserie serves both French and Spanish cuisine, including tapas.

For a key to hotel price categories see p174

Apex City of London Hotel

MAP H3 ▪ 1 Seething Lane EC3 ▪ 020 7702 2020 ▪ www.apexhotels. co.uk ▪ ££

The four-star Apex has rooms with state-of-the-art facilities and a smart restaurant. Special offers are often available. Two more Apex hotels are there in the city – on Fleet Street and on Copthall Avenue.

DoubleTree by Hilton London West End

MAP M1 ▪ 92 Southampton Row WC1 ▪ 020 7242 2828 ▪ www.hilton.com ▪ ££

Behind the Edwardian façade of this veteran Bloomsbury hotel are smart rooms, with state-of-the-art facilities and luxury suites with a separate lounge area. There is also a good restaurant.

Hotel La Place

MAP D2 ▪ 17 Nottingham Place W1 ▪ 020 7486 2323 ▪ www. hotellaplace.com ▪ ££

This townhouse in Marylebone is quirky and unique. Decor in the 20 rooms and Le Jardin wine bar is chintzy and ornate. A full English breakfast is included in the room rate. The owners take great care of their guests.

Malmaison

MAP G2 ▪ 18–21 Charterhouse Sq EC1 ▪ 020 3750 9402 ▪ www.malmaison. com ▪ ££

Located in Smithfield, this boutique chain hotel is charming and reasonably priced. Apart from the comfortable rooms, it offers a gym, a chic brasserie and a lounge bar.

Meliá White House

MAP D2 ▪ Albany St NW1 ▪ 020 7391 3000 ▪ www.melia.com ▪ ££

Close to Regent's Park, Oxford Circus and Piccadilly Circus, this classic four-star hotel was originally built as a block of model apartments in 1936. After its refurbishments, the hotel boasts 581 spacious and comfortable rooms, a restaurant, cocktail bar and a bar with a terrace open in summer as well as a shisha lounge.

Mercure London Bridge

MAP R4 ▪ 71–9 Southwark St SE1 ▪ 020 7902 0800 ▪ www.all.accor. com ▪ ££

Situated close to the Tate Modern, Borough Market and The Shard, this hotel boasts a smart contemporary design plus a high level of facilities, including Marco's New York Italian restaurant by celebrity chef Marco Pierre White.

myhotel Bloomsbury

MAP L1 ▪ 11–13 Bayley St WC1 ▪ 020 3004 6000 ▪ www. myhotels.com ▪ ££

Just off Tottenham Court Road, this hotel is a blend of Eastern and Western styles. The staff is attentive and the rooms are light and contemporary with a bohemian feel, in sync with the Bloomsbury area.

Park Lane Mews Hotel

MAP D4 ▪ 2 Stanhope Row, Park Lane W1 ▪ 020 7493 7222 ▪ www.parklanemews hotel.net ▪ ££

Located in Mayfair, this four-star hotel is just minutes away from Harrods, Oxford Street, Buckingham Palace and Hyde Park. The decor is smart and traditional. The restaurant and lounge are perfect for relaxing in after a busy day.

The Resident Kensington

MAP A5 ▪ 25 Courtfield Gardens SW5 ▪ 020 7244 2255 ▪ www.resident hotels.com ▪ ££

This "luxury budget" hotel offers free Wi-Fi and mini-kitchens with complimentary Fairtrade tea and Nespresso coffee machine in every room. Its 65 rooms, each of which is decorated in contemporary style, range from singles and luxury bunks to family rooms.

Thistle Trafalgar Square

MAP L4 ▪ Whitcomb St WC2 ▪ 020 7523 5064 ▪ www.thistle. com ▪ ££

The Thistle Group has eight hotels in London. This one is next door to the National Gallery, close to Leicester Square, so staying here will save on transport costs. Rooms are stylishly furnished with all mod cons.

Inexpensive Hotels

Church Street Hotel
29–33 Camberwell Church St SE5 ■ Tube Oval, then 12, 36 or 436 bus ■ 020 7703 5984 ■ www.church streethotel.com ■ £
Enjoy a vibrant slice of Latin America in this cheerful Hispanic-themed establishment in South London. Many art galleries, pubs, and live music venues dot the area. There is no Tube station nearby. However, central London is only 30 minutes away by bus.

easyHotel Victoria
MAP D5 ■ 34–40 Belgrave Rd SW1 ■ 020 7834 1379 ■ www.easyhotel.com ■ £
The company behind easyJet offers a fleet of budget hotels with small, functional rooms. Expect no frills as they are the cheapest en-suite double rooms in town. There are three more easyHotels in central London (in South Kensington, Paddington and Old Street) and also at Heathrow, Luton and Croydon. TV and Wi-Fi cost extra.

Qbic
MAP E2 ■ 42 Adler St E1 ■ 020 3021 3300 ■ www. qbichotels.com ■ £
With bright and quirky decor, this budget hotel offers rooms with comfortable beds at great value. The hotel also offers bikes for hire.

Bedford Hotel
MAP M1 ■ 83–95 Southampton Row WC1 ■ 020 7636 7822 ■ www. imperialhotels.co.uk/ bedford ■ ££
One of six large, good-value Bloomsbury hotels run by Imperial London Hotels, the Bedford's advantages are a good restaurant and a sunny lounge and garden. It has simple yet comfortable rooms, some of which overlook the garden.

Columbia Hotel
MAP B3 ■ 95–9 Lancaster Gate W2 ■ 020 7402 0021 ■ www.columbiahotel. co.uk ■ ££
With a delightful leafy setting overlooking Hyde Park and Kensington Gardens, the Columbia is cosy family-run hotel. Originally townhouses, one of which was used as an American Red Cross Hospital during World War I, the hotel offers interconnected and four-bed rooms for families.

Fielding Hotel
MAP M2 ■ 4 Broad Court, Bow St WC2 ■ 020 7836 8305 ■ www.thefielding hotel.co.uk ■ ££
Named after the novelist Henry Fielding and ideally situated right opposite the Royal Opera House, this charming hotel is a warren of oddly shaped rooms, with showers and basins tucked in corners. Outside there is all of Covent Garden to breakfast in. All rooms are equipped with amenities such as digital TV, Wi-Fi and air conditioning.

Millennium Gloucester Hotel
MAP B5 ■ Harrington Gardens SW7 ■ 020 7373 6030 ■ www.millennium hotels.com ■ ££
Located at a minute's walk from the tube station, this hotel close to attractions such as Kensington Palace, the Royal Albert Hall and Hyde Park. The modern rooms are spacious and reasonably priced. Three restaurant options offer Asian, Indian as well as classic British cuisine. Other facilities include a fitness centre and chargeable parking.

Morgan Hotel
MAP L1 ■ 24 Bloomsbury St WC1 ■ 020 7636 3735 ■ www.morganhotel.co. uk ■ ££
This family-run hotel has several rooms overlooking the British Museum and all have air conditioning. The cosy breakfast area has framed London memo-rabilia on the walls.

Z Soho
MAP L2 ■ 17 Moor St W1 ■ 020 3551 3701 ■ www.thezhotels.com/ soho ■ ££
Set in the heart of Soho, this hotel offers 85 tiny rooms, some with no windows, a small café and free Wi-Fi. It is close to Theatreland.

B&Bs and Hostels

At Home Inn Chelsea
MAP B6 ■ 5 Park Walk SW10 ■ Tube South Kensington, then 14 or 414 bus ■ 0799 084 4008 ■ www.athomeinn chelsea.com ■ £
Housed in an early 18th-century townhouse, this B&B offers two cosy guestrooms equipped with en-suite bathrooms, as well as tea and coffee making facilities. One of the rooms has a terrace. Minimum stay is two nights.

For a key to hotel price categories see p174

Clink261

MAP F2 ▪ 261–5 Grays Inn Rd WC1 ▪ 020 7833 9400 ▪ www. clinkhostels.com ▪ £
Clink hostels have double rooms and dorms maintained by a friendly staff. TV lounge, free Wi-Fi and self-catering kitchen are available. Though Clink261 has a bar, the nearby Clink78 has a livelier one. Charges include breakfast.

The Dictionary Hostel

MAP H2 ▪ 10–20 Kingsland Rd E2 ▪ 020 7613 2784 ▪ www.thedictionary hostel.com ▪ £
This party hostel located in Shoreditch offers free Wi-Fi. There's also a bar with evening entertainment, table football and a roof terrace. Dormitory and double rooms available.

Dover Castle Hostel

MAP G4 ▪ 6a Great Dover St SE1 ▪ 020 7403 7773 ▪ www.dovercastlehostel. com ▪ £
This privately run hostel offers great value-for-money accommodation for backpackers. There are 60 beds in total, which range from 4 to 12 per dormitory-style room. There's free Wi-Fi and lockers can be rented. The late-licensed bar has live music every Thursday.

Generator Hostel London

MAP E2 ▪ 37 Tavistock Place WC1 ▪ 020 7388 7666 ▪ www.stay generator.com/hostels/ london ▪ £
With decor somewhere between sci-fi and industrial chic, this youth-orientated hostel provides budget solutions for impecunious travellers. Private rooms are available as well as dorms. There's a café and bar, and the hostel arranges tours and other regular events.

Palmers Lodge Swiss Cottage

40 College Crescent NW3 ▪ Tube Swiss Cottage ▪ 020 7483 8470 ▪ www.palmers lodge.uk ▪ £
A converted Victorian mansion is an unlikely setting for a hostel, but this is budget accommodation at its most luxurious, with 24-hour reception and security, free Wi-Fi and car parking, plus an on-site bar and restaurant. There is another branch of Palmers Lodge, called Hillspring, in Willesden.

St Christopher's at The Village

MAP G4 ▪ 161–65 Borough High St SE1 ▪ 020 7939 9710 ▪ www. st-christophers.co.uk ▪ £
This is the largest of three hostels on this street run by St Christopher's Inns. It is also UK's first hostel with capsule beds fitted with curtains as well as USB chargers. There are other branches in Camden, Greenwich, Shepherd's Bush, Liverpool Street and Hammersmith. Private capsules, private dorms and mixed dorms are available along with complimentary buffet breakfast and free Wi-Fi. Belushi's bar is great for partying and there's a resident DJ at weekends.

YHA Earl's Court

MAP A6 ▪ 38 Bolton Gardens, Earl's Court SW5 ▪ 0345 371 9114 ▪ www.yha.org.uk ▪ £
Set in a Victorian building with a courtyard garden, the rooms in this backpackers' hostel are minimalist in decor. Guests have access to comfortable shared areas.

Arosfa Hotel

MAP E2 ▪ 83 Gower St WC1 ▪ 020 7636 2115 ▪ www.arosfalondon. com ▪ ££
In the heart of Bloomsbury, near the British Museum, this Georgian townhouse has been renovated as a comfortable B&B, with modern bathrooms in its small but cosy rooms. The owners are welcoming, and there's a pleasant guest lounge as well as a little garden at the back.

Aster House

MAP B5 ▪ 3 Sumner Place, SW7 ▪ 020 7581 5888 ▪ www.asterhouse. com ▪ ££
This B&B in a Victorian townhouse has just 13 rooms. It is within walking distance of the Science, Natural History and Victoria and Albert Museums. The buffet breakfast is served in the orangery.

B&B Belgravia

MAP D5 ▪ 64–66 Ebury St SW1 ▪ 020 7529 8570 ▪ www. bb-belgravia.com ▪ ££
Set within two Grade II listed Georgian townhouses, this B&B offers 17 en-suite rooms, as well as nine studios with

kitchenettes and a delivered continental breakfast. Guests have 24-hour access to a lounge with an open fire, a laptop, free Wi-Fi, a TV, a printer, daily newspapers and a coffee machine. There's also a garden. Guests can borrow bikes for free.

Smart Hyde Park View
MAP B3 ■ 16 Leinster Terrace W2 ■ 020 7262 8684 ■ www.smart hostels.com ■ ££
Situated just off Hyde Park, this is a comfortable variation on a hostel, offering double rooms with private bathrooms as well as traditional dormitories. It has branches in Camden and Russell Square too.

Hotels Out of Town

Hotel 55
55 Hanger Lane W5 ■ Tube North Ealing ■ 020 8991 4450 ■ www.hotel55-london.com ■ £
The decor of this hotel is bright and modern, with character. Dine in the in-house Japanese restaurant, Momo and unwind in the landscaped garden.

The Lodge Hotel
52–4 Upper Richmond Rd SW15 ■ Tube East Putney ■ 020 8874 1598 ■ www. thelodgehotellondon. com ■ £
Leafy Putney isn't that far from the centre of London, but this hotel has a calm out-of-town feel to it. Two Victorian mansions and a former coaching stable have been joined together to

provide 73 bedrooms along with a bar, lounge, gym and restaurant.

Martel Guest House
27 The Ridgeway, Golders Green NW11 ■ Tube Golders Green ■ 020 8455 1802 ■ www.martel guesthouse.co.uk ■ £
Hidden away along a quiet tree-lined road just a 5-minute walk from the tube station (15-minute journey to central London), this neat and clean guesthouse offers well-appointed rooms. The owner, Phil, is warm and friendly and helps with taxi rides and useful tips. A buffet breakfast is served in the dining room that overlooks a garden.

The Mitre
291 Greenwich High Rd SE10 ■ Train to Greenwich ■ 020 8293 0037 ■ www.themitre greenwich.co.uk ■ £
Originally a coaching inn belonging to the 18th century, this bustling pub with 24 en-suite rooms, including three family suites, is close to Greenwich's sights and transport links. Popular with locals, the pub serves good food, including hearty Sunday roasts. There is a conservatory and a garden but no parking.

Novotel London Stansted Airport
Stansted Airport ■ 01279 680 800 ■ www.all.accor. com ■ £
A modern hotel with standard facilities, this is just a 6-minute journey to the terminal at Stansted Airport via

shuttle bus, making it an ideal choice for early flights.

The Pilot
68 River Way, SE10 ■ 020 8858 5910 ■ www. pilotgreenwich.co.uk ■ ££
Tucked away from central London, this hotel offers a refreshing change from the city. The hotel flaunts a nautical theme, while the rooms are decorated with separate themes. It features a good bar and is a ten-minute walk away from The O2 (see p73), which hosts live music concerts.

Renaissance London Heathrow
Bath Rd, Hounslow ■ Tube Hounslow West ■ 020 8897 6363 ■ www. marriott.com ■ ££
With a 24-hour fitness centre and soundproofed rooms, this hotel with views of Heathrow's runways is handy for getting to the airport.

Sofitel London Gatwick
North Terminal, Gatwick Airport ■ 012 9356 7070 ■ www.all.accor.com ■ ££
Walk directly from Gatwick's North Terminal to this elegant hotel, which has a full range of facilities. It is linked to London by the Gatwick Express train.

St Paul's Hotel
153 Hammersmith Rd W14 ■ Tube Hammersmith ■ 020 8846 9119 ■ www. stpaulhotel.co.uk ■ ££
Housed in a handsome 1884 Victorian building, this boutique hotel is just a short walk away from the Eventim Apollo and Olympia London.

For a key to hotel price categories see p174

General Index

Acknowledgments

Author
Roger Williams is a London-born journalist and long-time Soho inhabitant. He has written and edited several dozen travel guides, including Dorling Kindersley's Eyewitness guides to Provence and Barcelona.

Additional Contributors
Vinny Crump, Joe Staines

Publishing Director Georgina Dee

Publisher Vivien Antwi

Design Director Phil Ormerod

Editorial Ankita Awasthi-Tröger, Michelle Crane, Rebecca Flynn, Rachel Fox, Fíodhna Ní Ghríofa, Freddie Marriage, Sally Schafer, Christine Stroyan

Cover Design Maxine Pedliham, Vinita Venugopal

Design Tessa Bindloss, Sunita Gahir, Marisa Renzullo, Jaynan Spengler

Picture Research Phoebe Lowndes, Susie Peachey, Ellen Root, Oran Tarjan

Cartography Subhashree Bharti, Suresh Kumar, Casper Morris

DTP Jason Little, George Nimmo, Joanna Stenlake

Production Olivia Jeffries

Factchecker Kate Berens

Proofreader Anna Streiffert

Indexer Kathryn O'Donoghue

Illustrator Chris Orr & Associates

Revisions Sophie Adam, Avanika, Marta Bescos, Dipika Dasgupta, Maria Edwards, Sumita Khatwani, Shikha Kulkarni, Darren Longley, Hayley Maher, Arushi Mathur, Bhavika Mathur, Meghna, Alison McGill, Gaurav Nagpal, Matt Norman, Bandana Paul, Vagisha Pushp, Lucy Richards, Rohit Rojal, Anuroop Sanwalia, Azeem Siddiqui, Neil Simpson, Jackie Staddon, Flora Spens, Hollie Teague, Manjari Thakur, Priyanka Thakur, Åsa Westerlund

Commissioned Photography Susie Adams, Max Alexander, Demetrio Carrasco, Geoff Dann, Mike Dunning, Steve Gorton, Frank Greenaway, John Heseltine, Ed Ironside, Colin Keates, Laurie Noble, Stephen Oliver, Rough Guides/Victor Borg, Rough Guides/Suzanne Porter, Rough Guides/Natascha Sturny, Rough Guides/Mark Thomas

Jean-Baptiste Rabouan 55cl; Quentin Bargate 42cl; Massimo Borchi 92b; Alan Copson 73clb; James Davies 141br; Demotix/Malcolm Park 40c; dpa/Peter Kneffel 32–3; Eurasia Press/Steven Vidler 4cl, 88b; Dennis Gilbert 15cl; Grady: Damian 55cr; John Harper 54br; Heritage Images 62bl; Roberto Herrett 147cra; JAl/Alan Copson 7tr; Pawel Libera 154t, Yang Liu 102–3, Loop Images / Dave Povey 104tr, Loop Images / Eric Nathan 77tl; Leo Mason 70tl, 71cr; Reuters 25br; Robert Harding World Imagery 96b; Napoleon Sarony 60tl; Hendrik Schmidt 61tl; Splash News 68crb Homer Sykes 112tr; Mark Sykes 144cr; The Gallery Collection 16cra, 16br, 58tl; Steven Vidler 57cr,142cr.

Dalloway Terrace: 117cra

Daunt Books: 138b.

Dean and Chapter of Westminster: Jim Dyson 34bl.

Dorling Kindersley: Max Alexander 116b; Courtesy of the Natural History Museum, London/John Downes 10clb, /Colin Keates 20cl; courtesy of the Royal Festival Hall, and Park Lane Group Young Artists' Concert 81tr; Courtesy of The Science Museum/Geoff Dann 10crb; Courtesy of Benjamin Pollock's Toyshop/ Max Alexander 109br; Courtesy of the Wallace Collection, London/Geoff Dann 134tr.

Dreamstime.com: Acmanley 91tr; Andersastphoto 98b; Tudor Antonel Adrian 150b; Ajv123ajv 3tr, 164–5; Altezza 4clb, 87cra; Anizza 119tl; Ardazi 107tl; Anthony Baggett 61br; Baloncici 59cl, 125tr; Bargotiphotography 135tr; Beataaldridge 54t; Michal Bednarek 108tr; Felix Bensman 27br; Christian Bertrand 73tr; Mikhail Blajenov 6cl, Bombaert 114b, 160bl, Dan Breckwoldt 126b, 129tr, 136b, Anthony Brown 56t, Andrew Chambers 119b; Claudiodivizia 143bl; Mike Clegg 130 cla, 161br, 162tr; Cowardlion 28-9c, Cowardlion 50clb; Johanna Cuomo 68bl, 79tl; Chris Dorney 7cr, 51 tl, 54t, 120b, 127cla, 142bl; Mark Eaton 155clb; Jorge Duarte Estevao 161tl; Eric Flamant 83cl; Michael Foley 36cla, Haircutting 152cl;

Jodi Hanagan 158cla; Sven Hansche 132-3; Anna Hristova 163bl; Imaengine 15b; Irishka777 113t; Dragan Jovanovic 128cra; Kmiragaya 4cla, 105br, 146tr, 153tr; Georgios Kollidas 126cra, Slawek Kozakiewicz 129clb, Jan Kranendonk 122b, Charlotte Leaper 118tl, 159tr; Lowerkase 10–1b, 26bl; Maisna 137cl; Ac Manley 115bc; Mark6138 87br; Mikecphoto 106cra; Krzysztof Nahlik 94tl; Nadirco 4b; Dmitry Naumov 42br; Nhtg 55tr; Dilyana Nikolova 2tl, 8-9; Radub85 63tr; Sampete 64tl; Pere Sanz 26cla; Sinoleo 141tr; Socrates 86cla; Spiroview Inc. 149bl; Stuart456 4cr; Thevirex 79bc; Alexandra Thompson 140cra; Travelwitness 64b; Tupungato 91clb, 100br; Paul Wishart 70cr; Yongong 135b.

Electric Cinema: 128bl.

Getty Images: AFP/Dan Kitwood 81cl; Bloomberg Anna Branthwaite 75tr; DeAgostini 30–1; DESPITE STRAIGHT LINES (Paul Williams) 36–7c; Tabatha Fireman 72t; Furture Light 65clb; Heritage Images 40tr, 45b; Gamma-Keystone / Keystone-France 19c; Leemage 120cra; NurPhoto 83cr; Pawel Libera 4t, 27cl; Max Mumby 38cla; Robert Harding World Imagery/Amanda Hall 38–9; Lizzie Shepherd 6tr.

Gordon's Wine Bar: 110b.

By permission of IWM (Imperial War Museums): Richard Ash 57tl.

Inn the Park/Peyton and Byrne: 123tr.

iStockphoto.com: MichaelUtech 95tr; violettenlandungoy 53cl

J Sheekey: 101cr.

The Jerusalem Tavern: 145tr

KU Bar: 96cra

La Fromagerie: 139cr.

National Portrait Gallery, London: 10cla, 18cr, 18bl.

The National Trust Photo Library ©NTPL: Andrew Butler 76bl.

The Trustees of the Natural History Museum, London: Kevin Webb 21tr, 20cr.

OXO Tower Restaurant/Harvey Nichols: Jonathan Reid 93cr.

Philip Way Photography: 44tr, 45cl.

Royal National Theatre: Philip Vile 70br.

The Royal Collection Trust © Her Majesty Queen Elizabeth II 2015: Crown © HMSO 41cl; Derry Moore 25tl.

Rules Restaurant: 74t.

Science Museum: 23crb, Greg Kinch 23tr

Courtesy of the Trustees of Sir John Soane's Museum/Caro Communications: Gareth Gardner 113br

St Paul's Cathedral: 42–3.

© Science Museum Group: 68t

Superstock: Stefano Baldini/age fotostock 19tr.

© Tate, London 2013: Norham Castle, Sunrise by Joseph Mallord William Turner 30cla; Carnation, Lily, Lily, Rose John Singer Sargent 31tr; Three Studies for Figures at the Base of a Crucifixion Francis Bacon 31crb; DACS, London 2016 /Whaam! (1963) Roy Lichetenstein 28br; /Three Dancers (1925) Pablo Picasso 28cla.

Tate Modern: Cildo Meireles Babel 2001 © Cildo Meireles 29tr

The City Barge Pub: 157tr.

Victoria and Albert Museum: 56bl.

Cover

Front and spine: **AWL Images:** Alan Copson.

Back: **Alamy Stock Photo:** robertharding tl; **AWL Images:** Hemis crb; **Alamy Stock Photo:** Sergey Borisov tr, Helen Dixon cla; **AWL Images:** Alan Copson .

Pull out map cover

AWL Images: Alan Copson.

All other images are: © Dorling Kindersley. For further information see www.dkimages.com.

Printed and bound in China

First edition 2002

First published in Great Britain by
Dorling Kindersley Limited
DK, One Embassy Gardens, 8 Viaduct
Gardens, London SW11 7BW, UK

The authorised representative in the EEA is
Dorling Kindersley Verlag GmbH. Arnulfstr.
124, 80636 Munich, Germany

Published in the United States by
DK US, 1450 Broadway, Suite 801
New York, NY 10018, USA

Copyright © 2002, 2021 Dorling
Kindersley Limited

A Penguin Random House Company

21 22 23 10 9 8 7 6

Reprinted with revisions 2004, 2005, 2006, 2007, 2008, 2009, 2010, 2012, 2013, 2014, 2015, 2016 (twice), 2017, 2018, 2019, 2021

A CIP catalogue record is available from the British Library.

A catalogue record for this book is available from the Library of Congress.

ISSN 1479-344X
ISBN 978-0-2415-0962-3

As a guide to abbreviations in visitor information blocks: **Adm** = *admission charge.*

MIX
Paper from
responsible sources
FSC™ C018179

This book was made with Forest Stewardship Council ™ certified paper – one small step in DK's commitment to a sustainable future. For more information go to www.dk.com/our-green-pledge